Shaw and Feminisms

The Florida Bernard Shaw Series

UNIVERSITY PRESS OF FLORIDA

Florida A&M University, Tallahassee
Florida Atlantic University, Boca Raton
Florida Gulf Coast University, Ft. Myers
Florida International University, Miami
Florida State University, Tallahassee
New College of Florida, Saras~*~
University of Cen*~ *
U~ *
U

Shaw and Feminisms

·····················

On Stage and Off

Edited by D. A. Hadfield and Jean Reynolds

Foreword by Rodelle Weintraub

University Press of Florida

Gainesville · Tallahassee · Tampa · Boca Raton

Pensacola · Orlando · Miami · Jacksonville · Ft. Myers · Sarasota

This book may be available in an electronic edition.

21 20 19 18 17 16   6 5 4 3 2 1

First cloth printing, 2013
First paperback printing, 2016

Library of Congress Cataloging-in-Publication Data
Shaw and feminisms : on stage and off / edited by D. A. Hadfield and Jean Reynolds ;
Foreword by Rodelle Weintraub.
p. cm. — (Florida Bernard Shaw series)
Includes bibliographical references and index.
Summary: A volume that gathers critical perspectives on Shaw's feminism and the
contradictions therein.
ISBN 978-0-8130-4243-5 (cloth: alk. paper)
ISBN 978-0-8130-6238-9 (pbk.)
1. Shaw, Bernard, 1856-1950—Criticism and interpretation. 2. Women in literature. I.
Hadfield, D. A. (Dorothy A.) II. Reynolds, Jean. III. Weintraub, Rodelle. IV. Series:
Florida Bernard Shaw series.
PR5367.S735 2012
822'.912—dc23
2012031674

The University Press of Florida is the scholarly publishing agency for the State
University System of Florida, comprising Florida A&M University, Florida
Atlantic University, Florida Gulf Coast University, Florida International
University, Florida State University, New College of Florida, University
of Central Florida, University of Florida, University of North Florida,
University of South Florida, and University of West Florida.

University Press of Florida
15 Northwest 15th Street
Gainesville, FL 32611-2079
http://www.upf.com

Funding to assist in the publication of this book was generously provided by the David and Rachel Howie Foundation.

To LWC
Mentor, colleague, friend

Contents

Foreword xi
Rodelle Weintraub

Acknowledgments xv

Introduction 1

PART I. THE WOMEN IN SHAW'S PLAYS

1. Shaw's Athletic-Minded Women 19
Tracy J. R. Collins

2. Shaw and Cruelty 37
Lawrence Switzky

3. Shutting Out Mother: Vivie Warren as
the New Woman 56
Ann Wilson

4. The Politics of Shaw's Irish Women in
John Bull's Other Island 73
Brad Kent

PART II. SHAW'S RELATIONSHIPS WITH WOMEN

5. Bernard Shaw and the Archbishop's Daughter 95
Leonard W. Conolly

6. Writing Women: Shaw and Feminism
behind the Scenes 112
D. A. Hadfield

7. Feminist Politics and the Two Irish "Georges":
Egerton versus Shaw 133
Margaret D. Stetz

8. The Passionate Anarchist and Her Idea Man 144
Virginia Costello

PART III. SHAVIAN FEMINISM IN THE LARGER WORLD

9. *Mrs Warren's Profession* and the Development of
Transnational Chinese Feminism 171
Kay Li

10. Shaw's Women in the World 177
John M. McInerney

11. The Energy behind the Anomaly: In
Conversation with Jackie Maxwell 199
Interview and editing by D. A. Hadfield

Bibliography 211
Michel Pharand

Contributors 225

Index 227

Foreword

In 1977 when *Fabian Feminist: Bernard Shaw and Woman* was published, women's studies was in its infancy. Coincidentally, the National Women's Studies Association was founded in 1977. Although the first program in women's studies was begun in 1970 at San Diego State College (now San Diego State University) of California, it was not until the 1980s that colleges and universities established departments of women's studies that were not merely a program in some other department such as American studies. A generation and a half of women has matured since those beginnings.

In 1981, Michiko Kakutani in her *New York Times* article "G.B.S. and the Women in His Life and Art" (27 September 1981) complained that Shaw had been adopted as a kind of father figure by certain proponents of women's liberation, singling out Rodelle Weintraub and *Fabian Feminist* for contributing to that idealization. Rather than finding Shaw to be a feminist father figure, Kakutani accused him of "employing the misogynist vocabulary of Schopenhauer and Nietzsche in his plays, describing woman as a predatory animal intent on imprisoning her male prey." What woman did she mean besides Ann Whitefield in *Man and Superman*? And Ann was hardly one of Shaw's New Women. Although Shaw claimed to have "stood up for the intellectual capacity of women," Kakutani wrote, he reserved creativity for the male. (See part 2 of this volume.) She further claimed that he romanticized women, although he did provide "a new role model for thousands of Victorian women." Among Shaw's women who happened to be on the New York stage that season were Candida in *Candida*, Lina Szczepanowska and Hypatia Tarleton (possibly another one of those predatory women) in *Misalliance*, and Eliza Doolittle in *My Fair Lady*, the musical adaptation of *Pygmalion*.

The response to Kakutani's views—whether challenge or confirmation—has been long overdue, despite a number of studies of Shaw's relationships with women and involvement in women's issues. Margot Peters's *Shaw and the Actresses* (1981) examines his relationships with actresses, and J. Ellen Gainor's *Shaw's Daughters: Dramatic and Narrative Constructions of Gender* (1992) focuses on analyses of Shaw's plays. In "Shaw's Life: A Feminist in Spite of Himself" and *Bernard Shaw: The Ascent of the Superman*, Sally Peters discusses Shaw's views on women in a number of contexts, including his family, his marriage, his friendships with women, the women who populate his plays, and his advocacy for women's suffrage. A. M. Gibbs, in his *Bernard Shaw: A Life* (2005), provides an extensive discussion of Shaw's relations with women and their influence on his prose fiction and dramatic writings, and Gibbs includes an entire chapter concerned with Shaw's connections with feminism, on- and offstage.

But no book has focused solely on Shaw's position in historical feminism. Opening this volume and breaking new ground, we find an article on athleticism in Shaw's New Women. Following are discussions about his curious employment of cruelty and pain on and off the stage, another look at the mother-daughter relationship of Kitty and Vivie Warren, the echoes of Ibsen's *A Doll's House* in the plays, and until now the overlooked Irish women, one of whom is named Nora (as in Ibsen), in *John Bull's Other Island*.

Did Shaw practice what he preached? The essays in part 2, "Shaw's Relationships with Women," which focus on Shaw and actual New Women, not stage presentations, open a window into his discomfort with the real thing. How supportive of these real-life New Women was he? Did he encourage them to speak and to act for themselves? Even those of us well acquainted with Shaviana will be surprised by the article about Shaw and the anarchist Emma Goldman.

The final section of *Shaw and Feminisms* examines some aspects of Shavian feminism in the larger world, from transnational Chinese feminism to American ambivalence toward women such as Hillary Clinton as powerful public figures. The volume ends with an interview with Jackie Maxwell, artistic director of the Shaw Festival in Niagara-on-the-Lake, Ontario, Canada. The festival, begun in 1962 with a production of *Candida*, Shaw's own *Doll's House*, celebrated its half century in the 2011 season by performing it again. Other theaters outside of England that perform Shaw regularly are the New York Gingold Theatrical Group's Project Shaw, the Washington D.C. Stage Guild, and ShawChicago.

Michel Pharand's bibliography of writings on Shaw and women brings us up to date on the publications on the topic of Shaw and woman.

Confirm and/or challenge? Is G.B.S. still the father figure of women's liberation, or, when viewed in the twenty-first century, does the father have feet of clay? Coeditors Dorothy Hadfield and Jean Reynolds are to be commended for producing this work and helping us view Shaw from some new perspectives. As the "mother" of *Fabian Feminist*, I am proud of "my daughters," this next generation of scholars who have enabled this comprehensive look at Shaw in the light of modern feminism and feminist theory. Thanks also go to the men and women contributors whose work will expand your knowledge as it did mine.

Rodelle Weintraub
Newark, Delaware

Acknowledgments

The Society of Authors, on behalf of the Bernard Shaw Estate. Previously unpublished material: Copyright © 2012 The Trustees of the British Museum, The Governors and Guardians of the National Gallery of Ireland, and Royal Academy of Dramatic Art.

The John Hay Museum at Brown University for permission to quote from the Mary Hamilton letters.

The British Library for permission to quote from the manuscript for "Mrs. Daintree's Daughter" by Janet Achurch.

Candace Falk for permission to quote from *The Emma Goldman Papers: A Microfilm Edition*, 69 reels (Chadwyck-Healey Inc., 1991).

Some of the papers in this collection were germinated at various conferences and symposia co-sponsored by the International Shaw Society over the last few years. We would like to thank the participants at these events for their support, spirited discussions, and collegiality. We must also thank the International Shaw Society, especially Richard F. Dietrich and Leonard Conolly, for putting these programs together, and for their unflagging enthusiasm for all things Shavian.

A special thank-you goes to Rodelle Weintraub, who edited *Fabian Feminist*—the first landmark collection on Shaw and feminism—three decades ago and who showed tremendous generosity and support for a new volume to reflect a new generation of feminist scholarship.

We are grateful to Amy Gorelick and the team at University Press of Florida, especially Marthe Walters and Jonathan Lawrence, for the care with which they saw this book through the editing process.

The finished volume has also benefited from the astute suggestions of the readers who evaluated the manuscript for the University Press of

Florida. We thank them all for their expertise and improvements, and we readily acknowledge that any remaining errors or infelicities are our own.

And gratitude overflows, as always, to our families for their patience and support during this project.

Introduction

"I say, Archer, my God, what women!" (qtd. in Weintraub 156). Although Robert Louis Stevenson was reacting excitedly to the women in *Cashel Byron's Profession*, he could have been referring to any of Bernard Shaw's plays. The plays, like the novels, are replete with extraordinary women who slap, think, argue, study, manipulate, control, work, nurse, chase, fly, juggle, cross-dress, seduce, save souls, and inspire men. While this diverse cast of female characters may not seem a significant achievement to a twenty-first-century audience—why wouldn't we expect female characters to do these things?—Shaw's original audiences would not have had our luxury of more than a century of feminist thought to challenge the essentialist assumptions of biological determinism and religious ideologies that advocated "natural" female inferiority. Shaw's "secret" for writing such exceptional female characters—"I have always assumed that a woman was a person exactly like myself, and that is how the trick is done" (qtd. in Weintraub 114)—was itself still a revolutionary idea.

Shaw was born into the era of high Victorianism, a period marked by a profound paradox for women. While the most powerful figure in the empire was a woman, Queen Victoria considered her personal crowning achievement to be her absolute, dutiful submissiveness to her husband. At the same time as their monarch modeled perfect feminine submission to masculine authority in her marriage, Victorian women were also simultaneously being relegated to the home by increasing urbanization and the entrenchment of a social and economic middle class. As Sue-Ellen Case has explained (318–20), the tidy organization of life into two categories—public (the domain of men) and private (the domain of women)—has inflected modes of narrative and cultural authority since Aristotle, and throughout the nineteenth century this ideology of "separate spheres" was certainly pervasive: men circulated in the "public" sphere of business, professions, and politics, while women were confined to the "private" sphere of family, children, and home. Throughout the middle of the century, Coventry Patmore published various editions of his long poem *The Angel in the House*, which codified the ethos of the age. Written for his own wife, Emily, *The Angel in the House* celebrates the excruciatingly idealized vision of the wife and mother, a woman whose considerable purities and virtues were marked above all by an absolute submissiveness to her husband's will. The poem engendered very little response at its initial publication, but it became increasingly popular as an ideological counterforce to the feminism that was gaining traction as a social and political force toward the end of the century.

Shaw began writing his largely unsuccessful novels in 1876, but he didn't write his first play, *Widowers' Houses*, until 1892. So, while he was born into the height of Victorian "separate spheres" gender ideologies, he emerged as a dramatic author at the time that those ideologies were on the wane, challenged by an increasingly adamant and organized early feminism. Middle-class women who had opportunity and, often, financial necessity were gaining entry into certain professions, allowing them to achieve independence and financial autonomy. Access to education, changes in property laws, and a population surplus of women led to increased agitation for economic, personal, and political equality with men.[1] "The woman question" dominated public discourse in novels and periodicals, although, as Shaw noted, it was slow to appear on the theatrical stage. Rushing into the void, Shaw became the first British playwright to seriously stage debates around "the woman question," and the extraordinary range of female characters that populate his plays literally embody various perspectives and positions in the debate. Nor did he confine his explorations on female emancipation to the theater: both onstage and off, Shaw invested vast amounts of time and energy to thinking and writing about women—their legal status, their domestic problems, and their relationships. Shaw was a strong advocate for social change, noting, for example, that what the marriage laws were "really founded on is the morality of the tenth commandment, which Englishwomen will one day succeed in obliterating from the walls of our churches by refusing to enter any building where they are publicly classed with a man's house, his ox, and his ass, as his purchased chattels" (*Getting Married* 17).

However, the so-called first-wave feminism of the late nineteenth century became increasingly identified with the issue of universal female suffrage, and it largely lost its momentum with the achievement of that goal in the late nineteenth and early twentieth centuries.[2] A global economic crisis and two world wars helped to divert attention away from lingering systemic inequities that women still faced, like access to professional work, the right to control their own bodies, and pressures to confine themselves to marriage and motherhood. During the Depression era, women often suffered unemployment and economic hardship alongside their male counterparts, and during wartime they enjoyed significantly increased employment opportunities, albeit mostly in the manufacturing sector, when the men were pressed into military service. These "equalities," however, represented less a philosophical shift than a practical one; they were not achieved for women per se but merely as by-products of particular moments of crisis. Ironically, the same state that had required its women to leap into the breach to keep the wheels of industry turning smoothly when their fathers, brothers, husbands, and sons went off to war also expected them to happily relinquish their jobs and their autonomy and return quietly to a life circumscribed by childcare and domestic chores when the men returned and the postwar socioeconomic structure returned to "normal." In the United States, Rosie the Riveter[3] apparently exchanged her kerchief for an apron, left the factory, and became the "suburban housewife . . . the dream image of the young American women and the envy, it was said, of women all over the world" (Friedan 13).

Perhaps not surprisingly, this revival of the "angel in the house" ethos proved unsustainable. In her seminal feminist text, *The Feminine Mystique*, Betty Friedan documents the disjuncture between the "dream image" of woman idealized in media portrayals and the lived experience of unfulfilled desire for real women. By the 1960s, women had once again renewed their attack on social, cultural, and economic discrimination. During this period of second-wave feminism, proponents of the women's liberation movement confronted separate spheres ideology directly, summing up the imbrications of the two in the slogan "the personal is the political." Identifying inequities in both their private and public lives, feminists advocated for increased career choices for women, control of their own bodies and reproduction, and equal rights in all aspects of civil society. In the United States, women's rights advocacy became intertwined with a larger concern over civil rights, officially addressed through the

Presidential Commission on the Status of Women established by President Kennedy in 1961, and facilitated through organizations such as the National Organization for Women (est. 1966). In Canada, the 1967 Royal Commission on the Status of Women developed into the National Action Committee on the Status of Women (est. 1972) to implement recommendations and policies to promote women's equality. Consciousness-raising groups and women's rallies created a collective sisterhood of galvanized energy and action around a broad range of social and political goals.

Although Shaw had died in 1950, before this women's liberation movement had really taken hold, he would have sympathized with many of its goals. He believed that domesticity should be a choice rather than a destiny for women, insisting that confinement in the home was stifling and stultifying. In the preface to *Getting Married* (1908) he complained that "most women are so thoroughly home-bred as to be unfit for human society" (26). In that same play he broached a very nascent version of the arguments around women's right to control reproduction. Without actually addressing the profoundly controversial topics of birth control and abortion, Lesbia Grantham in *Getting Married* effectively critiques the social system that insisted on coupling motherhood with marriage and assumes she will accept both as her patriotic duty: "I ought to have children. I should be a good mother to children. . . . But the country tells me that I cant have a child in my house without a man in it too; so I tell the country that it will have to do without my children. If I am to be a mother, I really cannot have a man bothering me to be a wife at the same time" (119). Even from his earliest plays, he had very aggressively—and at the time scandalously—recognized the relationship between the personal and the political. In *Mrs Warren's Profession*, Kitty overpowers her daughter's liberal feminist assumptions by asserting that in a society where women were systemically kept financially dependent on men, marriage was no better than legalized prostitution: "What is any respectable girl brought up to do but to catch some rich man's fancy and get the benefit of his money by marrying him?—as if a marriage ceremony could make any difference in the right or wrong of the thing! . . . I always thought that it oughtn't to be. It *cant* be right, Vivie, that there shouldn't be better opportunities for women. I stick to that: it's wrong. But it's so, right or wrong; and a girl must make the best of it" (124–25).

A self-proclaimed "world-betterer," Shaw saw that solving women's problems was a key to social reform. Yet he may have fallen victim, to some extent, to his own propensity for paradox and contradiction. As the years went by, he often expressed disappointment at his failures as a reformer: he told biographer Archibald Henderson, "I have produced no permanent impression because nobody has ever believed me" (qtd. in Bentley 128). In 1932 he sighed, "I have solved practically all the pressing questions of our time, but . . . they keep on being propounded as insoluble just as if I had never existed" (qtd. in Bentley 130).

Whether or not Shaw could identify any direct influence of his dramatic or political campaigning on policies and opportunities for women in his lifetime, there is no doubt that many of the ideas for which he was a pioneering champion have become acceptable and accepted. Writing her introduction to *Fabian Feminist* in 1977, at the crest of the second wave, Rodelle Weintraub pointed out, "The gradual turnabout in popular thought that has resulted in many people deciding that much of Shaw is now out of date and 'old hat' suggests how successful he and his like-minded contemporaries were" (11). Society has come around to many of Shaw's positions about the legal, social, and domestic status of women, so that most women—at least in the West—today take for granted the universal suffrage, expanded legal rights, access to careers, and choices about domestic life that many of Shaw's contemporaries still experienced as contested ground.

However, in the decades since *Fabian Feminist* appeared, the optimistic egalitarianism that it seems to celebrate has significantly failed to materialize. Critics of second-wave feminism exposed the way its ethos of homogeneous collectivity neglected specific constituencies: "despite the best of intentions, the collective 'we' generated by the movement tended to be exclusive rather than inclusive. In brief, in assuming the 'essential' priority of (inter) sexual difference, feminism generated a 'we' that failed to take account of how it might simultaneously be inscribed through discourses of class (middle), sexuality (hetero) and above all 'race' (white)" (Aston and Harris 6). Recognizing the validity of this critique, a "third wave" of feminism emerged, characterized by an openness and broadness that recalls a descriptive phrase Eric Bentley employed in his classic study of Shaw: "the Shavian inclusiveness" (xvi). The idea of a singular "feminism" has given way to multiple "feminisms" as third-wave feminists recognized a need for diversity, committing to include women who might have felt neglected by earlier feminist movements: women from diverse racial and ethnic backgrounds, women from working classes, and lesbians, for example, have brought new tools and new insights for discussions about women's rights and women's identities. Feminist issues are similarly diverse, considered to include almost anything that impinges on women's construction of identities, including economics, sex abuse, legislation, culture, and history.

Nonetheless, the very diversity that can be considered third-wave feminism's necessary intervention and strength has also rendered it vulnerable to a certain entropy and disintegration. As Janelle Reinelt points out, the "lack of meaning of the term 'woman' . . . has meant that there is no mobilizing term under which heterogeneous women can identify and organize. By the mid-1990s, feminism had a hard time forming a focal point because identifying with any common properties held by all women seemed impossible" (18). It seems that, without the positive assertion of a concerted response, the critiques of second-wave feminism, to paraphrase Shaw, "keep on being propounded as insoluble just as if [the third wave] had never existed."[4] The focus on rejecting the limitations of the feminism of a particular moment has overwritten the emphasis on feminism as an evolving and productive movement, opening a space where renunciation can turn easily to repudiation: "Indeed it appeared to be in the very nature of feminism that it gave rise to dis-identification as a kind requirement for its existence. But it seems now, over a decade later, that this space of distance from feminism and those utterances of forceful non-identity with feminism have consolidated into something closer to repudiation rather than ambivalence, and it is this vehemently denunciatory stance which is manifest across the field of popular gender debate. This is the cultural space of post-feminism" (McRobbie 15). This is the space where "feminism" becomes "the f-word," a puritanical, restrictive ideology that ostensibly seeks to limit the freedoms that young women feel entitled to. Like Shaw's Vivie Warren, who has unquestioningly accepted and derived benefit from an education that has been paid for by a socioeconomic system she claims the intellectual right to denounce, women growing up in a postmodern world that offers them hitherto-unknown freedoms and opportunities feel entitled to reject and renounce the history of feminist interventions that have made this position possible. Angela McRobbie argues that this is a backlash all too easily and eagerly promoted by the media: "The media has become the key site for defining codes of sexual conduct. It casts judgement and establishes the rules of play. Across these many channels of communication feminism is routinely disparaged" (16).

Since this disparagement is often ostensibly framed ironically, however, for the benefit of younger, more media-literate consumers, popular media encourage female complicity with our own sexual commodification: to dissent is to mark oneself as too stodgy and old-fashioned to get the joke. "Thus the new female subject is, despite her freedom, called upon to be silent, to withhold critique in order to count as a modern sophisticated girl," writes McRobbie. "Indeed this withholding of critique is a condition of her freedom. There is quietude and complicity in the manners of generationally specific notions of cool, and more precisely, an uncritical relation to dominant commercially produced sexual representations which actively invoke hostility to assumed feminist positions from the past, in order to endorse a new regime of sexual meanings based on female consent, equality, participation and pleasure, free of politics" (18).

"Free of politics" and free of history, it seems easier to sell the idea that feminism has achieved its goals and outlived its usefulness. Yet this assumption rests uneasily in a world where, despite repeated campaigns, the United States has yet to ratify the Equal Rights Amendment—an amendment that was initially proposed by first-wave feminists in 1923, and finally passed in 1972, during feminism's second wave. Despite popular perceptions to the contrary among young women, a significant wage gap still exists: a report published by the Canadian Parliament in 2010 confirmed that women still consistently earn about 70 percent of what men earn when other contributing factors are accounted for; moreover, these findings are common across "all the countries that are members of the Organisation for Economic Co-operation and Development" (Cool 1). In Britain, to celebrate the centenary of International Women's Day on March 8, 2011, the charity coalition EQUALS launched a television commercial featuring Judi Dench and Daniel Craig in their James Bond movie characters outlining the pervasive gender inequities that still exist. Perhaps, to loosely paraphrase Mark Twain, the rumors of feminism's irrelevance have been greatly exaggerated.[5]

If feminism's future is imbricated with its revisions and reassessments of its past, it seems useful to revisit one of its original, foundational political and literary figures. In many ways, perceptions of Shaw's relevance have followed the feminist tides. Although he has had steady and stalwart support from publishers—for example, in the University of Toronto Press's Shaw Correspondence series and the University Press of Florida's Shaw series—his plays have virtually disappeared from educational curricula and major theatrical stages around the world. One notable exception to this dramatic neglect has been the Shaw Festival in Niagara-on-the-Lake, Ontario, a summer theater festival that began humbly in the early 1960s and has grown into a world-renowned ensemble company. In an interview for this book, Jackie Maxwell, the Shaw Festival's first female artistic director, acknowledges that one of the festival's major challenges lies in rehabilitating Shaw's reputation, to put him back "on the radar" for the last two or three generations who might know him as the "out of date and 'old hat'" character that Weintraub suggested—if they know him at all. For Maxwell, who has a substantial background working in feminist theater, Shaw is far from antiquated; characterizing his plays as "eerily prophetic," she sees the Shaw Festival "at a cusp" where there is a serious need to put Shaw's plays back into the forum of public debate because his "really progressive and interesting and thorny plays . . . still ask questions and shed light on things that are really worth looking at."

And there is evidence that the tide is, indeed, turning. Shaw societies are active in the United States, Canada, the United Kingdom, India, and Japan, and York University in Toronto has undertaken a major research project to create a comprehensive online scholarly and teaching resource for the entire oeuvre of Shaw's plays.[6] In the United States, two new theater projects have emerged—ShawChicago and Project Shaw in New York—to join Canada's Shaw Festival in showcasing Shaw's plays, and recently, productions of Shaw's plays were also seen on the stage of major theaters and large commercial stages in the United Kingdom and New York. In the scholarly world, annual conferences and symposia are regularly attracting new scholars from around the world, where Shaw's feminism and representations of women continue to figure prominently among the conference papers, articles, and the occasional monograph written on Shaw. However, no book since Weintraub's *Fabian Feminist* in 1977 has attempted to collect materials covering various aspects of Shaw's work and influence and put them into dialogue with contemporary feminist thinking. This volume attempts to address that neglect.

While the contributors to this book pursue a fairly wide range of interests, the resulting essays trace a surprisingly coherent narrative line. Feminism and Shavian thinking come together in three postmodern themes that can often be seen in Shaw's depictions of women: ambivalence, identity, and incompleteness. These themes open the door to a fresh look at Shaw and his views of women. Shaw was never at a loss for things to say about the always vexing question of women's identity, including the factors that may—or may not—make women different from men. Despite his frequent insistence that he saw women and men as fundamentally the same, his plays nonetheless often present intrinsic differences between the two—an ambivalence and ambiguity that has shaped and continues to shape feminist thought and action. This ambivalence is perhaps even clearer offstage in his many relationships with women. As feminist scholars actively pursue materials that have previously been deemed historically insignificant, the collision between the personal and the political in these relationships emerges quite vividly and in directions that sometimes seem quite at odds with his public face. Nonetheless, as Shaw himself said—demonstrating that same feminist ambivalence—"If history repeats itself and the unexpected always happens, how incapable must Man be of learning from experience." Moreover, even as this contemporary reconsideration calls the extent of Shaw's feminism into question, it is important to remember that for many of the actresses and agitators of his age, Shaw played a major role in the early stages of feminism. To derogate his work in hindsight is to dismiss as naive the enthusiasm with which "leading ladies" like Lillah McCarthy embraced his interventions into the "woman question" debates:

> I played Ann Whitefield in "Man and Superman." She was a "new woman" and she made a new woman of me. The women of the previous day, on or off the stage, had been of the stage, stagey. Ann was of the earth, earthy. . . . A real woman on the stage! No wonder people were scandalised! . . . Women, many of them, have told me that Ann brought them to life and that they remodeled themselves upon Ann's pattern. . . . Shaw, with his love of paradox, must have been delighted when he thought that the Court—symbol of all that is decorous and decent—was become the scene of women's emancipation; a double emancipation, for Ann set the leading lady—and with her all the ladies of the theatre—free, and she set the world of women free. (63–64)

Respecting these women means recognizing and acknowledging the radical directions that Shaw's work pointed them toward. Similarly, revisiting Shaw is useful only if we consider what possibilities we can find in Shaw's writings that might point women to new directions for the future.

The essays in part 1, "The Women in Shaw's Plays," deal with Shaw's plays from a variety of angles. In "Shaw's Athletic-Minded Women," Tracy J. R. Collins explores Shaw's answer to the "womanly woman" he so often disparaged. Collins notes that the Shavian New Woman is well known for her intelligence, education, and independence. What has not yet been explored are the physical qualities that characterize Shaw's progressive female characters, a neglect that Collins ties to a larger feminist interest in the role of the body. Reminding readers that if economic and political realities are manifested on the bodies of women, the political significance disappears when the reader dismisses the body in the text, Collins directs her gaze toward the explicit athleticism and physicality that Shaw's emancipated women characters always exhibit to examine the relationship between physical and political liberation.

Lawrence Switzky's "Shaw and Cruelty," on the other hand, shows Shaw making use of masculine dominance over traditionally feminine values. Like others from the Victorian period, Shaw regarded inflicting pain as a necessary masculine prerogative. In *The Philanderer*, Switzky argues, Shaw advances the notion that woman's role is to receive pain, suffering so that men can advance their knowledge. Shaw "feminized" his audiences by inflicting pain on them, unsettling their conventionalism and complacency, but also sensitizing them to suffering and convincing them that the masculine priorities of science and knowledge are not worth the price of suffering.

Ann Wilson's "Shutting Out Mother: Vivie Warren as the New Woman" examines *Mrs Warren's Profession* as a play that questions the New Woman's autonomy by emphasizing the performative nature of social and gender roles. In the play's finale, Vivie may believe she has achieved an absolute independence from her mother, but Wilson argues that Vivie underestimates the extent to which her ability to perform the identity of the New Woman depends on Mrs. Warren's performance of traditional middle-class respectability. For Shaw, Wilson suggests, the New Woman was merely a new type of middle-class womanhood rather than a radical new mode of femininity.

Next, Brad Kent focuses his attention on one of Shaw's more underexamined plays, *John Bull's Other Island*, pointing out that the play's lack of critical attention from feminists is especially bewildering "given the primacy of women as symbols of the nation" (a point also addressed by Wilson). Kent reads the women of *John Bull's Other Island*, especially Nora, as a corrective to the romanticized myths in Irish nationalist literature and cultural revival, arguing that the disenfranchised women demonstrate the potential for political agency through their alignment with influential men and through the trope of hospitality, a quality of domestic life that has a corollary in the political sphere of relations between nations. Kent acknowledges, however, that the portrayal of women in *John Bull's Other Island* can be viewed as profoundly ambivalent and conflicted, perhaps reflecting Shaw's complex relationships with representations of the feminine on both the national and personal levels.

Part 2, "Shaw's Relationships with Women," focuses on Shaw's dealings with four contemporary women: an actress, two aspiring playwrights, and a political anarchist. As Margaret Stetz explains, "Like many a male feminist, [Shaw] was an advocate for the New Woman, so long as *he* was the one giving voice to that character, and so long as she was merely a literary character, not a flesh-and-blood figure who refused to please . . . in other words, so long as she did not dare to resemble himself or behave the way he did toward others." The essays in this section draw extensively on previously unpublished materials to present a new perspective on the interpersonal politics of Shaw's feminism.

In "Bernard Shaw and the Archbishop's Daughter," Leonard W. Conolly examines Shaw's friendship with actress Mary Hamilton. Drawing on previously unpublished letters that Shaw wrote to Hamilton, Conolly documents a charming relationship between the playwright and the actress who caught his attention when she played the first Minnie Tinwell in *The Doctor's Dilemma* (1906) and appeared as the Parlour Maid and Violet in early productions of *Man and Superman* at the Court in 1906–7. Shaw's kindly encouragement of Hamilton, however, contrasts sharply with the vehement disparagement of Achurch, Egerton, and Goldman chronicled in the next three chapters, highlighting his unease with women who insisted on defining freedom and independence on their own terms.

In "Writing Women," D. A. Hadfield focuses on Shaw's friendship with a much more famous actress, Janet Achurch, who was well known as an accomplished presenter of Ibsen's and Shaw's women. But Achurch also aspired to playwriting, and Shaw (who would enthusiastically mentor actor/writer Harley Granville-Barker) took a different tack with Achurch the playwright. Acting and writing, he insisted to her, were incompatible, and in examining the way Shaw discouraged and undermined Achurch's attempts at playwriting, Hadfield raises "the possibility that [Shaw's] success in writing women was built in no small part on his ability to keep them from writing themselves." Excerpts from Achurch's unpublished and unproduced play, "Mrs. Daintree's Daughter," allow Janet Achurch, playwright, to speak for herself for the first time since she wrote her play more than a century ago.

Shaw's troubled relationship with aspiring playwright Achurch finds a more openly hostile parallel in the relationship between Shaw and George Egerton, as documented by Margaret D. Stetz in "Feminist Politics and the Two Irish 'Georges': Egerton versus Shaw." Reginald Golding Bright was a fledgling critic and theatrical agent and a favored protégé of Shaw's when he married "George Egerton" (Mary Chavelita Dunne), an outspoken feminist author closer to Shaw's age than her husband's. Egerton had gained significant literary notoriety with the 1893 publication of her short-story collection, *Keynotes*, but after the marriage she turned her attention to playwriting. As with Achurch, Shaw had little encouragement for her theatrical aspirations, and even fewer kind words for a woman who insisted on the right to express her opinion as doggedly as Shaw expressed his. Like Hadfield, Stetz allows Egerton's voice to emerge from the unpublished and uncirculated materials she includes, especially her play "The Backsliders," written in part to mock and discredit Shaw's "false" feminist pretensions.

In the final essay in this section, "The Passionate Anarchist and Her Idea Man," Virginia Costello explores Shaw's confrontational encounters with Emma Goldman, the freethinking anarchist (1869–1940). Costello points out that in most of his relationships with political women, Shaw usually had the upper hand, offering advice to women who admired his brilliant achievements. However, Goldman, who wrote extensively about Shaw and admired his plays, accused Shaw of not living up to the radicalism he advocated in his writings; Shaw, in return, preferred to forget that the two had ever met. Even more than in Hadfield's or Stetz's essay, Costello's account of this "peculiar relationship" derives from the woman's perspective: using unpublished materials from Goldman's archives, Costello shows us a unique image of Shaw as seen through the words of a passionate feminist anarchist.

Shaw, refusing from the start to embrace the "art for art's sake" philosophy that was popular with many of his contemporaries, always insisted that the theater had a sacred trust to engage, convert, and empower thoughtful people to correct the social, economic, and political injustices they should see around them. Part 3, "Shavian Feminism in the Larger World," examines Shaw's continuing impact on women in the world.

Kay Li explores the crucial role Shaw played in developing transnational Chinese feminism in the past century, showing how he enabled Chinese feminists and their supporters to assert themselves against the restrictions of the traditional Chinese patriarchal feudal society. Li argues that Chinese productions of Shaw's plays empowered Chinese women to reexamine their traditional Chinese patriarchal family system and to campaign for the right to vote.

John M. McInerney's "Shaw's Women in the World" considers the question of Shaw's relevance to women today. McInerney notes that Shaw still has much to say to American women who aspire to significant leadership roles, and indeed, to women already in those positions, like Hillary Clinton and Sarah Palin, who are navigating their way "through social obstacles, storms of opposition, and conflicting currents" in a society that is still apparently uncomfortable with the appearance of women as powerful public figures.

This section concludes with an interview with Jackie Maxwell, artistic director of the Shaw Festival (Niagara-on-the-Lake, Canada). Maxwell discusses the challenges and rewards when twenty-first-century actors and directors at the festival encounter and embody Shaw's women. While audiences and actors today can take for granted many of the feminist reforms that Shaw advocated, the current popularity of the festival and even the shift to a slightly younger demographic suggest that Shaw and the questions his plays pose are still tremendously relevant to contemporary society. As a committed feminist herself, Maxwell is also making a concerted effort to revive plays written by Shaw's female contemporaries, reclaiming them from historical obscurity and bringing their voices back into a dialogue with Shaw's claims about what women have wanted, then and now.

Shaw scholars have a long history of conscientiously documenting writings by and about Shaw on various topics. Readers interested in looking further into the topic of Shaw and feminism will find the appendix, a bibliography updated from a list previously published by Michel Pharand, of tremendous interest.

Taken together, these essays illustrate Shaw's continuing relevance to women as they continue to probe their role in today's complex world. Whether we find inspiration or caution in his feminist ideas and practices,

Shaw can still speak to us today. As each wave of feminism crests and falls, we can expect women to continue to find much that is wise, misguided, prophetic, and provocative in Shaw's astounding literary output.

Notes

1. George Gissing treats the effects of these social and demographic changes in his novel, *The Odd Women*. The title refers to the phrase assigned in the late nineteenth century to these "surplus" women. In 2010 the Shaw Festival premiered a play called *Age of Arousal* by Canadian playwright Linda Griffiths, which was loosely based on Gissing's novel.

2. In the United Kingdom, property-owning women over the age of thirty were declared eligible to vote in 1918 (for men, the age was nineteen or twenty-one); it was another decade before women in the UK achieved voting rights equal to men's. In Canada some women became eligible to vote in certain provinces as early as 1884, and all women were given the franchise at the federal level in 1918; however, it took until 1940 for the final province (Quebec) to grant female suffrage in provincial elections. In the United States, the timeline for suffrage similarly varies by state, but by 1920 the Nineteenth Amendment effectively finished the process by prohibiting states to discriminate on the basis of sex. Our thanks to Tony Gibbs for pointing out that universal suffrage was attained in New Zealand in 1893 and in South Australia in 1893; local voting privileges were given to female property owners in South Australia in 1861.

3. Rosie the Riveter was a fictional character created to encourage women to join the workforce during World War II. She was usually depicted wearing blue coveralls, with a red and white dotted kerchief over her hair, flexing her right arm and making a fist with her right hand.

4. See Aston and Harris, who provide another good overview of "postfeminism's" deliberately constructed relationship to second-wave feminism.

5. Jennifer Pozner has christened this "False Feminist Death Syndrome."

6. For more information on this project, see "The Orion-Shaw Project" at shaw.yorku.ca.

Works Cited

Aston, Elaine, and Geraldine (Gerry) Harris. "Feminist Futures and the Possibilities of 'We'?" *Feminist Futures?* Ed. Elaine Aston and Geraldine Harris. Houndsmills, Basingstoke, Hampshire: Palgrave Macmillan, 2006. 1–16.

Bentley, Eric. *Bernard Shaw*. New York: New American Library, 1985.

Case, Sue-Ellen. "Classic Drag: The Greek Creation of Female Parts." *Theatre Journal* 37.3 (1985): 317–27.

Cool, Julie. *Wage Gap between Women and Men*. Social Affairs Division, Parliamentary Information and Research Service. Publication No. 2010-30-E. Canada: Library of Parliament, 29 July 2010. http://www2.parl.gc.ca/Content/LOP/ResearchPublications/2010-30-e.pdf, accessed 26 February 2011.

Friedan, Betty. *The Feminine Mystique.* New York: Dell, 1963.

McCarthy, Lillah. *Myself and My Friends.* Keystone Library edition. London: Thornton Butterworth, 1934.

McRobbie, Angela. *The Aftermath of Feminism: Gender, Culture, and Social Change.* London: Sage 2009.

Pozner, Jennifer. "The 'Big Lie': False Feminist Death Syndrome, Profit, and the Media." *Catching a Wave: Reclaiming Feminism for the 21st Century.* Ed. Rory Dickerson and Alison Piepmeier. Boston: Northeastern UP, 2003. 31–56.

Reinelt, Janelle. "Navigating Postfeminism: Writing Out of the Box." *Feminist Futures?* Ed. Elaine Aston and Geraldine Harris. Basingstoke, Hampshire: Palgrave Macmillan, 2006. 17–33.

Shaw, Bernard. *Getting Married; Press Cuttings.* Harmondsworth, Middlesex: Penguin, 1986.

———. *Mrs Warren's Profession.* Ed. L. W. Conolly. Peterborough, Ont.: Broadview, 2005.

Weintraub, Rodelle, ed. *Fabian Feminist: Bernard Shaw and Woman.* University Park: Penn State P, 1977.

I

The Women in Shaw's Plays

1

Shaw's Athletic-Minded Women

• • • • • • • • • • • • • • • • • •

TRACY J. R. COLLINS

In "The 'Unwomanly Woman' in Shaw's Drama," Sonja Lorichs's contribution to *Fabian Feminist: Bernard Shaw and Woman*, edited by Rodelle Weintraub, Lorichs noted that "Shaw, with his usual foresight, anticipated the development of women into something quite different from the Victorian 'womanly woman,' and in several of his plays insists that this development must be through education" (100). As Lorichs points out, Shaw's plays frequently demonstrate his dramatic support for the purposeful education of women, a proposition that was still the subject of some controversy and resistance among segments of late-Victorian society. But Shaw's ideas about the transformation of female identity actually go much further than Lorichs notes, into even more controversial territory than the more obvious claim for decent educational opportunities for women. What has yet to be examined is the extent to which just as many of Shaw's plays demonstrate his understanding that, in addition to intellectual education, the evolution of womanhood must also come from a fundamental physical fitness and athleticism.

For Shaw, the essential New Woman was usually an athlete. Irrespective of Shaw, in the last twenty-five years of analysis of the definition and theorization of the New Woman by scholars, none has addressed her essential athleticism. Moreover, the existing studies of Shaw's portrayals of the New Woman as politically and sexually liberated do not elaborate to consider as well his simultaneous inventions of the athletic and physically liberated woman. As recently as 2008, John Louis DiGaetani in *Stages of Struggle* describes Shaw as "clearly interested in what defines masculinity and what defines femininity despite the Victorian strictures on rigid sexual roles" (11), but focuses his discussion around his observation that "repeatedly in Shaw's plays, the main characters become variations of two of Shaw's favorite character types: masculine women and effeminate men" (10). DiGaetani certainly has carnal sexuality as his emphasis, but at no point does he explicitly notice that the "masculinity" of Shaw's female characters is created by their physical strength and fitness.

Shaw's repeated representation of athletic women emphasizes his interest in them and dramatizes how this quality would enable their progressive personality and politics. Himself an avid practitioner of physical fitness regimes, it is perhaps not surprising that Shaw demonstrated a strong consciousness of the bodies of his female characters. Shaw's own stamina, energy, athleticism, the admiration for fitness and athleticism, and the assertiveness that accompany possession of them predict the feminist personalities he created. Shaw also had real-life models of this empowered female personality. Amber Reeves, the founder of the Cambridge Fabian Society, was not only a brilliant student but was exceptionally physically fit, even taking up jujitsu.[1] From *Widowers' Houses* (1892) to *The Millionairess* (1934), Shaw's plays present female characters who are not only interesting representations of politically and socially emancipated and liberated people but are also required to be performed onstage as energetic, physically fit, active, and athletic.

Shaw clearly understood the need for athletic women as actresses to portray his women properly. When Shaw was trying to get Katharine Hepburn to star in *The Millionairess,* he is reported to have asked Lawrence Langner, "What sort of athlete is Kate? She has to do Judo." Langner's wife, Armina, replied that Hepburn was "a very good athlete." Shaw, not hearing correctly, replied, "I know she's a good actress. I mean is she strong?" to which Armina answered, "Is she strong? Why, she gets up and plays tennis every morning. She's one of the most athletic girls I know." Shaw then joked that it might not be wise for Hepburn to star in his play because she might kill her fellow actors if she were so strong (Cohen 3). Though Shaw wrote *The Millionairess,* with its athletic female heroine, in 1934, it was not the first such character in his works. For example, a few years earlier, Shaw had Orinthia in *The Apple Cart* (1928) rolling about on the floor in a wrestling match with the king (*BH* 6: 349). Going back even further, to his second play, Julia Craven burst onto stage in *The Philanderer* (1898) and straight into a wrestling match with Leonard Charteris (*BH* 1: 144). Shaw had been writing a version of this physically robust feminine personality from the beginning of his playwriting career. Even before the epithet "New Woman" was formalized in print in 1894, the female characters in Shaw's *Plays Unpleasant* (1898) had expressed their emotional and intellectual emancipation in explicitly athletic and physical terms, embodying their freedom and power in ways that critics have yet to address.

Shavian scholarship is not alone in overlooking the role of bodies in feminist identities. It is only within the last two decades that feminist theorists have begun reclaiming and revising the traditional female body. Some have attacked the ways in which the female body has been over-written by social constructions, while others focus on the multiplicity of bodies, thereby challenging the notion of any stereotypical female body. Perhaps no one has done this more effectively than Elizabeth Grosz in her seminal work, *Volatile Bodies: Toward a Corporeal Feminism* (1994). Grosz asserts that for a feminist theoretical approach to the body to succeed it must "avoid the impasse posed by dichotomous accounts of the person which divide the subject into mutually exclusive categories of mind and body. . . . While dualism must be avoided, so too, where possible must biologistic or essentialist accounts of the body" (21–23). Ultimately, feminists have begun to look for the ways in which the body emerges in, disrupts, reflects, or redirects contemporary narrative discourses. "If economic and political realities are manifested on the bodies of women, the political significance disappears when the reader dismisses the body in the text" (Smith and Watson 36). Simply put, the body cannot be ignored. People are their bodies. It is, indeed, the entirety of the subject personality—certainly in any analysis that rejects dualist theories of human nature. This non-dualist premise currently characterizes the most reputable behavioral and scientific anthropologies and psychologies.[2]

So far only Shirley Castelnuovo and Sharon Guthrie in *Feminism and the Female Body: Liberating the Amazon Within* (1998) find that feminist theorists who have set out to reclaim the female body do not escape a crippling emphasis and implication of Cartesian dualism. They examine the work of feminist theorists who claim to transcend this dualism, such as Elizabeth Grosz, Luce Irigaray, Iris Young, Frigga Haug, and Judith Butler. According to Castelnuovo and Guthrie, the assumption underlying the work of these theorists "is that a focus on the body automatically results in a non-dualistic analysis. If we look closely at their liberatory analyses, however, we find that they have not actually done what they claim to do: eliminate dualism" (32). Not addressing the strong textual presence of bodily empowerment causes this particular turbulence in the New Woman feminist argument. Emphasizing only cognitive activities without realizing that in order to empower and encourage women cognitively they must be transformed physically ignores a crucial aspect of New Woman discourse. As Castelnuovo and Guthrie write: "Transformation of the female self requires bodily transformation as well" (32). "The mind and body must be conceived of as a unity in understanding the social construction of gender and sexuality and in developing and embodying feminist perspectives" (35).

Building on this insight about the united mind and body, Castelnuovo and Guthrie set out to "cultivate and celebrate an Amazonian presence among women" (1), to rehabilitate and return respect to the "Amazon" personality. They define an Amazon as "a warrior," but not a warrior "with a blade or gun in hand." Instead they define her warrior-like qualities in terms of her challenge to hierarchies of gender:

> She has developed her bodily and mental skills to their fullest capacity and she directs her energies toward achieving equality for women. Consequently, she has the power and commitment to equalize the fields on which hierarchical gender relations are played out. Moreover, because she is aware of the need to protect herself physically, she has the potential to minimize, if not eliminate, the physical power imbalances between herself and the men with whom she interacts; and she knows that, when necessary, she has the right to defend herself. She is a woman who represents a significant challenge to patriarchal domination. (2)

Castelnuovo and Guthrie use the contemporary female bodybuilder as one example of this modern Amazon. They agree that women's competitive bodybuilding is a singular site of female resistance to patriarchal constructions.

With their focus on the contemporary, Castelnuovo and Guthrie fail to realize that the twenty-first-century female bodybuilder/"Amazon" has at least one ancestor: the historical New Woman of the 1890s, who was also characterized by physical fitness combined with mental fitness. In the great majority of cases, these virtues were complementary in the New Woman or she was not a New Woman. The simplicity of this conflation was not lost on Shaw as he staged his own version of the New Woman throughout his career, but until now the proposition represented in the writing of Castelnuovo and Guthrie has not been brought to the study of the nature of the New Woman in general or of Shaw's New Woman in particular.

Reading the physically fit and athletic female body in Shaw's plays is important because at a time in history when women's bodies were essentialized and bodies were literally asked by society to disappear into private invisibility, Shaw chose to write plays that not only brought attention to the physical female body but also explicitly named and assigned the ways that their bodies could be used and were being used as agents of emancipation and change.[3] More often than not, the female body in his plays was an instrument of subversive practice in her pursuit of a social and political emancipation.

In the *Plays Unpleasant* collection, Shaw presents three examples of strong and athletic women. *Widowers' Houses, The Philanderer*, and *Mrs Warren's Profession* were plays intended to give constructive advice to the late-Victorian world as Shaw saw it. On his way to challenging his audience, he created female characters who are intellectually exceptional and physically forceful. *Widowers' Houses* depicts Blanche Sartorius as such a woman. She is described as a "well-fed, good-looking, strongminded young woman . . . and none the worse for being vital and energetic rather than delicate and refined" (*BH* 1: 49). Her father notes that she has a "strong character and . . . physical courage, which is greater than that of most men, I can assure you" (89). Despite the conventional marriage plot of this play, Shaw creates in Blanche the first of the many woman characters in his plays who were strong enough intellectually and physically to make their own rules and create their own futures. Not only does Blanche physically terrorize her maid, but in the final scene she uses her strength to intimidate Harry Trench. Thus, Shaw represents a robust Blanche calling upon the personality of her athleticism to impose her will. For Blanche, the power of her physical presence gives her a new discursive site from which to express the liberatory needs of her emerging New Woman personality, but her unbridled use of bullying force makes her otherwise a difficult character to sympathize with. Shaw's inability to present Blanche as a more admirable role model might suggest that Shaw himself was still coming to terms with the force of the intellectually and physically liberated woman that he had unleashed. He also might have been warning readers that, even in a woman, physical power can easily turn to cruelty if not tempered by self-control.

Shaw's second play, *The Philanderer* (1893), provides almost as explicit a description of an athletic New Woman, the late-Victorian version of a liberated woman. But in *The Philanderer*, the ideal liberated woman emerges from the amalgamation of three characters: Julia Craven, Sylvia Craven, and Grace Tranfield all possess particular aspects of the prototypical New Woman Shaw is characterizing. Shaw chooses to focus upon their physical bodies in order to display their liberated personalities. Grace Tranfield, a thirty-two-year-old widow who is attracted to the philandering Leonard Charteris, is old enough to have learned to control her body. For example, when Julia first sees her with Charteris, she runs at Grace, who "preserves her self-possession" (*BH* 1: 144). She "enters briskly like a habitually busy woman" (183). Charteris calls her a "thoroughbred" and finds that she "doesn't scream and cry every time" her heart is "pinched" (184). Grace has no desire to be coddled by a man. She conducts her daily affairs for her own benefit and not for a man or children. She likes Charteris because he is fun, but she has no intention of marrying him. She is an early compilation of the marriage-as-prostitution trope that Shaw defines in so many of his plays. She is "an advanced woman," a woman who "belongs to herself and to nobody else" (142), and embodies that self-possession physically and emotionally.

Sylvia Craven is another potential New Woman, but unlike Grace Tranfield, Sylvia Craven's fitness is shown through her choice of clothing. We meet her for the first time at the opening of act 2. She is "sitting in the middle of the settee before the fire, reading a volume of Ibsen. She is a pretty girl of eighteen, small and trim, [and associated with athleticism because she is] wearing a mountaineering suit of a Norfolk jacket and breeches with neat stockings and shoes" (167). Her vesture, brought about exclusively because of liberated women's recent embrace of male clothing and male sports, is the costume that became a familiar uniform of the New Woman. In contrast to her sister Julia, the gentlemen at the club she belongs to declare that she is full of Ibsen (169). A generation younger than Grace, Sylvia displays her inclinations toward emancipation more assertively by wearing this practical costume that signals an affinity for physical activity. Her movements are also described as energetic and aggressive. She is described as "self-assertive" (167). She "snatches" up her detachable skirt and "flounces" out the door (168). At the club she insists that she not be referred to as Sylvia but by her last name as the men generally are accustomed to doing. Charteris roguishly responds by slapping her on the shoulder as he says, "I forgot. I beg your pardon, Craven old chap" (179).

Julia Craven is the most elaborate example of the physically strong and athletic woman in this play. Where Grace displays mental strength and liberal ideas, and Sylvia displays her emancipation through her clothing, Julia performs these same qualities in physical energy. Her first entrance on the stage, an interruption of an assignation between Charteris and Grace, is noted with a "violent double knock" at the door (143). When she enters the rooms, she "comes straight at Grace. Charteris runs across behind the sofa and stops her. She struggles furiously with him" (144). The encounter ends with her "striking him in the face as she frees herself" (144). By the end of the first act, she has pushed and shoved and run and blocked entrances and exits of both Charteris and Grace. The second act begins much the same way. Julia's entrance is a game of the "huntress and her prey" as she chases Charteris about the club (177). During this act she frees herself from the grip of Charteris and pushes him into a chair. The third act once again repeats this mode of action. Julia shakes Charteris, grabs his lapels, and reaches up to slap him (200, 219). Being athletic alone, however, is not enough. In the end Julia wins a physical struggle with Charteris but loses the political high ground because she ends up marrying in a conventional sort of way by the end of the play. Her remarkable physical fitness and athletic ability do not get her the longed-for freedom of choosing that someone like Grace achieves. All three of these women interact with Charteris, who may be a stand-in for Shaw. Should he choose the woman strong in mind, in potential, or in body? Thus, the problem that Shaw begins to present in *Widowers' Houses* he engages much more fully in *The Philanderer*. But here he stages the three personalities separately; as "unpleasant" as this play is, Shaw still has not yet shocked the audience by offering in a single woman character one who has the very public business sense and contempt for traditional beliefs that Grace has, with the physically liberating costume and meditative disposition of Sylvia, and with the outright physical strength, athleticism, and determination of Julia. His audiences would have to wait until his next play.

Perhaps Shaw's most memorable physically fit and emancipated female in the *Plays Unpleasant* collection comes in the character of Mrs. Warren's daughter, Vivie, in *Mrs Warren's Profession* (1893). Vivie has the poise, self-control, and intelligence of Grace Tranfield, the sartorial costume and reading list of Sylvia, and the physical fitness and athleticism of Julia. Vive has achieved emancipation in proportion to her athleticism. Vivie is athletic. She rides a bicycle and plays lawn tennis (*BH* 1: 272, 277). She is physically well conditioned, as she demonstrates by comparing her slim wrists with "the rolls of fat" on her mother's (307). She has fit legs and strong lungs, and can walk seemingly forever (307). She is so strong that she causes grown men to wince by her apparently unconsciously bone-bruising handshake, and she can throw lawn furniture around like matchsticks (273, 274, 282). The puckish Shaw almost subverts the meaning of this radical combination of superior human qualities, describing her as "an attractive specimen of the sensible, able, highly-educated young middle-class Englishwoman. Age 22. Prompt, strong, confident, self-possessed. Plain business-like dress, but not dowdy" (273). Vivie, when the label becomes available in 1894, will be an example of the New Woman. Presciently, in this incarnation Shaw makes her explicitly physically strong and athletic. At the same time, Shaw depicts her as choosing her destiny with a fierce independence when she decides against a traditional Victorian feminine existence. By the end of the play she has made the conscious choice to live without a man, in marriage or otherwise. She is earning her living in a business that uses her skills, and she engages in whatever activities with whomever she wants, including living in what might turn out to be a lesbian relationship with her similarly independent business partner.

In *Misalliance*, by contrast, Shaw offers Lina Szczepanowska and Hypatia Tarleton as young women raised in different familial traditions, the acrobatic Szczepanowska clan fostering in their daughter the empowerment and freedom through physical conditioning that the sheltered daughter of the Tarleton's Underwear empire can only yearn for. By the time Shaw wrote *Misalliance* (1909), his treatise on parenting, he had already established himself as a formidable playwright. In addition, he was associated with progressive ideas in England. His theory of parenting, and especially how to rear a female child, was radical. The interesting thing about Shaw's notion of parenting in this particular play has most to do with his ideas on the education of children, which he asserts should not dismiss one aspect of their development in favor of another. At the beginning of the play we are presented with Johnny Tarleton and Bentley Summerhays. Each represents one half of the theory of the ideal person. Johnny is "all body and no brains" (*BH* 4: 145). Bentley is "all brains and no more body than is absolutely necessary" (146). But for Shaw, the fates of both young men reinforce Shaw's theory that mind and body are not separate, for either the ideal male or female of the species.

The female child of the Tarleton family is Hypatia. She is "a typical English girl of a sort never called typical: that is, she has . . . swift glances and movements that flash out of a waiting stillness, boundless energy and audacity held in leash" (150). In Hypatia, Shaw has created a charismatic female personality, but not one who would be understood as typical by the public. She is interesting because few people at the time knew how to recognize that girls had energy and bodies that would choose activity and exercise just as their male counterparts did. In this context, Hypatia tries very hard to be a "typical" English girl, all the while feeling like a pent-up animal. Her education has also been typically philistine and British in that it has ignored her body. Hypatia reminds her mother that she also does not know as much about her body as she should: "There was a physiology and hygiene class started at school; but of course none of our girls were let attend it" (159). Shaw understands not only that females have bodies that need and desire to be active, but also that they should be given opportunities to know their gender's biology. In the absence of these opportunities, Hypatia spends the first half of the play lamenting her situation and arguing for a more active life. She likes Lord Summerhays because he called her a glorious young beast: "I like that. Glorious young beast expresses exactly what I like to be" (181). Hypatia's speech outlines the situation that women inherit and that women such as Hypatia then struggle to escape: "I'm fed up with nice things: with respectability, with propriety! When a woman has nothing to do, money and respectability mean that nothing is ever allowed to happen to her. I dont want to be good; and I dont want to be bad: I just dont want to be bothered about either good or bad: I want to be an active verb" (181–82).

If Hypatia's parents have sheltered her to keep her out of trouble, their fears are misplaced: Hypatia has no desire to be a "bad" girl. Rather, she wants to be a woman who has done something in her life. She wants to be active, telling Lord Summerhays, "I mean to make a fight for living" (182). Marshaling the "fight" of an "active verb" in the body of a "glorious young beast," Hypatia will seek intellectual and political freedom with her corporeal self. She must be allowed to live an active life, to run around, to do physical labor, and even to smoke. In short, she must be allowed to have the freedom to do with her body what she desires. Mr. Tarleton wrongly believes he has made a mistake in allowing his daughter a liberal education. He does not think for a moment that his daughter's life has been at all an inactive one. At the same time, he realizes that "superabundant vitality is a physical fact that cant be talked away" (185). Shaw's diction here is unequivocal. He insists that Hypatia's personality is founded in a "physiology" and the "physical fact" of a "superabundant vitality." These are the properties of an athlete.

After Mr. Tarleton notices that Hypatia wishes "adventures to drop out of the sky" (185), one does just that. Easily one of the most electric female characters in the Shavian gallery is Lina Szczepanowska, the Polish, cross-dressing, acrobatic airplane passenger. Shaw assigns to a foreign woman the task of demonstrating to the members of the house, as well as to the audience, what a truly free female could look like. Immediately upon arrival Lina is mistaken for a man because of her male-associated aviator's clothing. Nonetheless, her presence eloquently testifies that if a woman is to have a body that is active and free, she must have the appropriate clothing. She must be wearing pants, boots, and even goggles. Upon being offered a gown for dinner, Lina responds with a matter-of-fact refusal: "I'm quite comfortable as I am. I am not accustomed to gowns; they hamper me and make me feel ridiculous" (196).

Next, for a woman to be free, she must be allowed to take risks. Lina explains her family tradition of risking their lives: "Not a single day has passed without some member of my family risking his life—or her life" (195). Women are no different from men in this pursuit. It is pertinent that the next detail Shaw offers is about Lina's family profession. She comes from a family of acrobats. Lina is not a teacher or a financial actuarist like Vivie Warren. She has a profession that requires physical fitness and great athleticism. Most importantly, her profession involves balance, both practically and symbolically, in order to be successful on the tightrope: a truly free woman must have a balance between her body and her mind.

Shaw seems to have anticipated by some one hundred years the arguments of Castelnuovo and Guthrie, that "transformation of the female self requires bodily transformation as well. The mind and body must be conceived of as a unity" (32). As an exemplum, Lina explains that the best way to quiet the soul is to read the Bible while juggling six balls in the air all the time one is reading (200). The Bible and juggling are mantras for the mind and the body. Through them it is possible for a person, regardless of gender, to integrate the self, a balance that Lina has been able to achieve.

After being courted by every man in the house, Lina voices Shaw's explanation of women's position in his current society: "It is disgusting. It is not healthy. Your women are kept idle and dressed up for no other purpose than to be made love to. I have not been here an hour; and already everybody makes love to me as if because I am a woman it were my profession to be made love to" (248). In fact, the physical fitness of each household member is called into question by Lina. Each time a man has difficulty with her rejection, she advises him to straighten out his mind by exercising his body and then drags him off to the gymnasium. Next Lina describes the life of a truly free woman: "I am an honest woman: I earn my living. I am a free woman: I live in my own house. I am a woman of the world: I have thousands of friends: every night crowds of people applaud me, delight in me, buy my picture, pay hard-earned money to see me. I am strong: I am skilful: I am brave: I am independent: I am unbought: I am all that a woman ought to be" (249).

Lina offers her life not only as a role model for Hypatia Tarleton but as a role model, as well, for the men in the house, for the audience, and for all of England. A liberated woman who is by nature physically fit and athletic, Lina is by far the most engaging person onstage throughout the play, one who in turn inspires Hypatia to focus her own considerable physical energy into achieving a self-determined emancipation from the family home. In *Misalliance*, Shaw concertedly elaborated his theory that physical fitness and athleticism would empower twentieth-century women toward liberation.

The century, nevertheless, is young, and Shaw is far from finished: *Fanny's First Play* (1911), like *Misalliance*, stages an education for England's youth in the value of expressing women's emancipation through physical actions. In his preface to the play he asks, "Is it any wonder that I am driven to offer to young people in our suburbs the desperate advice: Do something that will get you into trouble?" (*BH* 4: 345). Shaw then uses a female to write the play that will model this moral to modern youth, and it is a female child whom Fanny uses as the youth to receive Shaw's lesson. As a metatext, a play within a play, Fanny O'Dowda has written a script featuring Margaret Knox, a young woman who has been imprisoned for fighting a policeman while attending a concert at a gallery. She was attacked and physically roughed up by the police. Through it all, she held her own.

Afterwards she learned, "I know now that I am stronger than you and papa. I havent found that happiness of yours that is within yourself; but Ive found strength. For good or evil I am set free; and none of the things that used to hold me can hold me now" (396). Her pleasant disposition, family money, and social position could not set her free. It is her belief in the strength of her own physical body that can. She found she could physically hold her own in the world and survive the serious physical stress of two weeks in prison. Policemen twisted her arms, attacked her, and shoved her. So she punched a policeman in the mouth and knocked out two of his teeth. She fought back, defended herself and her right to be out in the evening and to enjoy herself without a chaperone. Significantly, in order for Margaret to gain equality, she has to be physically assertive and skillful—even pugilistic.

While it is always assumed that Margaret will marry, her physical prowess ensures that she will control the terms of her marriage; she will not be bullied into it by any man. Margaret goes to visit Bobby Gilbey, the man her parents seem to have arranged for her to marry, but they both have since learned that they really are not in love. It is clear they are good friends, and that they will not marry. After hearing about her escapades, her going out to the gallery and talking with a French lieutenant, he asks her why she went out in the first place, and she assures him "I didn't do it for a lark, Bob: I did it out of the very depths of my nature. I did it because I'm that sort of person" (406). What sort of person is she? When Lieutenant Duvallet, the Frenchman with whom Margaret began to dance at the gallery, calls on Margaret at Bobby's house, he sees the two of them wrestling, boxing each other, and pushing each other. Afterwards Margaret chides Bobby, saying, "Monsieur Duvallet will think I'm always fighting," but Duvallet quickly compliments her: "Practicing jujitsu or the new Iceland wrestling. Admirable, Miss Knox. The athletic young Englishwoman is an example to all Europe" (409). Margaret's father later arrives and is met by Juggins, the footman. Mr. Knox is anxious about his daughter's marriage prospects, but Juggins advises Mr. Knox that to worry about his daughter getting married is futile: "Your daughter, sir, will probably marry the man she makes up her mind to marry. She is a lady of very determined character" (430). Shaw has also made it clear that Margaret's acquisition of personal and political emancipation will be greatly dependent upon her physical strength and athleticism. Fanny will marry whom she wants not because of her parents' indulgence but because no man can force her to do otherwise. The personality Shaw created for Fanny is one in which she would literally beat her way out of any marriage she did not choose for herself. And, significantly, Margaret is an alter ego for her creator: Fanny O'Dowda, author of the play, has had her own encounter with the police. As Trotter declares in the epilogue, "You cant deceive me. That bit about the police was real" (440).

Shaw imagined other strategies in his recommendation that a woman should possess physical fitness and toughness in order to obtain any sort of independence. Two of his plays about cross-dressing female soldiers make this point dramatically by literally writing these women as men. In *Annajanska* (1917), a seventeen-page play about a cross-dressing female, the Grand Duchess Annajanska is a physically strong woman. At the beginning of the play she is escorted, as a prisoner, into the office of General Strammfest. Shaw describes her entrance: "The Grand Duchess bursts into the room, dragging with her two exhausted soldiers hanging on desperately to her arms. The two soldiers make a supreme effort to force her to sit down. She flings them back so that they are forced to sit on the bench to save themselves from falling backwards over it" (*BH* 5: 238). Annajanska threatens to beat three soldiers about the head and reports how she bit one of them. This all sets up the dramatic irony that Shaw will present in the dramatization of her physical "acrobatics."

After a great deal of arguing with the General about how she has been consorting with a common soldier, well beneath her station, Annajanska describes to the General the time she was taken to the circus as a child: "It was my first moment of happiness, my first glimpse of heaven. I ran away and joined the troupe [of acrobats]. They caught me and dragged me back to my gilded cage, but I had tasted freedom; and they never could make me forget it" (247). He is shocked: "Freedom! To be the slave of an acrobat!" She reminds him that as a female member of the court she was already physically enslaved by her requirement "to be exhibited to the public"—"Oh, I was trained to that. I had learnt that part of the business at court"—and longed to mark her political emancipation in physical terms.

When the General protests that "You had not been taught to strip yourself half naked and turn head over heels," Annajanska assures him, "I *wanted* to get rid of her swaddling clothes and turn head over heels. I

wanted to, I wanted to, I wanted to. I can do it still. Shall I do it now?" (247). Once again, Shaw returns to the image of the acrobat—the human exemplar of miraculous athleticism—to facilitate the woman's desire for emancipation. All Annajanska wishes to do is be free. In her character Shaw demonstrates, as he began to do with Sylvia Craven's costume some thirty years earlier, that being acrobatically free from her clothes is liberating, as Lina Szczepanowska's acrobatics inform her passion for independence. The sublime acrobat's habit for physical liberation cannot tolerate the tyranny of social inferiority and political slavery.

The Grand Duchess's final acrobatic move is metaphoric as she reveals herself to the General as the cross-dressed soldier she was reported to have run away with earlier. The Duchess asks the General if he is sure that the soldiers in his command would not sooner rally to her call than to his. He responds, "Only if you were a man and a soldier!" (250). Of course, the irony is that he does not realize she is both of these. Annajanska asks him, "Suppose I find you a man and a soldier?" The General is sure she is referring to the acrobat that she ran away with, not realizing that she is the real acrobat here. When the General goes to the window to find the man she says "is here," Annajanska "takes off her cloak and appears in the uniform" of the soldier (250). The paternalistic chauvinism of the General is then vanquished. Annajanska is strong and athletic, but she has had to look like a man in order to be seen as having these qualities. She could do so because she was an acrobat, physically and philosophically.

Annajanska was, of course, not Shaw's only cross-dressing female soldier. Near the start of his career, he had already introduced the type in *The Man of Destiny* (1895), where The Lady also learns "the sensation of freedom from petticoats" (*BH* 1: 655) dressed as a soldier.

And at the height of his dramatic power, Shaw created his most famous cross-dressing soldier, a woman who well understood the need to look like a man in order to be seen as having the qualities normally associated with one. Of all his plays, *Saint Joan* is the one likely most readily associated with the idea of a physically fit and athletic female who sought freedom from traditional gender politics. Joan is physically strong enough to keep up with the male soldiers. She can ride horses, wear armor, and carry a sword, although because it is sacred, she must not strike a blow with it (*BH* 6: 121). The sublimity of the athletic female body makes athleticism with weapons vulgar at best. This physical fitness is necessary to legitimize her intelligence and leadership abilities, the qualities that ultimately allow her to escape her woman's life of domestic duties and farm chores to lead her entire "nation" to freedom and independence.

Joan herself recognizes the significance of her transformation through the talismanic alchemy of trans-gendering, repeatedly resisting any attempts to re-feminize her. In scene 3, for example, Joan declares, "I am a soldier: I do not want to be thought of as a woman" (121). When one of the men accuses her of being a woman after all, she retorts, "No: not a bit. I am a soldier and nothing else" (144). At the climax of her trial, this willful regendering becomes one of the most serious accusations against her, and she explains at length: "what can be plainer commonsense? I was a soldier living among soldiers. I am a prisoner guarded by soldiers. If I were to dress as a woman they would think of me as a woman; and then what would become of me? If I dress as a soldier they think of me as a soldier, and I can live with them as I do at home with my brothers" (177).

Even her accusers are forced to acknowledge the wisdom of this "commonsense" strategy for achieving the privileges of a male simply by masquerading as one. In *Saint Joan*, where a woman can "become" a man by training and dressing her body as one, we see another questioning by Shaw of the male/female binary. Shaw allows the abstraction of her warriorhood to become the site of the play's problems—which assemble the traditional inventory of binaries—of opposed theologies, opposed nationalities, and confoundingly opposed gender roles. *Saint Joan* is an allegorical argument for gender equality, troped on Joan's physically fit soldier's body.

Shaw renewed his attack upon the male/female binary in the athletic body of Epifania Fitzfassenden. In *The Millionairess* (1934), published in *Plays Extravagant*, Shaw allowed himself, in this his self-styled "extravagant" phase, to imagine that men and women actually could be thought of as equals. In the play, Shaw begins to analyze issues of leadership and the "born bosses" that is the declared topic of *The Millionairess* and the title of its preface. Yet, instead of analyzing this issue by using a male as the "born boss," he places a female in that position. To represent that Epifania is emancipated and privileged, Shaw describes her as "a tragic looking woman, athletically built, and expensively dressed" (*BH* 6: 883). Her clothing signals her social standing and her athletic abilities, which are soon demonstrated and mark her as an independent woman and "captain of industry." Her athleticism is revealed when we learn that her father believed all women should be able to defend themselves, and so she was taught judo. As the play begins, Mrs. Fitzfassenden finds herself meeting with her lawyer because her husband has found another woman. Moreover, to suggest the confusion and mixing of the male/female gender prerogatives, Epifania declares that "Alastair is physically attractive: that is my sole excuse for having married him" (904). The play acts out the career of an athletic, socially and professionally liberated woman. Therefore, it is now the passive male body that Shaw will depict as an object. The female athletic body in this play is the active body.

The Millionairess is a play about marriage. Therefore, in making the reversal of Epifania to the status of a wealthy male, Shaw allows her the same types of speeches that are traditionally allowed to men. She reflects, "it is convenient to be married. It is respectable. It keeps other men off. It gives me a freedom that I could not enjoy as a single woman" (912). These lines express ideas that are more commonly associated with men. Shaw finally confirms Epifania's lack of a gender signifier through her interactions with the Egyptian doctor. A medical doctor, more than anyone, should be able to identify and analyze the physical bodies of patients.

After Epifania pushes her erstwhile lover, Adrian Blenderbland, down a flight of stairs, the doctor is called in and makes this assessment of Epifania: "Enormous self-confidence. Reckless audacity. Insane egotism. Apparently sexless." She yells back, "Sexless! Who told you that I am sexless?" The doctor explains, "You talk to me as if you were a man. There is no mystery, no separateness, no sacredness about men to you. A man to you is a male of the species" (927). This apparent "sexlessness" or genderlessness that the doctor observes is the ironic key to the ultimate feminism of Epifania's body. Strong, confident, independent, she can decide to be married or not and can decide whom she will make love to even while she is married. Epifania's transcendence of a traditionally female gendered body enables this. Significantly, it makes her marriage to the doctor therefore an uncommon one—one based in real identities, free of idealism and the false illusions of gender. Unshackled from the bonds of traditional, submissive femininity, she is free to take her position in a love relationship as a true equal of her partner.

While many of his contemporaries were still coming to terms with the New Woman's insistence on ideological, political, and financial independence, Shaw was already recognizing how closely these achievements were tied to constructions of the female body. In direct contrast to the slander of the Victorian stage that made actresses indecent because they put their bodies on display, Shaw made women's bodies a vital aspect of the argument for feminist emancipation. For Shaw, the sign of an ideologically fit mind was a physically fit body, and his female characters stage his developing awareness of the extent to which women's liberation must be simultaneously intellectual and physical. Shaw explores his particular forms of athletic feminism through early characters such as Blanche Sartorius, Grace Tranfield, Sylvia and Julie Craven, and Vivie Warren. Some, like Hypatia Tarleton and Margaret Knox, learn how to express their emancipation through their physicalities, while others, like Lina Szczepanowska, Annajanska, Saint Joan, and Epifania Fitzfassenden, more confidently assume their right to move about freely in a traditionally male-dominated world. He uses these active strong bodies as thereby empowered to question traditional gender roles. Shaw goes a step further in questioning the traditional role of women as weak and passive by creating a woman like Miss Mopply, the patient in *Too True to Be Good* (1932). She pretends to be an invalid because that is the role her overprotective mother has encouraged—or required—her to play. But Shaw introduces one of his strangest characters, a giant microbe inhabiting her body, to literally speak for her body, assuring the audience that the apparent invalid is "naturally as strong as a rhinoceros" (*BH* 6: 437) but has been weakened by an enforced lack of physical activity and fresh air. The microbe's diagnosis proves to be correct, and when the need arises to protect something she values, Miss Mopply is able to summon her strength to jump out of bed in the middle of the night, kick the burglar in the solar plexus, lift Sweetie the nurse and send her flying into the air. Sweetie has already shown her disdain for Miss Mopply's invalid pose, refusing to coddle her and insisting that the only medicine her histrionic patient needs is a mouthful of kitchen salt, but the nurse is nonetheless "dazed by the patient's very unexpected athleticism" (444). Interestingly, it is the male burglar who recognizes that, given the option, Miss Mopply would choose to live a life of adventure and activity rather than the enforced passivity of a protected, upper-class woman.

Shaw wrote enough plays to represent the theory that a woman who would be independent necessarily had to be an athlete. Then he used this female athletic character to speak feminist narratives that attacked traditional gender roles. Shaw had the luxury of longevity. Feminists have had the benefit of this time as well to explore the multiple aspects in which feminist representations manifest themselves. This analysis of how Shaw depicts his female characters as physically fit and athletically strong demonstrates a feminism rooted not in the vicissitudes of chance opportunity in a modern industrialized civilization but rather in the inspiring alternatives of an egalitarian social physiology rooted in the fitness and athleticism of women.

Notes

1. I would like to thank Professor Tony Gibbs for reminding me of Reeves and for his generous advice regarding this essay.

2. For a narrative of the history of feminists theorizing the female body, especially in terms of autobiography, see Smith and Watson's *Women, Autobiography, Theory: A Reader* (1998).

3. Certainly, it is significant that theatrical productions are always all about the bodies of the performers. Fitness, grace, and athleticism are always an essential element of actors' dramatic performance. But for Shaw's socially, politically, and morally radicalizing work, the athleticism of his heroines is necessary to counterbalance the energy, durability, and athleticism of the darker characters and forces against which they contend in their progressive struggle toward emancipation.

Works Cited

Castelnuovo, Shirley, and Sharon Guthrie. *Feminism and the Female Body: Liberating the Amazon Within*. London: Lynne Reinner, 1998.

Cohen, Patricia. "The Theatrical Katharine Hepburn, in Journals and Letters." *New York Times* 3 Oct. 2007.

DiGaetani, John Louis. *Stages of Struggle: Modern Playwrights and Their Psychological Inspirations*. Jefferson, NC: McFarland, 1998.

Grosz, Elizabeth. *Volatile Bodies: Toward a Corporeal Feminism*. Bloomington: Indiana UP, 1994.

Lorichs, Sonja. "The 'Unwomanly Woman' in Shaw's Drama." Weintraub 99–113.

Shaw, George Bernard. *The Bodley Head Shaw Collected Plays with Their Prefaces*. 7 vols. London: Reinhardt, 1970–74.

Smith, Sidone, and Julia Watson, eds. *Women, Autobiography, Theory: A Reader*. Madison: U of Wisconsin P, 1998.

Weintraub, Rodelle, ed. *Fabian Feminist: Bernard Shaw and Woman*. University Park: Penn State P, 1977.

2

Shaw and Cruelty

• • • • • • • • • • • • • • • • • • •

LAWRENCE SWITZKY

> I believe no one has ever pointed out the sadistic element in Bernard Shaw's
> work, still less suggested that this probably has some connection with Shaw's
> admiration for dictators. . . . It is important to notice that the cult of power tends
> to be mixed up with a love of cruelty and wickedness *for their own sakes.*
>
> George Orwell, "Raffles and Miss Blandish" (1944)

When Shaw oversaw the second publication of *The Quintessence of Ibsenism*, the lectures on Ibsen's plays that he had delivered before the Fabian Society during the summer of 1890, he promised that some additional chapters at the end would describe "the change in the theatre since Ibsen set his potent leaven to work there" (*Three Critical Essays* 10). One of the most significant of these innovations, as Shaw points out in "The Technical Novelty in Ibsen's Plays," is that Ibsen deliberately inflicts pain on his audiences. By giving us "ourselves in our situations" (144), as opposed to the escapist fantasies of melodrama or the distant royals of Shakespeare, Ibsen perfected the "terrible art of sharpshooting at the audience" (145): his plays "are capable of hurting us cruelly and of filling us with excited hopes of escape from idealistic tyrannies, and with visions of intenser life in the future" (144). The coupling of injury and inspiration is a Shavian signature, a dire duty and a life-giving pleasure. As he reflects on his own playwriting practice as a beneficiary of Ibsen's influence, Shaw pronounces that he too is "teaching and saving" (145) his audiences, commanding their attention as surely as a dentist or the Angel of the Annunciation. Theatrical enchantment, writes Shaw, ought to be deployed to soften the blow, but not to disarm it: a skilled dramatist "may use all the magic of art to make you forget the pain he causes you or to enhance the joy of the hope and courage he awakens" (145). But socially effective art nonetheless depends on a substratum of cruelty.

Where Orwell may have overstated his diagnosis of Shaw's sadism is in the accusation that Shaw pursued "cruelty and wickedness *for their own sakes.*"[1] A more accurate depiction of Shaw's procedures, and Orwell's as well, is that both believed that cruelty deployed instrumentally is an acceptable practice. Shaw's occasional use of other terms for his reformist operations ("discomfort," "unpleasantness") should not distract us from the potentially unsavory question of how pain is instrumentalized in Shaw's drama. In the dedicatory epistle to *Man and Superman*, Shaw effuses that it "annoys me to see people comfortable when they ought to be uncomfortable," and he insists on bringing his audiences to "a conviction of sin" (8). Dentists and Angels of Annunciation are not hard to locate in the Shavian canon: the latter in *The Simpleton of the Unexpected Isles*, the former through the ministrations of Valentine in *You Never Can Tell*. Michael Holroyd notes that Shaw once wrote to a dentist, comparing their professional roles as pain givers: "I cannot give anaesthetics, but I do it [cut out carious material] as amusingly as I can" (qtd. in Holroyd 217).

Shaw's attitudes toward the deliberate infliction of pain were conditioned not only by contemporaneous developments in theater but also by advances in experimental science and feminist activism. The denial of anesthesia to vivisected animals was a hotly contested question in the medical circles of Shaw's day as well as the dramaturgical ones. The social historian Coral Lansbury notes, for instance, that stoicism before pain was deliberately conditioned in medical students to toughen them for the grisly duties they would have to perform: "the cries of vivisected animals helped to habituate the student to the pain of a human patient—an argument which continued after the introduction of anaesthesia" (12). Stanton Garner has claimed that Continental naturalism, one of the greatest influences on Shaw's early dramaturgy, was explicitly concerned with harnessing technologies of somatic disclosure to modernize the theater, and that Émile Zola, author of the 1881 manifesto "La naturalisme au le theatre" ("Naturalism in the Theatre"), participated in "theatrical vivisection."[2] Who gets to carry out the deployment of pain in Shaw's plays and the persuasiveness of their justifications for their ethical and social experimentation is often an unresolved question. One place to start answering that question is to note that one of the most significant transitions in Shaw's dramaturgy is the switch from men to women as the administrators of necessary pain: whereas Sartorius in *Widowers' Houses* (1892) or Undershaft in *Major Barbara* (1905) are the Mephistophelean bearers of painful social realities, Lina Szczepanowska drags the screaming Bentley Summerhays to a gymnasium in *Misalliance* (1909), while Ariadne in *Heartbreak House* (1916) "rags" her puerile cousin Randall until he cries. Shaw began to think about the right to administer cruelty as a gendered phenomenon early in his career and continued to trouble the relationship between science, sex, and pain throughout his plays.

The play in which Shaw examines cruelty in terms of gender and the naturalist "vivisectional theater" most explicitly is his second "unpleasant" play, *The Philanderer*; and it is also the play in which the problem of a dramaturgical method that depends on instrumentalizing pain is placed most strenuously under the microscope. That cruelty is a masculine phenomenon in Shaw's journeyman text is partially a consequence of the fact that the executors of pain in the play, Leonard Charteris and Dr Paramore, are members of new and, in the play's terms, masculinized professions: the modern realist philosopher and a doctor who is also a research physiologist. Both are also characterized as "vivisectors" in the course of *The Philanderer*, a job description that Shaw associated with the unjustified use of instrumentalized cruelty in his prose treatises. Because of Shaw's fervent association with the largely feminist anti-vivisection movement and his intimate knowledge of vivisectionist practices, vivisection gave Shaw both a language to discuss the operations of instrumentalized pain as well as a model to resist as he constructed his own dramaturgy.

The *Philanderer* cost Shaw a great deal of pain to write, as its tortured composition history lays bare. At the suggestion of Lady Colin Campbell, Shaw abandoned a final scene set several years after the initial action of the play (though he could not bring himself to "commit it to the fire" as he intended), and he cut out a number of subplots, allegedly to shorten the play to an acceptable running time. Sensitive scholarly responses to *The Philanderer* view it largely as an interesting mess, a preview of Shaw's artistic evolution: a proto-discussion play junked before it came to fruition

(Brian F. Tyson); a provocative rehearsal of gendered relationships developed more poignantly in later plays (Alfred Turco Jr.); or as an experiment in fusing autobiography and the problem play genre in a frank depiction of "the degrading of love" (Julius Novick).[3] It deserves our attention because of its unusual candor regarding the maneuvers of figures who claim to instrumentalize pain for the cause of social progress, as Shaw himself did, and the female victims of these maneuvers. Furthermore, Shaw conceived of sensitivity to pain as a feminine trait, and part of Shaw's dramaturgical program was an attempt to "feminize" his audiences.

Vivisectional Cruelties

Shaw's public support of the anti-vivisection movement began as early as 1885 with satirical depictions of dog torture in his serialized novel *Cashel Byron's Profession*, and lasted until 1949, the year before his death, when G. H. Bowker published a collection of his essays and speeches, *Shaw on Vivisection*. While vivisection, a major component of experimental science and a staple of demonstrations in medical classrooms, was largely associated with Continental practices, anti-vivisection found its most fervent supporters in England. One notable feature of the anti-vivisection movement was the unusual opportunity for leadership roles that it offered female supporters: Richard French, a historian of British vivisection, estimates that women accounted for 40 to 60 percent of patrons, vice-presidents, and members of executive committees of anti-vivisection societies (239). Frances Power Cobbe, the most recognizable figurehead for the movement in the 1880s and 1890s, was also the founder of the Society for the Protection of Animals Liable to Vivisection, more commonly known as the Victoria Street Society. Although she supported feminist activism, Cobbe subscribed to conservative notions of gender. Women, she argued, ought to be allowed a more active role in the public sphere (as a trial run for earning suffrage rights) because they could contribute feminine qualities otherwise lacking in masculine politics—chiefly religious and moral sensitivities lacking in male politicians. Cobbe advocated the usefulness of female work particularly "in some gratuitous labour of love for the poor, the sick, the ignorant, the blind; for animals; in short, in any cause of humanity; but, above all, in the cause of their own sex, and the relief of the misery of their own sisters" (qtd. in French 242). The anti-vivisection cause parted ways with other groups like the Royal Society for the

Protection of Animals because it championed allegedly feminine values, eschewing scientific progress in favor of moral and religious duties, and favoring "emotionalist" appeals that, as Harriet Ritvo has argued, jarred against the cool equipoise of public statements by physiologists.[4]

While Shaw notably showed his public support for the anti-vivisection cause, he took care to dissociate himself from charges that he unconditionally supported it as a feminist cause. In the 1911 preface to *The Doctor's Dilemma*, which is also one of Shaw's most tenacious descriptions of cruelty, he describes an Anti-Vivisection meeting at Queen's Hall in London in which, in addition to hunting sportsmen, he encountered the hypocrisy of ladies "wearing hats and cloaks and head-dresses obtained by wholesale massacres, ruthless trappings, callous extermination of our fellow creatures" (*Dilemma* 44). Shaw's account of the group's "hysterics of indignation at the cruelties of the vivisectors" (45) sums up his repulsion regarding these morally suspect and, by virtue of their "hysterical" emotional displays, feminized figures.

If Shaw was unwilling to let his female compatriots off the hook, though, he was, by his own accounts, unequivocally opposed to vivisection as a symptom of latent cruelties in British society. Shaw's discussion of vivisection, the cutting open of animals for experimentation and/or demonstration, is, at heart, a critique of unjustifiable methods of knowledge acquisition. Cruel research methods are the product of cruel researchers, and Shaw's most pressing indictment of scientists who engage in vivisection is finally an exposure of character traits that they would otherwise like to conceal behind a veneer of professional respectability: "The paths to knowledge are countless. One of these paths is a path through darkness, secrecy, and cruelty. When a man deliberately turns from all other paths and goes down that one, it is scientific to infer that what attracts him is not knowledge, since there are other paths to that, but cruelty" (*Dilemma* 57).

Cruelty is a poor choice among many methodological options, a clue to pathology in the scientist. The cruelty of vivisectors is the misapplication of Ibsenite sharpshooter techniques, sadism that degenerates rather than advances human welfare. Shaw's own cruelties in revealing this tendency in human character are, on the other hand, justified by the promise of social benefit. Indeed, Shaw pictures the consequences of his attack on the unquestioned virtue of the medical community as "a transport of virtuous indignation" (*Dilemma* 58), a moral convulsion that indicates that his arrow has hit its mark. The strangeness of the maneuver is that Shaw believes in a homeopathic response to cruelty: a "love of wickedness and cruelty *for their own sakes*" can only be dispelled by the instrumental application of more cruelty.

In light of Shaw's efforts to distinguish himself from the wrongheaded execution of cruelty, it is disheartening to discover that Shaw blithely described his own philandering relationships with women in the 1880s and 1890s as a species of "vivisection." In a troubling letter he wrote to Bertha Newcombe in 1896, a painter who had hoped to marry him, he dismissively refers to "vivisection" as a clichéd set piece of feminine hyperbole: "Your sex likes me as children like wedding cake, for the sake of the sugar on top. If they taste by accident a bit of crumb or citron, it is all over: I am a fiend, delighting in vivisectional cruelties, as indicated by the corners of my mouth" (*Letters* 620).[5] Shaw's devilish smile indicates his inhumane delight, his alleged attraction to cruelty in wooing and then abandoning lovers. But one might just as accurately locate his cruelty in the dismissive comparison of Newcombe to a selfish child, or the cavalier attitude Shaw adopts toward the otherwise serious topic of vivisection. Beatrice Webb, whose diaries record the formation of the "Fabian Junta" during the same period, advised Newcombe, also one of her friends, that despite any temporary heartbreak, it was just as well to be rid of Shaw, since he treated women with "a vulgarity that includes cruelty and springs from vanity" (Webb 111). If Shaw really was experimenting on women in ways that were analogous to vivisection, how could he compartmentalize his conviction that vivisection was an inadmissible method of knowledge acquisition?

The answer may be that he couldn't, and that *The Philanderer* is an attempt to resolve questions about cruelty as a romantic and a dramaturgical strategy that could not be broached more directly. Arnold Silver has noted that in Shaw's art "a marked sadistic streak can coexist with beneficent impulses" (Silver 51). The discomfiting adjacency of altruism and viciousness and the play's obsessive re-staging of efforts to heal that also wound lend *The Philanderer* its peculiarly barbed tone. The play notoriously germinated from a real-life event on 4 February 1893 that Shaw recorded in his diary. According to Shaw, Jenny Patterson, the woman who had deflowered him in 1885, burst in on him and the actress Florence Farr and caused "a most shocking scene." Alfred Turco proposes that Shaw subjected himself to the sort of homeopathic cruelty that he prescribed for his audiences by writing *The Philanderer*, bringing himself to a "conviction of sin" (despite the evidence of the Newcombe letter, which was written three years later) by humanizing Jenny Patterson in the character of Julia Craven and demonizing himself in the character of Leonard Charteris. Whatever therapeutic value Shaw may have received from dramatizing his unresolved feelings of guilt, he also used *The Philanderer* to develop an emerging poetics of cruelty that he had earlier ascribed to Ibsen. Although, in trying to shoehorn the play into a cogent narrative of his career, Shaw classified it as a problem play about unjust marriage laws, his description of the production of an unpleasant "atmosphere" in his "topical comedy" is closer to the mark—an atmosphere in which women and "feminized" men are subjected to the unjustifiably cruel designs of experiments both scientific and emotional (*Unpleasant* 26). The atmosphere that Shaw refers to obtained not only in the self-congratulatory world of advanced thought emblematized by the Ibsen Club in the play, however, but also in the dramatic traditions that Shaw worked to reinvent.

Dramatic Cruelties

The Philanderer is relentlessly concerned with the European theater's historical use and misuse of depicted suffering. It begins in a drawing room whose walls are hung with "theatrical engravings and photographs" representing a history of romantic, melodramatic, and pseudo-Ibsenite performers and dramatists, from Kemble and Mrs. Siddons through "*Henry Arthur Jones, Sir Arthur Pinero, Sydney Grundy, and so on, but not Eleonora Duse nor anyone connected with Ibsen*" (*Unpleasant* 99). These are the heroes of Cuthbertson, a theater critic and the champion of the old gender roles that *The Philanderer* allegedly exists to call into question. Before the beginning of the play, Cuthbertson has encountered an old friend (and romantic rival), Colonel Craven, and has cryptically explained to Craven that he passes his life "in witnessing scenes of suffering nobly endured and sacrifice willingly rendered by womanly women and manly men" (118). Craven, significantly, believes that his old friend is "something in a hospital" (121). But Cuthbertson is instead a supporter of melodrama, a genre that traffics in fantasies about victimization, power, and the apparently providential subjection of both heroes and villains to pain in a grand scheme of suffering and redemption.

The instrumental deployment of suffering in stage melodrama was, as Peter Brooks has trenchantly observed, in service of unveiling a "moral occult" in an otherwise ethically inscrutable universe: "Melodrama starts from and expresses the anxiety brought by a frightening new world in which the traditional patterns of moral order no longer provide the necessary social glue. It plays out the force of that anxiety with the apparent triumph of villainy, and it dissipates it with the eventual victory of virtue. It demonstrates over and over that the signs of ethical forces can be discovered and can be made legible" (Brooks 20).

Linda Williams has added the important corollary that a key feature of melodrama is "the sympathy for another grounded in the manifestation of that person's suffering," and that politically motivated melodrama can encourage pathos at witnessed pain in order to establish sympathy for marginalized groups.[6] Melodrama as a tool for social orientation, then, is a schizoid genre that inflicts pain on the persons or groups it both wants to expel and to redeem, and there are pleasures (both of moral certainty and of a more prurient nature) in the spectacle of suffering. In *The Philanderer* it is less a revealed "moral occult" than a hidden "gender occult" that Cuthbertson enjoys in the sentimental depictions of pain in melodrama. Outside the melodramatic stage depictions of "manly men and womanly women" that he champions, however, Cuthbertson finds gender legibility far more difficult to establish. In a discussion with Dr Paramore about what defines a man within the more fluid precincts of the parodic Ibsen Club in the second act of the play, Cuthbertson is flummoxed by a lack of adequate definitional tools:

PARAMORE. Er—by the way, do you think is Miss Craven attached to Charteris at all?

CUTHBERTSON. What! that fellow! Not he. He hangs about after her; but he's not man enough for her. A woman of that sort likes a strong, manly, deep throated, broad chested man.

PARAMORE. [*anxiously*] Hm! a sort of sporting character, do you think?

CUTHBERTSON. Oh, no, no. A scientific man, perhaps, like yourself. But you know what I mean: a MAN. [*He strikes himself a sounding blow on the chest.*]

PARAMORE. Of course; but Charteris is a man.

CUTHBERTSON. Pah! You dont see what I mean. (127)

Perseveration in Shaw ("man . . . man . . . man"), the loss of linguistic flexibility, is often a clue to intellectual morbidity. Here, it is more specifically a challenge to the definitional security of melodrama, which devolves here into mere deixis: in Cuthbertson's terms, you know who a man is because you can point to him on a stage in an attitude of suffering (or pound your chest in a display of masculinity: *this* is a man). Off the melodramatic stage, deixis is a far shakier method of disclosure, since scenes of suffering and sacrifice cannot be reliably produced on demand.

Craven's confusion of Cuthbertson with "something in a hospital" is fruitful in other ways as well. As Elin Diamond has argued, melodrama often conceived of itself as a quasi-medical genre, combining the "intensely judgmental ethos that pervades medical opinion on the hysteric" with "figural projections between the doctor and the hysteric" (10). Onstage a crusading doctor or a doctor figure, representing truth, health, and morality, exists to unmask the fallen (or falling) woman, identifiable through the overblown physical gestures (gnashing teeth, wringing hands) that characterized both hysteria and melodrama. According to Diamond's account, the movement from melodrama to naturalism re-locates the process of diagnostic clarification rather than expunging it. The realist actor "produces symptoms addressed to spectators, who gradually understand their meanings" (30). In either genre, the performance of pain produces a sequence of legible signs for spectators, who are absorbed in the pleasure of interpreting pathologies and rendering diagnoses. Cruelty is contained by and within the operations of the drama and unleashed in service of the linked procedures of moral knowledge and medical classification.

The instrumental deployment of cruelty has a history in theatrical practice predating Ibsen that Shaw could, and did, harness for his own purposes. But whereas the target of cruelty had been onstage figures suffering for the instruction, moral reassurance, and the darker enjoyment of audiences, Ibsenite drama makes audiences themselves the victims of cruelty. The crucial shift from watching and judging pain to experiencing pain is one of the key innovations that Shaw discovered in Ibsen and applied to his dramaturgy. Yet, while the other *Plays Unpleasant—Widowers' Houses* and *Mrs Warren's Profession*—seek to inflict audience suffering by exposing the complicity of spectators in slum-landlordism, prostitution, and the systematic corruption that licenses these practices, *The Philanderer* is an exposure of the social behaviors that constitute cruel behavior more broadly.

J. Ellen Gainor has observed that *The Philanderer* progresses through three different ideological dispensations (represented by pictures on the walls of each scene): the Old Order with its Victorian memorabilia in the first act, the New Order of the Ibsen club that uses advanced views on gender roles as a cover for its sexual intrigues in the second act, and the positivistic dispensation of Paramore's office in the third act (54). Each of these three realms, which overlap despite their distribution into separate scenes, is the staging ground for cruelty toward women, animals, and "feminized" men. These uses of cruelty are underwritten by claims of reciprocal benefit, though Shaw punctures the alleged humanitarianism of nearly every character who exploits pain instrumentally by citing this rationalization.

The most overt justifications of instrumental cruelty are set forth by the philanderer Leonard Charteris and Dr Paramore, who are paired as "vivisectors" and as suitors for Julia Craven—the former unwilling, the latter ungainly. Charteris, who stage-manages the action of the play, arranges two experiments in the course of the play. The first is an attempt to get Grace Tranfield to marry him (and thereby fend off the amours of Julia Craven); the second is to persuade Julia to marry Dr Paramore. In perhaps the most heated exchange between Julia and Charteris, however, we learn that these are only the most recent in a series of experiments that Charteris has conducted on Julia:

> JULIA. How have you the face to turn round like this after insulting and torturing me?
> CHARTERIS. Never mind, dearest: you never did understand me; and you never will. Our vivisecting friend [Paramore] has made a successful experiment at last.
> JULIA. [*earnestly*] It is you who are the vivisector: a far crueler, more wanton vivisector than he.
> CHARTERIS. Yes; but then I learn so much more from my experiments than he does! and the victims learn as much as I do. Thats where my moral superiority comes in. (168)

Julius Novick has read this exchange as a coded reference to sexual intercourse, where Charteris's cruelty consists in sleeping with women and then trifling with their affections (xvii). "Vivisection" in this sense carries the ciphered connotation of sexual penetration. But the ghastly richness of vivisection as a practice, and Shaw's association of it with injurious methods of knowledge acquisition, heightens the epistemological stakes of Julia's accusation.

Charteris claims that his cruel acts, libidinal or otherwise, are morally justifiable because there is a reciprocal benefit to his investigations: "the victims learn as much as I do." As dubious as this claim may be, Charteris contradicts himself several lines later because, he insists, Julia is uneducable:

> CHARTERIS. Oh, what I have learnt from you! from y o u! who could learn nothing from me! I made a fool of you; and you brought me wisdom: I broke your heart; and you brought me joy: I made you curse your womanhood; and you revealed my manhood to me. (169)

Implicit in the claim of reciprocal benefit is the promise of mutual growth, but Charteris's parallelism exposes his method as parasitism: one suffers while the other gains. The culmination of this gain-and-loss is a pride in masculinity that exists only at the expense of feminine self-hatred. It may not be going too far to conclude that Charteris believes that the one is dependent on the other—that the revelation of manhood can only take place when womanhood is cursed.

The simple structure of *The Philanderer*, with two suitors for Julia and two lovers for Charteris, invites us to compare vivisectors and to test Julia's claim that Charteris is crueler than Paramore. Dr Paramore's cruel medical experiments consist of cutting open ducts in the livers of guinea pigs without any regard for the suffering of the animals. But his more significant act of onstage cruelty is subjecting Colonel Craven, Julia's father, to a diagnosis that has, ironically, improved his health (to Shaw's vegetarian, teetotaling sensibilities) by making him give up meat and alcohol. Perhaps the more resonant cruelty inflicted by Paramore is his cultivated disregard for the feelings of his patient. When his discovery is challenged by a report in a medical journal, Paramore cannot sympathize with Craven's relief, but blames him for not feeling his own injury: "all invalids are selfish" (143). The reciprocal benefit promised by Paramore's experiments (i.e., the advancement of scientific knowledge) disguises desires for personal pride and career advancement.

One working definition of cruelty in *The Philanderer* is that it belongs to practices that create an asymmetrical distribution of pain. Paramore wants to inflict pain and privation without experiencing any pain himself. Charteris benefits from the same asymmetry, as he reveals in a discussion with Grace: "As a philosopher, it's my business to tell other people the truth; but it's not their business to tell it to me. I dont like it: it hurts" (140–41). Moreover, masculine professional roles enable this asymmetrical distribution of pain. As a former military officer, Colonel Craven is also implicated in cruelty: "How many camels and horses were ripped up in that Soudan [sic] campaign where you won your Victoria Cross?" (148) asks Dr Paramore. Rather than enabling reflection on the cruelty of both careers, however, the comparison between them finally establishes a sort of freemasonry between cruel professionals based in shared masculine stoicism.

The difference between giving pain (a masculine trait) and receiving pain (a feminine trait) is one way of distinguishing gender roles in *The Philanderer*. If Charteris's experiments on Julia have enhanced his manhood even as they denigrated her womanhood, Paramore's application of his (formerly) successful experiments have "feminized" his patient as well. Craven has lost his "manly taste" (145) for beefsteak, much as the caprices of medical diagnosis have denied him the ability to "die like a man when I said I would" (145). In the long run, this loss of "manliness" improves Craven's health. But the method of bringing Craven to his forcible loss of masculine traits is troubling even if the outcome is desirable. To be a victim of vivisectional cruelties is to be rendered abjectly feminine: in Julia's case, she has learned to curse her womanhood; in Craven's case, he has become "feminized" because he is unable to make choices for himself and has, by his own account, suffered as a result of those choice.

As ostensibly negotiable as gender roles may seem to be in *The Philanderer*, there are clearly identifiable masculine and feminine behaviors that the characters onstage (and, perhaps, the audience of the play) can recognize with lesser and greater degrees of perceptiveness. Acting like a man entails the infliction of cruelty with a stoic indifference to the pain involved. This stoicism is licensed by professional roles that supposedly demand empathic distance (doctor, military officer, philosopher). Acting like a woman, on the other hand, involves the deployment of highly conventionalized feminine emotions, many of them identified with duplicity. Julia, the chief bearer of these signs, performs pain strategically, making use of familiar melodramatic codes. In an altercation with Grace over Charteris's affections, for example, Julia suddenly "[*throws*] *herself tragically on her knees at Grace's feet*" (155) and then, "*trying her theatrical method in a milder form*," becomes "*reasonable and goodnatured instead of tragic*" (155). Grace, whose father is after all a critic of melodrama, instantly recognizes these signs and accuses Julia of treating her "like a man, to be imposed upon by this sort of rubbish" (155).

Calling someone out on this sort of role-playing, as Grace does to Julia, or disrupting the gender identity that allows a person to give coherence to his or her character, as Paramore does to Craven, both constitute forms of cruelty. Arguably, these are even admissible forms of instrumental cruelty. In fact, though, Shaw's own cruel designs in the play aim to recapture a stereotypical feminine sensitivity to suffering, not unlike the views advocated by Frances Power Cobbe. In other words, Shaw's post-Ibsenite theater attempts to make his audiences more "womanly."

Shaw's Theater of Cruelty

Melodrama and naturalism are stage genres that claim to confer moral and medical legibility. If these anterior genres clarify a confusing world, however, Shaw's plays, even though they seem bound to the stage conventions they inherit (and parody), are mimetic of the inscrutability of everyday life. It might be more accurate, in fact, to say that Shaw is less prescriptive than he is intrigued by the ways in which readings of the social world are either enabled or thwarted. Shaw's stage directions, which in *The Philanderer* are extensive even by his usual novel-like standards, are one clue to the meanings behind obscure gestures. The most significant, and troublesome, of these directions is the coda that Shaw added to the 1898 published edition of the play: "*Charteris, amused and untouched, shakes his head laughingly. The rest look at Julia with concern, and even a little awe, feeling for the first time the presence of a keen sorrow*" (177). These directions follow the first sympathetic encounter of the two heroines, as Grace catches a fainting Julia, and creates two onstage groups: "untouched" Charteris, and the rest of the characters, who feel "the presence of a keen sorrow." This is not the first time that the "awe" of genuine emotion has confronted a want of feeling: in fact, the play begins with Charteris's distance juxtaposed with Grace's feeling: "*His amative enthusiasm, at which he is himself laughing, and his clever, imaginative, humorous ways, contrast strongly with the sincere tenderness and dignified quietness of the woman*" (100).

The Philanderer is a treacherously theatrical play, in which real and feigned emotions are often indistinguishable. In fact, many of Shaw's stage directions indicate the trustworthiness of an emotional display for his reading audience: *"with sincere feeling"* (129); *"earnestly"* (168); *"very earnestly"* (171). These sorts of directions would be unnecessary if emotional responses were legible and commensurate with intentions. Duplicitous "female" emotions, conventionalized by the traffic between the stage and the social world, are one aspect of stereotypical womanliness unequivocally attacked by the play. But the susceptibility to suffering, and the sincere attentiveness produced by it, are an aspect of femininity that is preserved and even, in snatches, championed by the play. The perception of suffering, in fact, is one way of decoding the social world: by "feeling the presence of a keen sorrow," the figures onstage (and perhaps the audience of the play) can detect Charteris's cruelty behind the engineered marriage of Julia and Paramore.

The anxious composition history of the play demonstrates that Shaw was trying to bridge the gap between melodrama and Ibsenite drama in the play, between suffering as spectatorial delectation and pain that could be a clue to the interior lives of characters and a stimulus for reform. In the heavily edited first draft of *The Philanderer*, Shaw included a subplot in which Paramore has located the Cravens' lost dog, Toody (or Doody), and has saved it from vivisection. Brian F. Tyson, one of the few commentators on the excisions, speculates that Shaw removed the dog plot because it seemed too melodramatic and indebted to the coincidence-driven style of W. S. Gilbert, "the paradox of the cruel vivisector who is as much a sentimentalist at heart as Gilbert's Pirate King [in *The Pirates of Penzance*]" (74). The dog plot, however, also establishes a more humane and, significantly, a more "womanly" Paramore. In his draft, Shaw establishes Paramore's reaction to the "silky black and white Skye terrier" as a spontaneous movement from cruel disinterest to feeling: "If it had been the usual troublesome, frightened cur, I should never have given two thoughts to it, but it was not frightened in the least: it put the most implicit confidence in me. . . . I actually had to go over the whole theory in my mind, right up to the point where the experiment was to come in, before I could bring myself to set to work. I was on the very point of fastening him down when he grew a little anxious, and looking up at me in the most natural way, put his paw on my arm and gave two little barks" (*Philanderer* 217).

The progress of Charteris's conversion story, from theoretical self-reassurance to literally being "touched" by the dog he is about to vivisect (he "put his paw on my arm") is a *mise-en-abyme* of Shaw's method: a change from stoic detachment to painful interruption to reconsideration and a change of action. Julia, who listens to this account, is convinced that Paramore has murdered her dog, and lets out a torrent of abuse characteristic of melodramatic womanliness. But later Charteris accuses Paramore of being "womanish" on other grounds:

> Womanish, my dear fellow, womanish. I always suspected you vivisecting people of being womanish. . . . What does a woman do? She concentrates all her feelings on some one person whom she likes and who belongs to her. She'll sacrifice everything for the man she loves; but Heaven help the man she dislikes. That's just like you. You have taken a fancy to this particular dog; and I can imagine you petting it and stuffing it with lumps of sugar, and then going into your laboratory and coolly inoculating some wretched mongrel with hydrophobia or freezing it stiff and slicing its nerves as though they were cucumbers. (*Philanderer* 227–29)

The praise of Charteris's catholicity also appears in the published play, when Sylvia, Julia's sister and a thoroughgoing believer in the "unwomanly woman," realizes that "he doesnt care a bit more for one woman than for another" (136). But Charteris's Platonic attitude, as he rephrases Sylvia's words, also means that he doesn't "care a bit less for one woman than another" (136), a vicious egalitarianism that uses advanced views ("you never bother about them being only women") as a cloak for a familiar masculine stoicism and disregard. Paramore's "feminization" may be merely preliminary, but it is at least a kind of responsiveness to pain, an awakening that may bear fruit in the future. Whatever Shaw's reasons for cutting the subplot may have been, the "feminized" Paramore remains encoded in the draft of *The Philanderer* as an example of productive pain that shapes that final, complicated coda, the felt effects of which promise to extend beyond the horizon of the play.

In her reading of *The Philanderer*, J. Ellen Gainor proposes that "unmanliness," since it "remains unexplained . . . thus is an enigmatic, tantalizing state" that "may emerge as the only unexamined, and therefore unattacked, status in the play" (59). But there is also a case to be made for the resonance of "womanliness," despite its putative dismissals, as a source of value in the play. Womanliness is negatively characterized as a reservoir of deceptive signs, a melodramatic attitude of self-sacrifice, or the hypocritical exclusivity of love at various moments. But, as Shaw's final tableau demonstrates, it is also susceptibility to being "touched," both in knowing a "keen sorrow" and the physical support that Grace gives to Julia. By honoring a conservative strain in Victorian feminism, Shaw may sacrifice some of his prestige as a "gender-blind" activist. On the other hand, Shaw might be read as a revolutionary scavenger who re-purposes an apparent female weakness—sensitivity to suffering—as a harbinger of moral evolution, a trait audiences need to feel the combination of pain and inspiration that is Shaw's description of socially effective drama.

Shaw's fascination with and repulsion by vivisection, a bad use of instrumental cruelty, is a thread that runs throughout his playwriting. Claude Bernard, the most notorious experimental physiologist of the nineteenth century, wrote a passage that anti-vivisectionists made famous through quotation: "If I were to look for a simile that would express my feelings about the science of life, I should say that it was a superb hall, glittering with light, to which the only entrance is through a long and horrible kitchen" (qtd. in Lansbury 160). It is not difficult to hear an echo of this passage in Adolphus Cusins's skepticism that a munitions factory might be the gateway to social reform in *Major Barbara*: "Then the way of life leads through the factory of death?" (152). Vivisection is also the grisly metaphor that John Tanner employs to describe the war between the sexes in *Man and Superman*: "To women, [the artist] is half vivisector, half vampire. He gets into intimate relations with them to study them, to strip the mask of convention from them, to surprise their inmost secrets, knowing that they have the power to rouse his deepest creative energies, to rescue him from his cold reason, to make him see visions and dream dreams, to inspire him, as he calls it. He persuades women that they may do this for their own purpose whilst he really means them to do it for his" (61–62).

Again, Shaw presents an account of personal advancement disguised as a claim of reciprocal benefit, which Tanner believes himself entitled to as a philosopher—or, as he puts it, as a member of the "artist-man" profession. Ann Whitefield's instrumental use of cruelty, while trapping Tanner within his own design, concludes the marriage plot, guarantees the future of the race, and, moreover, binds her in an argumentatively productive relationship with Tanner that is, one imagines, a fusion of pain and pleasure. The right to inflict cruelty, in this case and others, involves reciprocal benefit and reciprocal suffering, a backlash that partakes in the sting.

Shaw most often attributes sensitivity to the effects of cruelty to women because they have not been corrupted by the routinization of cruelty demanded by the male professional world. By imagining that his audiences could become "womanly" in the best sense, Shaw may not have radically challenged the definitions of masculine and feminine behavior that were prevalent in his own era. But he did generously reimagine spectators as subjects who were capable of gender-bending transformations and hybrid blendings of masculine and feminine traits.

A belief that habituated insensitivity to cruelty is reversible is one of the keynotes of Shaw's dramaturgy. As often as Shaw is linked with his inheritor Bertolt Brecht, one might also establish a genealogy to Antonin Artaud, pioneer of the Theatre of Cruelty in Paris in the 1930s. While Artaud's hostility to spoken language is hardly amicable to Shaw's project, Artaud's desire to break apart the calcification of habit through the instrumental deployment of pain is strikingly similar. Artaud proposes sonic reform in stage language "to restore its possibilities for physical shock, to divide it and distribute it actively in space, to use intonations in an absolutely concrete manner and to restore their power to hurt as well as really to manifest something" (239). Shaw's formal conservatism, at least on a surface level, should not distract us from his own deliberate attempts to "shock" and "hurt" his audiences, to restore to them some of their feminine empathy and to strip them of their masculine indifference. *The Philanderer* is one of the first, and most committed, attempts to formulate a post-melodramatic dramaturgy that will utilize the suffering at the heart of Shaw's dramatic antecedents more effectively as well as more responsibly. Shaw's extraordinary artistic successes and profound humanitarianism should not distract us, though, from the underlying cruelty of his approach and the fragile, sometimes violated, distance between laughter and pain that places him in the vanguard of twentieth-century dramatic experimentation.

Notes

1. I am indebted to Richard Rorty's *Contingency, Irony, and Solidarity* (Cambridge: Cambridge UP, 1989), which features one of the seminal discussions of cruelty in literature, for this reference to Shaw. Though Rorty does not investigate this particular charge of sadism at any length, he does believe that Orwell envisioned Shaw as the inspiration for his Socratic sadist O'Brien in *1984*.

2. Stanton B. Garner Jr., "Zola, Medicine, and Naturalism," in *Modern Drama: Defining the Field*, ed. Ric Knowles, Joanne Tompkins, and W. B. Worthen (Toronto: U of Toronto P, 2003), 68. As Michel Pharand demonstrates in *Bernard Shaw and the French*

(Gainesville: UP of Florida, 2000), Shaw's propagandistic support of Zola's naturalism was coupled with disdain for Zola's pessimism, his lack of humor and of style. In an 1888 lecture titled "That Realism Is the Goal of Fiction," Shaw deliberately places naturalism second to more nuanced developments that were then developing: "Realism *in excelsis* transcends naturalism as far as Shelley transcends M. Zola. And I would contend that the lowest, merely fanciful fiction must advance towards Naturalism, whilst naturalistic fiction must advance towards Realism" (qtd. in Pharand 2–3). The movement toward theatrical "Realism" and away from unsavory elements that he detected in naturalism may have influenced Shaw's tortuously defended choice of "realism" and "idealism" as antithetical terms in *The Quintessence of Ibsenism.*

3. The essays I am referring to are Brian F. Tyson's "Shaw's First Discussion Play: An Abandoned Act of 'The Philanderer'" in *SHAW: The Annual of Bernard Shaw Studies* (12 [1969]: 90–103); Alfred Turco Jr.'s "*The Philanderer*: Shaw's Poignant Romp" in *SHAW: The Annual of Bernard Shaw Studies* (7 [1987]: 47–62); and Julius Novick's "General Introduction" to *The Philanderer: A Facsimile of the Holograph Manuscript* (New York: Garland, 1981), vii–xxvii. I will refer in particular to Tyson's discussion of the play's composition history later in my discussion.

4. Harriet Ritvo, *The Animal Estate: The English and Other Creatures in the Victorian Age* (Cambridge: Harvard UP, 1987), 162. According to Ritvo, despite leveling a "radical critique of Victorian materialism," by the beginning of the twentieth century the antivivisection movement "had become a fringe movement, appealing to an assortment of feminists, labor activists, vegetarians, spiritualists, and others who did not fit easily into the established order of society."

5. Julius Novick also notes that Beatrice Webb describes Shaw as a "vivisector" in her diaries. Novick xvii.

6. Williams is thinking principally of Harriet Beecher Stowe's *Uncle Tom's Cabin* and its theatrical and filmic incarnations, though her study includes a wide range of examples.

Works Cited

Artaud, Antonin. *Selected Writings.* Ed. Susan Sontag. Trans. Helen Weaver. Berkeley: U of California P, 1988.

Brooks, Peter. *The Melodramatic Imagination.* New Haven: Yale UP, 1976.

Diamond, Elin. *Unmaking Mimesis: Essays on Feminism and Theater* London: Routledge, 1997.

French, Richard D. *Antivivisection and Medical Science in Victorian England.* Princeton, NJ: Princeton UP, 1975.

Gainor, J. Ellen. *Shaw's Daughters.* Ann Arbor: U of Michigan P, 1991.

Holroyd, Michael. *Bernard Shaw.* New York: Random, 1997.

Lansbury, Coral. *The Old Brown Dog.* Madison: U of Wisconsin P, 1985.

Shaw, G. B. *Collected Letters.* Ed. Dan H. Laurence. Vol. 1. New York: Dodd, Mead, 1965.

———. *The Doctor's Dilemma.* New York: Penguin, 1946.

———. *Major Barbara*. New York: Penguin, 1960.

———. *Man and Superman*. New York: Penguin, 1957.

———. *The Philanderer*. New York: Garland, 1981.

———. *Plays Unpleasant*. New York: Penguin, 1946.

———. *Three Critical Essays*. London: Constable, 1932.

Silver, Arnold. *Bernard Shaw: The Darker Side*. Stanford: Stanford UP, 1982.

Tyson, Brian F. "One Man and His Dog: A Study of a Deleted Draft of Bernard Shaw's *The Philanderer*." *Modern Drama* 10 (1967): 69–78.

Webb, Beatrice. *The Diary of Beatrice Webb*. Vol. 2. Cambridge, MA: Belknap, 1982–85.

Williams, Linda. *Playing the Race Card: Melodramas of Black and White from* Uncle Tom's Cabin *to O. J. Simpson*. Princeton, NJ: Princeton UP, 2001.

3

Shutting Out Mother

Vivie Warren as the New Woman

• • • • • • • • • • • • • • • • • •

ANN WILSON

Near the end of *Mrs Warren's Profession*, the stage directions read: "*Mrs Warren goes out, slamming the door behind her*" (161).[1] This moment, the culmination of the strained relationship between Vivie Warren and her mother, clearly alludes to Nora Helmer's taking leave of her family at the end of Ibsen's *A Doll's House*. Vivie, whose strained face "*relaxes; her grave expression breaks into joyous content*" (161), then picks up a note from her suitor, Frank, reads it, and rips it up, saying, "And goodbye, Frank" (161).

Superficially, the end of *Mrs Warren's Profession* seems to signal the triumph of Vivie as an autonomous figure who has refused family in the form of her biological mother and the possibilities of family offered by Frank. The slammed door signals Shaw's reworking of issues concerning financial autonomy and womanhood that are key to *A Doll's House*, but also, through the obvious allusion to Ibsen's play, it emphasizes the importance of theatricality and performance in defining and perpetuating the social roles associated with gender. Vivie may seek to reject the roles of wife and daughter as defined by outdated Victorian conventions, but the New Woman identity she replaces it with is itself a role that has been scripted for her in print and onstage. Moreover, by emphasizing the similarities between mother and daughter throughout the play and at this climactic confrontation, Shaw strongly suggests that Vivie's ability to

successfully perform the role of the New Woman is far more deeply indebted to her mother's successful performance of middle-class femininity
than Vivie wishes to acknowledge.

Mrs Warren's Profession opens with Vivie onstage, and before she has
said a word, Shaw establishes a set of visual cues that signal that she is
an athletic and intellectual New Woman. Propped against the cottage is
a woman's bicycle, and within the reach of Vivie, who is lying in a ham-
mock, is a chair piled high with books and writing paper (87). Soon the
audience learns that Vivie excelled at mathematics at Cambridge, placing
third in her class to win a bet with her mother (90).

As a New Woman, Vivie strives for independence and so refuses the
normative standards of middle-class femininity, which placed a premium
on women being mothers who selflessly forfeited their own needs to meet
those of their husbands and children. The ethos of this mode of middle-
class, mid-Victorian femininity is conveniently summed up in the first
few lines of *The Angel in the House*, Coventry Patmore's poetic homage to
his wife, Emily:

Man must be pleased; but him to please
Is woman's pleasure; down the gulf
Of his condoled necessities
She casts her best, she flings herself. (9.1.1–4)

The ideal middle-class woman realizes herself by dedicating her life to
supporting others, particularly her husband, as if she were without aspirations of her own. For Patmore, if the husband fails, the proper wifely
response is to assume responsibility and accept the fault herself as a consequence of her failing to meet her duties, which include, moreover, unconditional devotion to her husband, even if her love is unreciprocated:

She leans and weeps against his breast,
And seems to think the sin was hers;
Or any eye to see her charms,
At any time, she's still his wife,
Dearly devoted to his arms;
She loves with love that cannot tire;
And when, ah woe, she loves alone,
Through passionate duty love springs higher,
As grass grows taller round a stone. (9.1.15–23)

Even before Shaw had Vivie reject this mode of femininity, he himself had already repudiated this idealized, "womanly woman" in his critical essay *The Quintessence of Ibsenism* (1891). "Although romantic idealists generally insist on self-surrender as an indispensable element in true womanly love, its repulsive effect is well known and feared in practice by both sexes" (56). He continues: "It is not surprising that our society, being directly dominated by men, comes to regard Woman, not as an end in herself like Man, but solely as a means of ministering to his appetite. The ideal wife is one who does everything that the ideal husband likes and nothing else. Now to treat a person as a means instead of an end is to deny that person's right to live" (58). Finally, he concludes: "The sum of the matter is that unless Woman repudiates her womanliness, her duty to her husband, to her children, to society, to the law and to everyone but herself, she cannot emancipate herself" (61). Were a New Woman like Vivie to marry, what sort of mother would she be? Presumably not the model of selfless maternity who could be described as "angel in the house." Vivie definitively signals the repudiation of idealized womanly conventions by rejecting Frank and ripping up the note from him, affirming that women like Vivie accept heterosexual relationships only on their own terms, without an obligation to marry and start a family. And, the woman who repudiates her womanliness may even be a woman who not only eschews the conventional terms of heterosexuality but actively flouts them by choosing to love another woman.

The profound resistance to the emancipation from idealized femininity that Shaw and Vivie espouse is implicit in a talk Virginia Woolf gave more than forty years after Shaw addressed the issue in print. In "Professions for Women," Woolf addressed the impact of the "angel in the house" with acerbic acuity:

> In those days—the last of Queen Victoria—every house had its Angel. And when I came to write I encountered her with the very first words. The shadow of her wings fell on my page; I heard the rustling of her skirts in the room. Directly, that is to say, I took my pen in my hand to review that novel by a famous man, she slipped behind me and whispered: "My dear, you are a young woman. You are writing about a book that has been written by a man. Be sympathetic; be tender; flatter; deceive; use all the arts and wiles of our sex. Never let anybody guess that you have a mind of your own." (357)

Well into the twentieth century, the Victorian Angel in the House still haunted the psyche of the professional woman asserting herself toward modernism.

The persistent power of this idealization of woman needs to be understood against broad social contexts and Britain's agenda of asserting its might as an imperial power. Middle-class women were crucial to the enterprise of Empire inasmuch as the family was the site of the transmission of the values of nation. In *Imagined Communities*, Benedict Anderson persuasively established the critique that now circulates as an accepted tenet in discussions of nation, that the project of nation building and of national identity is contingent on tropes of family. In speaking of nation—which has its etymological origin in the French verb *naitre* (to be born)—locutions include "motherland" and "mother tongue." As Anderson suggests, since patriotic duty includes the unconditional willingness to give one's life for the nation (7), this sense of sacrifice must necessarily have a corollary in the family, the trope on which the community of nation is modeled; national duty and filial duty thus become one. Against the spurious logic of both nation and family, the role of women, on the terms outlined by Patmore, is crucial because women, as mothers and wives, provide the model of selflessness that inculcates sons as model citizens who will selflessly give themselves to the project of nation, as their mothers did to their families. Women, as Shaw might say, are once again cast as the means to an end, this time in the project of male citizenship.

This ideology had its gaps, specifically in the way it left out daughters, especially those who might have anxieties around their relation to family life and citizenry. Daughters, like Virginia Woolf, were marked by their unease at seeing the extent to which the ideal of selflessness cost their mothers. Unlike sons, whose civic emulation of their mothers was validated and valorized by the nation, women lacked agency through the vote to participate in the public sphere as full citizens, while at the same time, being defined within the private sphere through their relationships with their families—as obedient daughters, wives, and mothers—meant they were idealized entirely through their abrogation of self. As a response to this self-negation, the New Woman is an expression of the desire of middle-class women to be independent on terms that allow for the assertion of agency and identity. The New Woman, in effect, represents the aspirations of middle-class women to forge roles for themselves within society as independent thinkers who were financially self-sufficient. Thus, the New Woman, as a cultural figure, simultaneously threatens notions of the middle-class family and the enterprise of nation because, if she has children, she cannot be counted on to model the crucial selflessness that is a foundation of citizenship.

The threat that this emerging option of femininity represented to the cohesiveness of the nation was not lost on those who opposed the New Woman. Almost as quickly as this mode of femininity appeared through representations in novels, short stories, and plays, as well as in periodical literature, it was countered by satiric representations of the New Woman as less than a woman. She was mannish, prone to preferences for wearing tailored blouses with ties, smoking cigars or cigarettes, and imbibing scotch. In Vivie, Shaw takes the visual cues that signal a mockery of the New Woman and turns them into an expression of independence. She tells Praed, a friend of her mother's, that she enjoys working and that when she tires of work, her idea of leisure is "a comfortable chair, a cigar, a little whisky, and a novel with a good detective story in it" (92). She is, as she tells Praed, "a perfectly splendid modern young lady" (93), not adding that the independence that she realizes is a site of cultural anxiety because, against such a spirit, how will the family—and by extension the nation—survive if women like Vivie become the norm?

While the New Woman represents a rejection of the conventions of family and its commensurate implications for citizenry, Shaw suggests in *Mrs Warren's Profession* that the erosion of the conventional middle-class family was under way even before the emergence of the New Woman as a recognizable figure within British culture. Vivie's mother, Kitty Warren, has supported her daughter financially but has been largely absent from the day-to-day rearing of her child, who spent her early years at school or with paid caregivers. Vivie did not miss her mother, telling Praed, "I hardly know my mother" (94).

Ironically, Vivie's assertion that she doesn't complain about the arrangements opens the unspoken possibility that she is not entirely satisfied with her upbringing, particularly given that she does not enjoy an affective bond with her mother. Her upbringing has featured very long gaps in her contact with her mother; she does not know, nor does she demonstrate an interest in, the identity of her biological father. Mrs. Warren takes on the role of the father while she displaces the role of providing nurture and instruction—the role to which mothers were assigned—to others who have been hired to rear Vivie. Although this unorthodox familial arrangement may have resulted in certain affective lapses between mother and daughter, Vivie's maturation into an independent, assured young woman nonetheless confirms the viability of this household structure.

Importantly, Vivie's contact with her mother is always in England. There, the mother circulates under the name of "Mrs" Warren, an honorific that accords her a measure of middle-class propriety by diverting attention from her marital status and the fact that she bore a daughter outside marriage. There is a strong sense in the play that Mrs. Warren's credibility in comporting herself as a middle-class woman is strained, lacking the modesty that is required of a woman who can be characterized as an "angel in the house."

Shaw hints that while Kitty Warren might want to circulate as a respectable woman through the use of "Mrs," she is unwilling to capitulate fully to the conventions of middle-class decorum in terms of her dress, and so attires herself in ways that accentuate hers as the body of a sexual woman. Shaw continues that Mrs. Warren is *"rather spoilt and domineering, and decidedly vulgar, but, on the whole, a genial and fairly presentable old blackguard of a woman"* (95). As Conolly comments in his notes to the Broadview edition of *Mrs Warren's Profession*, "blackguard" is used by Shaw as a cue that Kitty Warren's past is "dishonourable" (95). While that is undoubtedly true, the unfolding narrative also demonstrates that Shaw is sympathetic to Kitty Warren and her attempts to perform middle-class respectability. Here, the idea of social roles and their "performance" is key because Kitty is apparently utterly aware of the codes of propriety even if her performance of them is a bit rough.

The strain of the performance that might more accurately be described as "impersonation" is readable from the first time that Kitty Warren speaks. In telling Praed that it is his own fault that he has been kept waiting for her because he ought to have realized that she would arrive on "the 3:10 train," she reveals that she is not inclined to spare her friend by offering a demure apology for her chosen time of arrival (95). Further, she is somewhat bossy, telling Vivie to put her hat on and, in so doing, demonstrating a lapse of etiquette around performing introductions (95).

Mrs. Warren asserts her own will on terms that, although different from her daughter's, are nevertheless parallel. While Vivie has little direct knowledge of her mother, in many ways, from the outset of the play, she is presented as being her mother's daughter. She is loath to avail herself of the middle-class refinements purportedly offered by "high culture" and so is not inclined to go to concerts or art galleries which, on a trip to London, she endured for three days, "for civility's sake," and then, given her independent cast of mind, abandoned in favor of work (93). She particularly expresses disgust and impatience at the social performance of conventional values: when Praed admits that his generation substituted "gallantry copied out of novels, and as vulgar and affected as it could be. Maidenly reserve! gentlemanly chivalry!" for sincere interaction (90), Vivie responds by noting that such role-playing must have been "a frightful waste of time. Especially women's time" (90). In a sense, then, the tensions between mother and daughter escalate because each is intent on performing a variation of middle-class femininity: Mrs. Warren is intent on passing as middle class, although on her own terms; Vivie stages herself as the New Woman and so rejects the conventional model of middle-class femininity as atomized by Coventry Patmore.

As the narrative of *Mrs Warren's Profession* evolves, it is clear that at issue is class—specifically, Kitty Warren's aspiration to escape the grinding poverty of her working-class roots and create a life for herself as a middle-class woman. But the action of the play introduces Kitty Warren's dilemma: her performance of middle-class femininity appears contingent on her reclamation of motherhood, the role she has jettisoned in her attempt to secure financial solvency, the undergirding of being middle class.

Kitty Warren makes clear that she assumes she has a right, as Vivie's biological mother, to play the role of mother, but Vivie is far from inclined to accept Kitty's performance. On the evening of the second day of Mrs. Warren's visit with her daughter, the tensions between the two are palpable. Kitty is looking ahead to a great deal of mother-daughter bonding— a prospect that dismays Vivie: "Why? Do you expect we shall be much together? You and I, I mean?" (118). A few moments later Vivie castigates her mother's lack of fitness: "You are shockingly out of condition" (119)—a coded reminder that Vivie, as a New Woman, asserts her independence by engaging in physical activity while women like her mother, aspiring to ideals of middle-class femininity, view athleticism as manly and hence as something a genteel woman eschews.

But the stakes in Vivie's criticism exceed mere comment on the value of physical activity for good health. Vivie uses the comment, marked by its gratuitous cruelty, as a way of managing her relationship with her mother by keeping her at bay. As Vivie's earlier comment that she does not complain about her upbringing raised the possibility of its inverse—that she in fact harbors many unexpressed complaints—this comment raises the possibility that Vivie's apparent intention of keeping a distance from her mother masks the desire of the daughter for a loving and close relationship with the mother who has not been part of her life. This point becomes explicit when Vivie asks if Kitty Warren is her mother:

Then where are our relatives? my father? our family friends? You claim the rights of a mother: the right to call me fool and child; to speak to me as no woman in authority over me at college dare speak to me; to dictate my way of life; and to force me into an acquaintance with a brute whom anyone can see to be the most vicious sort of London man about town. Before I give myself the trouble to resist such claims, I may as well find out whether they have any real existence. (119)

Vivie may well be sincere in her expression of anguish about being a woman—a New Woman—who has no sense of her history; there is certainly no evidence in the text to indicate that she is being insincere. What is significant is the particular terms of her sincerity, which suggest that Vivie is invested in the notion of family. Shaw indicates that a New Woman, despite the satiric depictions of her in the popular press as being anti-family, retains the need for family and its bonds of love. Further, Vivie's expression of her anxiety over family and her awkwardness when her mother begins to cry leave the moment open to a reading that Vivie recognizes that she overplayed her expressions of pent-up anger through the gratuitously hurtful comments about Kitty's physical condition. Vivie's comments hurt her mother, with whom she might very likely crave a more loving bond than her upbringing has afforded her. But sincerity is not incompatible with performance: Vivie may be sincere in her position, but like her mother, she is nonetheless performing herself. The difference is that the role Kitty Warren aspires to play, the middle-class mother, is well established, while Vivie's roles as daughter of a mother she doesn't know and as New Woman created through cultural productions have less-realized scripts. With no social models to follow, Vivie must improvise.

Because well-rehearsed roles are lacking in Mrs Warren's Profession, the interaction between mother and daughter leaves each woman vulnerable and exposed, a trying condition for two women who prefer to be in control of situations. Unable to maintain absolute control in the face of the other's performance, each woman drops the persona she sincerely aspires to embody.

Kitty Warren's response to her daughter's performance is that "*she suddenly breaks out vehemently in her natural tongue—the dialect of a woman of the people—with all her affectations of maternal authority and conventional manners gone, and an overwhelming inspiration of true conviction and scorn in her*" (121). Against her mother's casting off the performance of middle-class motherhood, Shaw notes that Vivie "*is no longer confident; for her replies which have sounded sensible and strong to her so far, now begin to ring rather woodenly and even priggishly against the new tone of her mother*" (121). Thus, by displaying the cracking of the personae for both women, Shaw suggests that as Kitty Warren was performing motherhood, so Vivie, in her own way, was no less performing the role of the aggrieved daughter.

That evening Kitty grants her daughter's request to know something of her upbringing and struggle to escape poverty. Vivie asks her mother: "suppose we were both as poor as you were in those wretched old days, are you quite sure that you wouldnt advise me to try the Waterloo bar, or marry a laborer, or even go into the factory?" (125). Kitty's response is a fast, confident assertion:

Of course not. What sort of a mother do you take me for! How could you keep your self-respect in such starvation and slavery? And whats a woman worth? whats life worth? without self-respect! Why am I independent and able to give my daughter a first-rate education, when other women that had just as good opportunities are in the gutter? Because I always knew how to respect myself and control myself. Why is Liz looked up to in a cathedral town? The same reason. Where would we be now if we'd minded the clergyman's foolishness? Scrubbing floors for one and sixpence a day and nothing to look forward to but the workhouse infirmary. Dont you be led astray by people who dont know the world, my girl. The only way for a woman to provide for herself decently is for her to be good to some man that can afford to be good to her. If she's in his own station of life, let her make him marry her; but if she's far beneath him she cant expect it: why should she? it wouldnt be for her own happiness. Ask any lady in London society that has daughters; and she'll tell you the same, except that I tell you straight and she'll tell you crooked. Thats all the difference. (125–26)

Nonetheless, in recounting her story, Kitty Warren makes clear to Vivie that the choices she has made for herself are not ones she wants for her daughter: "But of course it's not worth while for a lady. If you took to it youd be a fool; but I should have been a fool if I'd taken to anything else" (125). Kitty's choices were made initially because she could see no other way to improve her life. Once she became a mother, continuing her business venture in prostitution is, from her perspective, her only means of ensuring that her daughter could be reared as middle class with access to an education that would ensure that Vivie would have secure prospects, including the ability to support herself financially. Kitty's telling of her story clearly affirms—to the audience, certainly, but to a degree to Vivie as well—that mother and daughter are not, despite appearances, dissimilar, because each values independence, including financial autonomy.

Vivie, in hearing her mother's story, gains a sense of her personal history and a seeming respect for the woman who wants to claim her rights as a mother. At the end of the evening, Vivie tells Kitty, "You have got completely the better of me tonight, though I intended it to be the other way. Let us be good friends now" (127). Act 2 ends with the following exchange:

VIVIE. Well, never mind. Come: goodnight, dear old mother. [She takes her mother in her arms].
MRS WARREN [fondly] I brought you up well, didnt I, dearie?
VIVIE. You did.
MRS WARREN. And youll be good to your poor old mother for it, wont you?
VIVIE. I will, dear. [Kissing her] Goodnight.
MRS WARREN [with unction] Blessings on my own dearie darling! a mother's blessing!
[She embraces her daughter protectingly, instinctively looking upward for divine sanction.] (127)

These closing moments of act 2 are sentimental. The apparent deep divides between Kitty and her daughter are seemingly resolved by Vivie's acceptance of her mother's story as enough to suture the differences between them that arose from the decisions that kept Kitty from being an active participant in her daughter's upbringing. While Kitty's telling of her story, like Vivie's earlier expressions of anguish at the terms of her upbringing, may be sincere, as suggested earlier, sincerity and performance are not antithetical in *Mrs Warren's Profession*. Kitty Warren may be sincere, but in telling her story she is performing, conscious of her audience—Vivie—and so editing out of her narrative the crucial bit of information that she remains active in her business ventures of running houses of prostitution in Europe. The failure to reveal that detail becomes the crux of the final exchange between mother and daughter and its terms of performance which, importantly, are predicated on the appearance of Kitty and Vivie in act 3.

The *morning* after Vivie learns of her mother's past, and so gains a sense of her own history, mother and daughter stroll to the rectory of the Reverend Samuel Gardner, the father of Vivie's suitor, Frank . . . and probably Vivie's father as well. They are preceded by Samuel Gardner and Crofts, *"followed by Mrs Warren and Vivie walking affectionately together"* (131). As if to emphasize the significance of the entry, Frank, who is waiting in the garden, comments, "Look: she actually has her arm round the old woman's waist. It's her right arm: she began it. She's gone sentimental, by God! Ugh! ugh! Now do you feel the creeps?" (132). Moments later Vivie and Frank have this exchange:

> FRANK. . . . But what on earth has happened to you? Last night we were perfectly agreed as to your mother and her set. This morning I find you attitudinizing sentimentally with your arm around your parent's waist.
>
> VIVIE *(flushing)*. Attitudinizing!
>
> FRANK. That was how it struck me. First time I ever saw you do a second-rate thing. (133)

The terms of the performance suggest that Vivie, through her entrance with her arm around her mother, stages her forgiveness of Kitty, the fallen woman who, because of dire poverty, made an imprudent choice to enter a life of prostitution. Vivie, during her conversation with her mother on the preceding evening, makes clear that she believes that each of us has the freedom to exercise choice:

> Everybody has some choice, mother. The poorest girl alive may not be able to choose between being Queen of England or Principal of Newnham; but she can choose between ragpicking and flowerselling, according to her taste. People are always blaming circumstances for what they are. I dont believe in circumstances. The people who

get on in this world are the people who get up and look for the circumstances they want, and, if they cant find them, make them. (121)

But Vivie's acceptance of her mother is contingent on her mother's account of her history, which, as noted earlier, leaves out the detail that Mrs. Warren is still in business. Vivie has accepted her mother as a woman who *owned* brothels, a fallen woman who saw the folly of her ways and has left her wanton life behind. Vivie's reception of her mother speaks to class, in terms that were readable to Shaw's audience: the pose is the progressive middle-class woman who extends the charity of acceptance to the fallen, working-class woman who has recognized her errors.

Vivie, as Frank predicts, soon loses her illusions about her mother when, in conversation with Crofts in the garden of the rectory, she discovers that her mother and Crofts are still in business.

Vivie, at least before Crofts, is not willing to renounce her mother fully, and so defends her mother to Crofts, saying, "My mother was a very poor woman who had no reasonable choice but to do as she did. You were a rich gentleman; and you did the same for the sake of 35 per cent. You are a pretty common sort of scoundrel, I think. That is my opinion of you" (139). With the reality of her situation sinking in, she admits that she has never asked the source of the money that has supported her: "I myself never asked where the money I spent came from. I believe I am just as bad as you" (140).

The terms of Vivie's coming to an awareness about how her mother provided for her daughter are personal, but Vivie is the metonym for the New Woman. Crofts atomizes those who have secured their social standing and high regard through questionable business ventures that allow them to contribute philanthropically, for example, through scholarships (140). Shaw's point is that social standing is contingent on capital and its exploitation of labor, a point to which he gives voice through Vivie, who says, "When I think of the society that tolerates you, and the laws that protect you! when I think of how helpless nine out of ten young girls would be in the hands of you and my mother! the unmentionable woman and her capitalist bully—" (140).

Crofts has made his point, harrowing to Vivie, when he tells her that she has lived on the profits of capital, "It paid for your education and the dress you have on your back. Dont turn up your nose at business, Miss Vivie: where would your Newnhams and Girtons be without it?"

(138). The plural of "Newnhams and Girtons" is significant as a moment when Shaw offers a prescient critique of the New Woman who, as a mode of middle-class femininity, is a consequence of the capital to which this mode of womanhood is indebted. Shaw, in suggesting that the New Woman is an effect of capital, implicitly challenges the dominant reaction to her as a figure who counters middle-class values. Shaw's implication is that the force of capitalism and its ideologies are so entrenched that dissident figures, such as the New Woman, merely *seem* to challenge the dominant structures of society, without actually doing so. Vivie, Shaw's figure of the New Woman in *Mrs Warren's Profession*, recognizes the terms of contradiction in which she lives. When Crofts, in anger, ends his conversation with her saying, "Damn you!" Vivie's response is "You need not. I feel among the damned already" (141).

By this point, Vivie is aware that her independence as a New Woman, contingent on her upbringing and education, is a consequence of the money that her mother—and Crofts—earned and continue to earn through employing women in prostitution. As the terms of the earlier parts of the exchange between Crofts and Vivie make clear, the issue is less the particulars of the business in which Crofts and Mrs. Warren are engaged and more its exploitative practices. Shaw suggests that, given that capital is contingent on the undervaluing of the labor of workers to generate profit, all capitalist enterprises are, de facto, modes of prostitution that depend on the exploitation of labor.

From a dramaturgical standpoint, Shaw could have ended *Mrs Warren's Profession* at the point in act 3 when Vivie declares herself "damned." But he does not, instead choosing to include act 4, which derives its theatrical power through the depiction of an angry exchange between Kitty Warren and her daughter. The final act of *Mrs Warren's Profession* echoes the exchange between mother and daughter in act 2, but with a crucial difference: Vivie has additional information about Kitty Warren that fuels Vivie's refusal to capitulate to Kitty's sentimental claims as her mother. Shaw's powerful dialogue risks the audience's losing sight of the context of the exchange between mother and daughter, and so of the stakes. Vivie, apparently deeply unsettled by what has transpired in the country, removes herself to London to take refuge in her place of work: the work which, as she mentioned in act 1, casts her, like her mother, as she who engages in business. Her sanctuary is disrupted, first by the appearance of Frank, who professes that his feelings for Vivie have not changed, and then by Praed, who is leaving for Italy and tries to convince Vivie to join him (147). Both men fail to win over Vivie and leave, setting the stage for Vivie's third visitor: her mother.

Kitty Warren visits her daughter with the intention of again claiming her rights to Vivie's affections on the grounds that she is Vivie's biological mother. Mrs. Warren has changed little in the course of the play; she is still the "*spoilt and domineering*" (95) woman she was in act 1. Her approach to her daughter indicates that she harbors an illusion that they can maintain a pro forma relationship as mother and daughter, as if the events of the preceding days have had no impact. Mrs. Warren still wants to perform the role of mother with Vivie playing the supporting role of daughter.

For Vivie, performing the role of Kitty Warren's daughter is impossible because her mother continues to make money through prostitution. Vivie returns her allowance, which shocks Mrs. Warren, who misunderstands the gesture as Vivie's dissatisfaction with her portion of her mother's wealth, and offers to make reparations by doubling it (156). She fails to appreciate that in light of the revelations that have occurred during the visit, Vivie wishes to sever all ties with her and go her own way, ceasing any further contact with her (156), and tries to dismiss her mother with a simple but forceful word: "Goodbye" (156). Against this cessation of relationships, Mrs. Warren first appeals to Vivie's capitalist instincts, emphasizing that through her business dealings she has amassed great wealth from which Vivie has benefited and will continue to benefit (157). That strategy fails, and so Mrs. Warren's recourse is to sentimentality: "We're mother and daughter. I want my daughter. Ive a right to you. Who is to care for me when I'm old? Plenty of girls have taken to me like daughters and cried at leaving me; but I let them all go because I had you to look forward to. I kept myself lonely for you. Youve no right to turn on me now and refuse to do your duty as a daughter" (159).

But Vivie holds her resolve to sever whatever nascent emotional bonds she might have established during her visit with her mother. She is clear about her reasons, saying: "I am my mother's daughter. I am like you: I must have work, and must make more money than I spend. But my work is not your work, and my way is not your way. We must part. It will not make much difference to us: instead of meeting one another for perhaps a few months in twenty years, we shall never meet: thats all" (159). Against her mother's protestations, she adds, "It's no use, mother: I am not to be changed by a few cheap tears and entreaties any more than you are, I daresay" (159).

In this statement, Vivie makes clear that she recognizes her mother's appeals are predicated on her *performance* of sincerity. Earlier, Vivie had accepted her mother's edited revelation of her past, which the daughter received as a recognizable narrative of a woman who was born into poverty and engaged in prostitution out of economic necessity. Vivie had accepted her mother's story, reading into its silence an assumption that her mother was no longer active within the business of prostitution. Vivie's supposition of what was unsaid reveals her investments because, although a New Woman, she accepts her mother by offering the largesse of privilege, suggesting that whatever independence she values, its terms are middle class. Vivie can accept Kitty as the fallen woman conditional on the supposition, which proves erroneous, that her mother is no longer a "prostitute and procuress," the two "infamous words" that circulate un-uttered in *Mrs Warren's Profession* (150). Hence, she is willing to enter the garden of the rectory, performing her forgiveness of her mother by walk-ing with her arm around her. Effectively, her embrace stages her charitable acceptance of her mother, whom she supposes has relinquished prosti-tution. Reinforcing her disillusionment around her mother's continued business practice is Vivie's recognition of her own complicity: that she is the woman she is because her mother's money—the sources of which she never queried—offered her the education that now affords her the oppor-tunity to be independent.

The final moments of *Mrs Warren's Profession* and their implications may be somewhat undercut by Shaw's choice to echo the ending of Ibsen's *A Doll's House*, in which Nora takes her leave of her family and, so, leave of the attendant hypocrisies that sustain the middle-class family. By echo-ing the ending of *A Doll's House*, Shaw risks that his audience will read the final scene through a filter of performance: Mrs. Warren is continu-ing her propensity to be self-staging. To a degree she does, but it is worth remembering that performance and sincerity are not incompatible in *Mrs Warren's Profession*.

Although the last moments of *Mrs Warren's Profession* feature a cre-scendo of action and escalating stakes between the characters, with Kitty Warren histrionically playing the wronged mother, that does not dimin-ish the implications of the scene and the critique of the New Woman in *Mrs Warren's Profession*. Mrs. Warren may well be sincere but know of no other ways of expressing herself except through the histrionic performance of sentimentality. But Vivie is her mother's daughter, and not herself immune to expressing her own sincere attitudes through performance, as she demonstrated by her arm-in-arm entrance with Kitty into the rectory garden, a sentimental staging of Vivie's forgiveness of her mother, the fallen woman.

A Doll's House ends with an empty stage, but *Mrs Warren's Profession* does not: Vivie remains onstage as the curtain comes down. The image is a powerful one, leaving Vivie alone to address what she has discovered about her past. Vivie's "Goodbye" is the curtain line to her relationship with her mother, but severing contact with her mother does not mean that she is motherless. While she has chosen to deny her mother, the woman who Vivie is, in a range of ways, is nonetheless her mother's daughter. The New Woman, as Shaw makes clear in *Mrs Warren's Profession*, is a figure who emerges within the context of middle-class values. She is a revision of the codes of middle-class femininity, a woman who has a mother whom she chooses to deny because she refuses her mother's values. *Wanting* to refuse values is not the same as actually refusing them: Vivie and her mother are alike in their values of independence and their propensity for staging themselves. Perhaps Vivie's harsh denial of her mother is a consequence of her seeing the reality that is unpalatable to her: Vivie Warren could not play the role of the New Woman without her notorious mother, a woman who strived to be seen in England as a woman of middle-class respectability so she could provide for her daughter and ensure that she, too, would not be condemned to a life of poverty. Whether or not she wishes to acknowledge it, the New Woman is deeply indebted to the middle-class values of her mother.

Note

1. All page numbers refer to the Broadview edition of *Mrs Warren's Profession*, edited by L. W. Conolly (Peterborough, Ont., 2005).

Works Cited

Anderson, Benedict. *Imagined Communities: Reflections on the Origin and Spread of Nationalism*. Rev. ed. London: Verso, 1991.
Patmore, Coventry Kersey Dighton. *The Angel in the House*. http://www.victorianweb.org/authors/patmore/angel/.

Shaw, G. B. *Mrs Warren's Profession*. Ed. L. W. Conolly. Peterborough, Ont.: Broadview Press, 2005.

———. *The Quintessence of Ibsenism. Major Critical Essays*. Harmondsworth: Penguin, 1986. 25–176.

Woolf, Virginia. "Professions for Women." *A Room of One's Own/Three Guineas*. Ed. Michèle Barrett. London: Penguin, 1993. 356–61.

4

The Politics of Shaw's Irish Women in *John Bull's Other Island*

• • • • • • • • • • • • • • • • • •

BRAD KENT

John Bull's Other Island is steeped in identity politics and is written by a Nobel Laureate renowned for his feminism. So it is strikingly odd that very little commentary has been devoted to its Irish women. The majority of critical responses focus on the deployment and explosion of Irish identity in the play to reveal Irishness as plural and fluid as opposed to an immutable and singular construct fashioned by either imperial or national discourses.[1] More recently, there has been concerted attention paid to English identity through examinations of Broadbent's character.[2] Critics have also begun to explore the importance of the underclassed Irish laborer Patsy Farrel and the English valet Hodson to the play's deconstruction of national identities by offering foils to the newly landed Irish farmers and the English businessman.[3] But despite the fact that the play has generated so much scholarly discussion, it has been completely ignored in feminist approaches to modern Irish drama.[4] Even works devoted to the issue of Shaw's feminism fail to either mention or adequately discuss *John Bull's Other Island* and his other Irish play, the one-act *O'Flaherty V.C.*[5] This situation is all the more startling given the primacy of women as symbols of the nation in both literature and the popular imagination.[6]

Rather than surmise why Shaw's readers have ignored the politics of his depiction of Irish women or probe the effects that this critical lacuna has had on reception of the play, this essay will analyze Shaw's Irish women in *John Bull's Other Island* by situating them in a broad literary history. In so doing, it becomes evident that Shaw was deploying and responding to archetypes that were well known and that would likely evoke specific reactions. His stagecraft is, of course, built on the premise of inciting his audience by overtly challenging their norms while holding their attention despite themselves through the palliative of his comedic wit. He hoped his views would eventually permeate the masses and lead to positive change. Given his reformist impulses, one must ask, as has been repeatedly done in relation to his depiction of Irish and English men, how his depiction of Irish women promotes a particular view of Ireland.

If much of the critical work devoted to the play has been focused on national identity politics, perhaps readers should not be surprised that its women have been largely ignored. One of the most common laments to begin studies of nationalism from feminist and women's studies perspectives is that the canonical titles of the field noticeably lack any serious discussion of how nationalism affects women and of women's varied responses to nationalism.[7] The result of this elision has been that the accepted canon is written from and forms a masculinist view to which women are relegated to secondary status, one that feminist critics claim is indicative of the actual marginalization and oppression women suffer in newly independent nationalist states. Examinations of women's relationships with nationalism therefore simultaneously challenge critical orthodoxies, political representation, and access to power.

In this respect, Nira Yuval-Davis and Floya Anthias were groundbreakers with the publication of *Woman-Nation-State* in 1989. In their introduction to the book they suggest five main ways that women participate in national processes. First, and most obviously, they biologically reproduce the nation through childbearing. They are the means through which the nation increases or decreases in size, some of this depending upon such factors as their roles according to cultural norms and expectations, incentive and punitive programs for having more or fewer children, and the availability of resources. Second, they reproduce the boundaries of the nation in terms of the relationship they and the fathers of the children have to the nation and the nation's definition of what constitutes one of its own in more tribal, sanguinary terms. Third, they ideologically reproduce the nation, in particular in their more traditional roles as cultural transmitters and those often in charge of childrearing. Fourth, they sig-nify national differences, especially through their symbolic figuration as the nation, essentially those for whom the men fight and whose honor needs protection. And fifth, they actively participate in the economic, po-litical, and military struggles of the nation via their roles in the workforce, campaigning and legislating, and warfare.[8] To a certain extent, the women of *John Bull's Other Island* demonstrate all of these aspects, but it is their symbolic figuration that is the most relevant in terms of identity politics and the literary tradition to which they belong.

Ireland has been represented as female in both imperial and national discourses throughout most of the modern era. Writing in 1911, only seven years after Shaw had composed *John Bull's Other Island*, Horace Plunkett attested to the prevalence of this female personification of the nation: "That Ireland, more than any other country, is spoken of as a woman is probably due to the appearance in our national affairs of qualities which men call womanly. And this impression is not merely the cheap attribu-tion of racial inferiority by the alien critic with which we are familiar, it is our feeling about ourselves" (1). The feminine personification of the Irish nation—variously incarnated as Mother Ireland, Cathleen ni Houlihan, Erin, the Shan Van Vocht, and Dark Rosaleen—is such a dominant trope in Irish literature that it is difficult to not read it into the female characters of many works of the pre-Independence period even where such an al-legory was not necessarily intended.[9]

Perhaps the most evident early use of this device appeared in Jonathan Swift's "The Story of an Injured Lady, Being a True Picture of Scottish Perfidy and English Partiality," written in 1706, the year before the Acts of Union that forged England and Scotland into the United Kingdom of Great Britain.[10] In this tale, England, depicted as a male suitor, turns his attentions away from Ireland to court Scotland, thereby leaving Ireland a woman scorned. Political union is thus allegorized in marital union, two separate but complementary entities coming naturally together to create an accordant whole. Swift's tale was updated some ninety years later by the Irish satirical newspaper *The Anti-Union* to stoke nationalist sentiment in the wake of the United Irishmen's failed rebellion of 1798, warning of the potential pitfalls of coupling with an ill-suited lover (Trumpener 134–37). Following the passage of the Acts of Union of 1800, which brought into being the United Kingdom of Great Britain and Ireland, the trope was then developed by other parties to make the union as harmonious as possible.

Irish literature of the post-Union period, most specifically the novel, became dominated by the genre of the national tale. Scholars date this literary form as appearing shortly after the French Revolution and having run its course by 1832 with the passage of the Reform Bill. In Ireland, its life is generally considered to fit within this period, stretching from 1800, the year of the Union, to 1829, the year of Catholic Emancipation.[11] The genre's life therefore aligns closely with the romantic period; this, together with the dating of its origins and its end with political change, marks it as a form intimately tied to reformational, if not revolutionary, forces.[12]

The national tale is defined as having several specific traits, some of which were in fact borrowed quite heavily from such established genres as exotic and historical tales.[13] Despite the limitation its name might suggest, a national tale was written for multiple audiences, specifically those situated in the metropole and the periphery. It describes local tradition, culture, and history in a way that seeks to instill pride and knowledge in those who are Irish and sensitivity and appreciation in those who are English. This generally occurs through three distinct phases: it begins with the journey of an ignorant Englishman to Ireland; it then provides much exposition and explanation of national character and culture; and it ends in a loving marriage between the traveler and a local woman. Through the second phase, it diagnoses the strengths and weaknesses of the past in trying to explain the state of the present. In some ways it is a conservative mode, aligned with the tale of the times in its pedagogical attempts at moral restoration and the drive toward the social harmony that is symbolized in the concluding marriage.

Although it had precursors, most notably Maria Edgeworth's *Castle Rackrent*, the first national tale was Sidney Owenson's *The Wild Irish Girl*.[14] Owenson's novel tells of Horatio, a young aristocratic libertine who is sent from the family's English castle to their Irish estate to repent for his wayward life, a punishment he considers worse than being banished to Siberia, the South Seas, or life among the Eskimos. Through his conversations with the locals, he learns to respect Irish culture and eventually marries Glorvina, the daughter of the chieftain whose family his own had dispossessed. The main struggle of the story comes from within Horatio, in his ability to overcome his metropolitan prejudices and gradually recognize the worth of Irish civilization, aided in no small way by Glorvina's beauty.

But critics should be warned against firmly casting the genre in the mode of its original. While *The Wild Irish Girl* certainly set the template and its immediate successors largely followed its conventions, the national tale experienced some changes over the course of its history. Most importantly, "its central political tendency shifts from a celebratory nationalism, which both recognizes cultural distinctiveness and believes in the possibility of transcultural unions, towards a more separatist position; continuing meditations on a history of cultural oppression makes rapprochement and reconciliation increasingly inconceivable" (Trumpener 146). The later national tales therefore have courtship difficulties, marital crises, and even divorces. The smooth conversion of the English man and the assumed happily-ever-after ending that follows marriage are shown to be shams, and the relationship's fluctuating fortunes point toward the need to renegotiate the political union, in due course leading to Catholic Emancipation in 1829.

One of the national tale's lasting legacies was institutionalizing the burden of representation in its allegorical depiction of the nation as an Irish woman.[15] By the time that Lady Gregory and W. B. Yeats collaborated to write their symbolist play *Cathleen ni Houlihan* in 1902, the feminine personification of Ireland was well established in the popular imagination. When the mysterious Old Woman arrives in the peasant cottage of the Gillane family, she informs them that she has been dispossessed by strangers, singing of her old lovers who have died for her and in the process bewitching the eldest son, Michael. She beckons Michael to sit close to her as she recounts stories of Ireland's heroic martyrs. Set on the west coast of Ireland in 1798, the nationalist resonances were felt by a populace who had vigorously celebrated the centennial of the Rebellion only four years earlier. The Old Woman tells Michael of how her friends are rising to take back her four green fields—the four provinces of Ireland. As she leaves, Michael's fiancée, Delia, arrives to finalize the plans for their imminent wedding, but Michael ignores his young sweetheart, drawn instead to the distant song of the Old Woman. In the end he pulls away from Delia and runs out the door toward Cathleen ni Houlihan. His younger brother enters, and when he is asked if he has seen an Old Woman walking down the road, he concludes the play: "I did not, but I saw a young girl, and she had the walk of a queen" (220). The power of the play lies in its compression, and the unseen though resonant image of the Old Woman transformed.[16]

Cathleen ni Houlihan thus more closely resembles the later national tales than the earlier ones, but with a decided edge. The Old Woman is ill treated, not courted by the English. Meanwhile, Michael runs out on his own marriage with Delia to go after the Old Woman, suggesting that the Irish people must defend Ireland; Delia's future is likewise sacrificed, signifying that Irish women can contribute to the national cause by giving their men to the country. This transparent call for martyrdom led Shaw to comment: "When I see that play I feel it might lead a man to do something foolish" (Gregory 444). Following the executions of the leaders of the Easter Rising in 1916, Yeats, too, famously wondered: "Did that play of mine send out / Certain men the English shot?" ("Man and the Echo" 11–12).

Shaw's comments directed at Yeats in his preface to *John Bull's Other Island* thus need to be reconsidered in this context. Shaw begins by claiming that the play was written in 1904 at Yeats's request "as a patriotic contribution to the repertory of the Irish Literary Theatre" (Shaw, "Preface" 13). But Yeats refused to stage it, Shaw readily admitting that the play was well beyond the theater's resources. This was certainly the case in terms of the Abbey's small stage and its lack of English actors to play Broadbent and Hodson.[17] Shaw, though, felt that the rejection of his play was likely due to Yeats getting "rather more than he bargained for": "It was uncongenial to the whole spirit of the neo-Gaelic movement, which is bent on creating a new Ireland after its own ideal, whereas my play is a very uncompromising presentment of the real old Ireland" ("Preface" 13). This comment has generally been read as Shaw's challenge to the Yeatsian construct of romantic Irishness, the famous "dreaming, dreaming, dreaming, dreaming" that irritates the play's Larry Doyle to no end (*John Bull's Other Island* 84).[18] But given that the allegorical use of Ireland is the most important device that Gregory and Yeats employ to urge and fashion a free Ireland in their hyper-nationalist *Cathleen ni Houlihan*, there should be some exploration of Shaw's own use of the trope, specifically through Nora and Aunt Judy, if *John Bull's Other Island* is to be understood as a response to the political aesthetics of the Irish cultural revival.[19]

Perhaps the reticence of critics to analyze the women of *John Bull's Other Island* stems from a perceived lack of importance that Shaw himself imparted to women in his play. A cursory examination of the preface, which is impressively half as long as the very lengthy play it precedes, has no meaningful discussion of women.[20] This masculinist perspective is emphasized in the opening stage directions, where the office of Doyle and Broadbent is described as "a room which no woman would tolerate, smelling of tobacco, and much in need of repapering, repainting, and recarpeting" (71). The world of business and politics—which their office represents through the map of South America in which the men's syndicate has financial interests, the poster advertising a steamship company, the portrait of Gladstone, and the caricature of Balfour and Chamberlain—is masculine territory.

This perspective has its complement in the opening directions of the second and third acts that confront the audience with natural Irish landscapes. In the move to Ireland, the man-made phallic round tower and the man-erected menhir rise from the feminine rolling hills. Later, in the garden of Cornelius Doyle's house, where Larry and Broadbent sit at opposite ends of a table having finished eating their breakfast, there is a "mutilated remnant of a huge plaster statue, nearly dissolved by the rains of a century, and vaguely resembling a majestic female in Roman draperies." She has "a wreath in her hand" and "stands neglected amid the laurels. Such statues, though apparently works of art, grow naturally in Irish gardens" (115). According to this description, the female form has, since roughly the time of the Acts of Union in 1800, become one with the Irish landscape; the two have literally dissolved into and grown out of one another. The natural world in which the men are attended to by Aunt Judy is therefore not only feminized, it is feminized in national terms when compared to the masculine English office. As the trope of female Ireland is inscribed in the stage directions, it is not too much to ask that the critic should consider Nora and Aunt Judy, the play's two female Irish characters, in this allegorical light.

Just as the hero of the national tale reluctantly travels from England, learns about and finally respects Irish culture and history, and ends by marrying an Irish girl, so Broadbent travels from England with his revolver to protect him from the savage locals, encounters Irish culture, and becomes engaged to Nora. Well, not quite. Whereas the middle phase is generally marked by an intellectual and sentimental engagement with Ireland that allows the marriage to occur on more equal terms which will increase the possibility of continued married bliss, Broadbent stumbles and forces his way into Nora's life. He never asks for a local interpretation of Ireland; instead, he relies on a Murray travel guide, a series that was published by and for Englishmen at the height of the Victorian imperial era. And he always misinterprets—willingly or not—local explanations and intentions as merely confirming his ideas of Ireland instead of challenging them.

In this regard, Shaw appears to suggest that England is incapable of ever understanding Ireland because it simply refuses to take the time or interest to do beyond what it must in order to fulfill its own goals. Broadbent attempts to charm Nora through flattery, noting that "all the harps of Ireland are in your voice," but she can only laugh at him (111). Frustrated, he seizes her arms and commands her to take him seriously, the violence of which leads her to take offense. When he worries that he has caused her concern because he has been traitorous to Larry, she is further annoyed: "What has Larry to do with it? It's an act of disrespect and rudeness to me: it shews what you take me for. You can go your way now; and I'll go mine" (111). And his blurted marriage proposal is categorically refused, Nora reproaching him to "get your sense back again" (113). However, the scene ends with Nora excusing Broadbent's behavior on the effects of his having imbibed poteen earlier in the evening.

While Broadbent's courtship of Nora makes for great comedy, it is one of the clumsiest and least satisfying in Shaw's oeuvre. Nora is constantly bemused and affronted by all that he does, whether it is in his English humor or bumbling efforts at romance. Even in the scene in which he offers his manly chest for her to cry upon, she is "incommoded and not at all enraptured by his ardor" (161). By the end of the play there are still no sparks on her side. If anything, she is degraded by Broadbent: she later complains that he has made her shake hands with the lower classes of men she never formerly acknowledged and, what's more, she will have to have tea with their wives in order to win votes so that Broadbent can stand as the new Member of Parliament.

Although Nora resonates with the audience through her allegorical representation as Ireland, she takes on another symbolic form for Broadbent. When he proposes to her the first time, they have talked for a matter of minutes. He is in love with the *idea* of Nora, of the exoticism and romanticism that she represents for him. In addition to symbolic capital, she most evidently has financial capital. While this is a pittance compared to what she would need to live in London and what Broadbent possesses,

Nora's dowry is important in that it distinguishes her from the people of Rosscullen.[21] By marrying her, Broadbent is more interested in the political and social capital that arises from her financial capital and her Irishness; together, these will legitimize his success. Keegan recognizes this in referring to Broadbent as the "conquering Englishman" (168). Having practically secured the riding's parliamentary seat and marriage to Nora within twenty-four hours of his arrival in Rosscullen, he aligns the political and the sexual in their future union.

Larry, then, functions as a foil for Broadbent in their relationships with Nora. As the Irishman who has some romantic connection with her, the allegorical use of a feminized Ireland asks that we consider Larry as figuring for the Irish people, those in competition with the English. Once again, we turn to Larry to grasp Shaw's own critique of the Yeatsian project. Of the Irishman, he says: "He cant be intelligently political. . . . If you want to interest him in Ireland youve got to call the unfortunate island Kathleen ni Hoolihan and pretend she's a little old woman. It saves thinking. It saves working. It saves everything except imagination, imagination, imagination, imagination; and imagination's such a torture that you cant bear it without whisky" (85). Larry thus rejects Nora and Ireland. Indeed, it has become commonplace for critics versed in the literary history of the representation of Ireland as female to regard Nora as "a diluted version of the *aisling* heroine, a Cathleen ni Houlihan gone pallid and limp" (Kiberd 57), but there is no extended discussion of what such a figure means or what the effects of it are on the play's politics. Nora is described as a "slight weak woman" who lacks "any symptoms of coarseness or hardness or appetite" with a "comparative delicacy of manner and sensibility of apprehension," having "fine hands" and a "frail figure." While Broadbent might consider her "attractive" and "ethereal," Larry views her as "an everyday woman fit only for the eighteenth century, helpless, useless, almost sexless, an invalid without the excuse of disease, an incarnation of everything in Ireland that drove him out of it" (99).

Perhaps focused on this description, one critic claims that Larry "has lost both Nora and the opportunity to represent Rosscullen in Westminster to Broadbent" (O'Flaherty 128). But Larry has *lost* nothing; he simply discards the sexual and political in refusing Nora and the seat that is first offered to him. Larry purposely sabotages these options to ensure that they will not be offered again. Even before he makes the trip across the Irish Sea, he explains to Broadbent that he will not be going back to visit the Irish nation, but to visit his father, Nora Reilly, and the rest of the people with whom he grew up. Ireland is a reality, not a concept for Larry. And the reason behind his reluctance to return is Nora. Despite the fact that he has been living abroad for eighteen years, Larry has remained aloof of his native land, never returning and ignoring Nora's missives. When she tried to engage him in correspondence at the outset of their separation, he stopped that practice by never responding punctually and by pretending that when he traveled her letters and parcels were lost in foreign post offices. In fact, he admits that he would give £50 to escape even seeing one of her letters (91–92). Nora and Ireland have no pull on Larry, notwithstanding her best efforts to charm and woo the exile; her efforts only serve to repel him. Larry takes more interest in the women of England for their marked differences to their Irish counterparts, thereby suggesting that he will not fall into an idealized nostalgia for Ireland but rather revel in his flight and remain overseas.[22] When he is convinced at the end of the first act to finally take the trip to Ireland, it is not because he wishes to supervise the work of the syndicate or to renew his personal relations, but because Broadbent reveals a budding interest in Nora. Before calling for Hodson to pack his bags, Larry remarks: "Oho! Here's a chance for Nora! and for me!" (94). Larry sees in Broadbent's interest the possibility for Nora to better her lot in life and, just as importantly, for him to finally be rid of any sense of responsibility for her and Ireland's well-being.

If readers are therefore to follow Shaw's implicit request at the outset of his preface to the play and read *John Bull's Other Island* as a literal and metaphorical response to Yeats and Lady Gregory, then Larry's rejection of Nora, his apparent indifference to her feelings, his refusal to communicate with her, and his reluctance to return to Ireland are a part of a didactic effort to convince the Irish people to reject the siren's call to martyrdom. While Michael Gillane enacts the sacrifice for the audience, Larry Doyle suggests that there are other options available to young Irishmen. Indeed, when nationalism is challenged by other interests, Shaw allows the latter to come out on top. For example, the exchange between the working-class Hodson and the peasant Matt Haffigan asks that all people become Home Rulers not out of any care for Ireland or national ideals but because the resolution of the national question at Westminster would allow a more pressing concern such as social welfare to become the focus of politics (137–40). Given Shaw's Fabian socialism, this would very much be in keeping with his political views.[23]

However, Broadbent's engagement to Nora and Larry's newfound freedom also point to the disturbing possibility that a rejection of nationalism simply leads to another form of exploitation through the practices of neoliberal economics, transnational capital, and multinational corporations. The political union of the two countries in this allegory will lead to disastrous results for the common people. As Keegan says at the end of the play, the syndicate will bankrupt the resort and buy it back from its ruined shareholders for shillings on the pound, then foreclose on its mortgages, force Haffigan to emigrate, use Doran to drive their slave-wage laborers, befuddle the people's minds with the booze they produce in the distilleries, make workers more efficient by opening a polytechnic, and charge tourists as much as they can (173–74). The success of the syndicate is possible through both its exploitative practices and the blinding effect it has on the locals who believe in Broadbent's empty rhetoric when he submits himself as a candidate for the election. He promises to keep their interests at heart, but he simply mimics the grand calls for national liberation in concluding his vapid appeals to peace, retrenchment, and reform: "I look forward to the time when an Irish legislature shall arise once more on the emerald pasture of College Green, and the Union Jack—that detestable symbol of a decadent Imperialism—be replaced by a flag as green as the island over which it waves" (133).

The apparent ambivalence in the portrayal of nationalism and the women of the play is not a result of Shaw's inability to craft a successfully unified argument against a romantic vision as much as it is a reflection of the deeply conflicted relationship he had with Ireland.[24] Shaw's casting of Nora in a romanticized light through Broadbent and a deromanticized light through Larry encompasses his own ambiguous feelings for the country that he had himself abandoned twenty-eight years earlier. But the writing of the play seems to have reawakened a love of his native land, which he began to visit almost annually for a good number of years. Significantly, six years earlier Shaw had taken an Irish woman as his wife.

Like Shaw and Charlotte's own relationship, the Irish women of *John Bull's Other Island* are barren of sexuality. Aunt Judy has likely never married or had children, having lived for many years with Cornelius Doyle to raise her motherless nephew Larry and the orphaned Nora. Well into her thirties, Nora is not described in sexually fecund terms, being slight and frail—although Broadbent promises her that with time his embraces will "plump out your muscles" and "set up your figure" (163–64). In fact, the men and the women are all bachelors, with marriage only a future prospect between two aging people with little hope of children issuing from the union.[25] In this regard, the futures of Ireland and of Anglo-Irish relations do not bode well, having apparently run their course. Larry describes Ireland in even more visceral terms: "First she was given to the rich; and now that they have gorged on her flesh, her bones are to be flung to the poor, that nothing can be done but suck the marrow out of her" (129). The only way to regenerate her, he claims, is for men of ability to take her to hand, for someone like Larry or Broadbent to make her useful. As Larry says to Nora: "Nora Reilly was a person of very little consequence to me or anyone else outside this miserable little hole. But Mrs Tom Broadbent will be a person of very considerable consequence indeed" (166). Instead of living an empty life in Rosscullen, she will find herself at the center of the world in Broadbent's London circles. Here, Larry tells her, "You will find your work cut out for you keeping Tom's house and entertaining Tom's friends and getting Tom into parliament; but it will be worth the effort" (166–67). The relationship is one in which her role will be to campaign on Broadbent's behalf, to ensure that he stands a chance for election and reelection. No one, not even Nora, raises the possibility of a maternal role in having children.

Shaw's critique of the sterility of national and neoliberal discourses—the one depopulating the country through adherence to sacrifice, the other depopulating the country through destruction of traditional ways of life and enforced emigration—converges in Broadbent's future marriage to Nora. The one potential savior of this situation is Nora herself: through her campaigning and socializing on her husband's behalf she could affect the direction of Anglo-Irish politics. Such women were at the fore of the Irish nationalist cause around the time of Shaw's play: one need only consider Lady Gregory, Maud Gonne, Alice Stopford Green, and the Countess Markiewicz as some of the many diverse pivotal figures, the first two even having played the role of the Old Woman in productions of *Cathleen ni Houlihan*.[26] Lady Lavery, another woman active in the movement, and one whom Shaw knew well, was involved in the negotiations that brought about the treaty to end the Anglo-Irish War in 1921. Preferring silent diplomacy to confrontational politics and public gestures, she hosted the

Irish delegates at her social soirees to help pave the way for smoother relations between the two parties. She was later memorialized for her efforts: her likeness, painted by her husband, John Lavery, graced Irish banknotes from 1928 to 1978, purposely symbolizing Mother Ireland and Cathleen ni Houlihan.[27] The figuration of Ireland as a female would then come to have both symbolic and financial currency in post-Independence Ireland.

The hospitality and social graces that Nora learns from Aunt Judy are important for how they will serve her to further political ends in London. Broadbent, in one of his many attempts to charm the locals, remarks upon Aunt Judy's "warm-hearted Irish hospitality" (147). From the time of his arrival in Rosscullen, she worries over his comfort, going so far as to refuse him the occasion to take a room at an inn and to offer him her own bed (106); she also harangues Larry for dragging the chairs outside for Broadbent and Larry to eat their breakfast for fear that they will catch their deaths in the cold air (117). In catering to the conquering Englishman, her hospitality allows him to feel welcome. Such acts of kindness to an Englishman by an Irish woman on the stage of this period, especially in a play written for the Abbey Theatre, would have certainly raised some eyebrows. However, the women are excluded from the discussion as to who will be the local candidate for the parliamentary seat (122–37), as might be expected given that women were still disenfranchised at this time and would be for more than another decade to come. Aunt Judy's quip that she would not give the seat to a man at all—"It's a few women they want in parliament to stop their foolish blather" (146)—is the only indication that either of the women is politically engaged, and it should be read for the good joke that it is rather than a suffragette's critique.

But Aunt Judy's and Nora's service to the men and their command of the domestic space allow them some political agency. As they clear the table of the breakfast dishes, they relate to Larry and Broadbent the social and economic changes that the Wyndham Land Act, passed in 1903, has had on the locals in its facilitation of the massive transfer of the land into Irish hands.[28] And when Cornelius Doyle wanders off to borrow more money from Broadbent, Aunt Judy dismisses herself to follow him out "with a resolute air that bodes trouble" for him (154). She has, she says, seen the negative effects of borrowing on credit, something that Cornelius has not learned despite having been formerly employed as an estate agent for the previous landlord. Her power is exerted behind the scenes, in the same way as Larry hints that Nora's will be exerted in London.

In this respect, the women of *John Bull's Other Island* move from being the flat allegorical figures of Ireland to discreet actors who can affect their own and their nation's destiny. Broadbent half-bullies and half-charms his blustery way into engagement with Nora, but she can and will make the most of it. She threatens Larry with as much when, just before she leaves the stage for the last time, she says, "if I have to keep his house for him, at all events I can keep you out of it; for Ive done with you; and I wish I'd never seen you. So goodbye to you, Mister Larry Doyle" (167). Regardless of Larry's initial rejection of her, she comes to reject him, already stating before her marriage and her first trip to England that she will assert her power as the head of Broadbent's house by selecting who will and who will not have social—and thereby economic and political—access to him. She will become what Larry has envisioned: a powerful woman who will help to get her husband elected.

Nora might have been named after Ibsen's famous heroine, but she will not live her married life as a mere plaything. Broadbent may regard her as such, but she has already displayed considerably more prenuptial feistiness than her Norwegian counterpart does before she finally closes the door behind her. The reader should beware of reading Shaw's allusions as simple templates or direct references; he plays with and explodes expectations too much throughout his oeuvre to accept the analogy at face value. Instead, he proposes a Nora who will define her place and exert her power, circumspect though she may be. She has shown her capacity to put Broadbent on the defensive and has even convinced him that he is drunk when he is not. *John Bull's Other Island*'s enactment of the development of the national tale in its shifting and gradually fleshed out gendered relations is an allegory in itself for the complexity of the political context of its time. But it is also a reflection of Shaw's own ambiguous relationship with Ireland and a testament to his repudiation of facile diagnoses and prescriptions. And, more importantly, it points to the transformative potential of women in the domestic and political spheres.

Notes

1. See, for example, Grene; Kiberd; and Jenckes.
2. See, for example, Schrank; and Cullingford, *Ireland's Others*.
3. See, for example, Gahan; and Kent.

4. See, for example, Harris; Sihra; and Johnson and Cairns. Harris's work does not even mention Shaw once; it is more properly a study of the drama of the Abbey Theatre in the modern period than of modern Irish drama. Although Sihra might be excused from including a discussion on Shaw because the book is largely devoted to recuperating women authors and challenging the masculinist canon of Irish drama, there are three essays wholly dedicated to the work of three male playwrights: Samuel Beckett, Stewart Parker, and Frank McGuinness. Shaw is mentioned twice: once as a part of the male-dominated canon and once as an abiding interest of Siobhán McKenna. In Johnson and Cairns's collection of essays, which is largely but not only concerned with drama, Shaw rates one mention, in which it is said that he differed from Yeats significantly as one who "offered powerful feminist analyses of the 'Woman Question'" (Cullingford, "Yeats" 47), yet Yeats and not Shaw is the focus of the study.

5. See, for example, Gainor. The earliest collection of essays on Shaw's feminism devotes all of four lines to Nora; it also offers about a half a page to *O'Flaherty V.C.* in an essay on mothers in Shaw's plays (Weintraub 9 and 154).

6. I include a brief discussion of the issue in an earlier article but only provide one page to raise the issue, as I was, like the other critics I mention, largely concerned with the deconstruction of masculine national identities (172–73).

7. See, for example, Yuval-Davis, *Gender & Nation*; Albanese; Yuval-Davis, "Gender and Nation"; Ranchod-Nilsson and Tétreault; and Racioppi and See. Werbner and Yuval-Davis's essay leads one to conclude that the masculinist focus of nationalism studies arises from nationalism's masculist tendencies since its rise in the modern era. A casual glance of works by such luminaries as Benedict Anderson, Walker Connor, Eric Hobsbawm, Elie Kedourie, Hans Kohn, Tom Nairn, and Anthony D. Smith attests to this claim.

8. The relevance of this typology is evident in how more recent studies approvingly cite and are dependent upon it. See, for example, Wilford; and Albanese.

9. See Innes.

10. Notably, John Arbuthnot, a friend of Swift's and a fellow member of the Scriblerus Club, is credited with popularizing the English national allegory of John Bull in his political pamphlets of 1712, collected and reissued as *The History of John Bull*.

11. See Burgess; and Ferris, "The Irish Novel."

12. The inclusion of Ferris's essay in *The Cambridge Companion to Fiction in the Romantic Period* bears this out.

13. For more on the genre's development, see Trumpener; Burgess; Ferris, "The Irish Novel"; Ferris, "Writing on the Border"; and Ferris, *The Romantic National Tale and the Question of Ireland*.

14. For an excellent critical edition containing both of these works, see J. M. Smith, *Two National Tales*.

15. This is a common term used in gendered studies of nationalism. See, for example, Yuval-Davis, *Gender & Nation*, 45.

16. For analyses of Yeats's gendered aesthetic politics, see Howes; and Cullingford, *Gender and History in Yeats's Love Poetry*. The play's composition history reveals another

layer of gendered politics: although Yeats claimed and was granted sole authorship of *Cathleen ni Houlihan*, it was originally penned by Lady Gregory with Yeats later helping to revise it. For more on its composition, see Pethica.

17. Ann Saddlemyer suggests that the Abbey's directors might also have feared "that a failure from such a big gun as Shaw would send their frail craft onto the rocks and perhaps prejudice later more possible favours from a powerful friend" (236).

18. All quotations from the play are taken from the 1931 Constable edition.

19. While he is open to reading the play and Nora's character in gendered nationalist terms, Ritschel focuses on *John Bull's Other Island*'s links to J. M. Synge's Nora in his *In the Shadow of the Glen*.

20. Shaw only speaks of "those working class members of the Church of England in London, who send their daughters to Roman Catholic schools rather than to the public elementary schools. They do so for the definite reason that the nuns teach girls good manners and sweetness of speech, which have no place in County Council curriculum" (24). His purpose in raising such a fact is to distinguish between Irish and English Protestantism, as Irish Protestants would never allow their children to attend a school of another denomination. Women, then, are simply said to contribute to national differences and are not considered as integral subjects that are worthy of analysis.

21. Larry mentions this very point to Broadbent before they leave England: "A girl with a dowry of five pounds calls it a fortune in Rosscullen. Whats more, £40 a year is a fortune there; and Nora Reilly enjoys a good deal of social consideration as an heiress on the strength of it" (91).

22. Barney Doran at one point asks: "Is it still Larry the bould Fenian?" Larry, however, has long since repudiated these beliefs as foolishness while admitting that he is perhaps even more foolish now (126–27).

23. For a recent examination of Shaw's relationship with Fabian socialism, see Carpenter.

24. A quick read through some of Shaw's writings on Ireland are enough to attest to the complexity of his relationship to his native country. See Shaw, *The Matter with Ireland*.

25. The one time that children are mentioned in the play, it is only to state that they will be exploited by the syndicate, forced to lug the golf bags of the wealthy tourists (168), hardly a positive and promising future.

26. For studies of some of the ways in which Irish women actively participated in politics, the cultural sphere, and military struggles for the nationalist cause, see McCoole, *No Ordinary Women*; Steele; Ryan and Ward; Coulter; and Ward.

27. For Lady Lavery's involvement in the treaty negotiations through her social soirees, see McCoole, *Hazel*.

28. For discussions of the importance of the Wyndham Land Act and its transformation of Irish society, see Pomfret; and Solow.

Works Cited

Albanese, Patrizia. *Mothers of the Nation: Women, Families, and Nationalism in Twentieth-Century Europe.* Toronto: U of Toronto P, 2006.

Anderson, Benedict. *Imagined Communities: Reflections on the Origin and Spread of Nationalism.* London: Verso, 1991.

Anthias, Floya, and Nira Yuval-Davis. Introduction. *Woman-Nation-State.* Ed. Nira Yuval-Davis and Floya Anthias. London: Macmillan, 1989. 1–15.

Arbuthnot, John. *The History of John Bull.* [1712]. Ed. Alan W. Bower and Robert A. Erikson. Oxford: Clarendon, 1976.

Burgess, Miranda. "The National Tale and Allied Genres, 1770s–1840s." *The Cambridge Companion to the Irish Novel.* Ed. John Wilson Foster. Cambridge: Cambridge UP, 2006. 39–59.

Carpenter, Charles A. *Bernard Shaw as Artist-Fabian.* Gainesville: UP of Florida, 2009.

Connor, Walker. *Ethnonationalism: The Quest for Understanding.* Princeton, NJ: Princeton UP, 1994.

Coulter, Carol. *The Hidden Tradition: Feminism, Women and Nationalism in Ireland.* Cork: Cork UP, 1993.

Cullingford, Elizabeth Butler. *Gender and History in Yeats's Love Poetry.* Cambridge: Cambridge UP, 1993.

———. *Ireland's Others: Gender and Ethnicity in Irish Literature and Popular Culture.* Notre Dame, Ind.: U of Notre Dame P, 2001.

———. "Yeats: The Anxiety of Masculinity." *Gender in Irish Writing.* Ed. Toni O'Brien Johnson and David Cairns. Milton Keynes, Eng.: Open UP, 1991. 46–67.

Ferris, Ina. "The Irish Novel, 1800–1829." *The Cambridge Companion to Fiction in the Romantic Period.* Ed. Richard Maxwell and Katie Trumpener. Cambridge: Cambridge UP, 2008. 235–49.

———. *The Romantic National Tale and the Question of Ireland.* Cambridge: Cambridge UP, 2002.

———. "Writing on the Border: The National Tale, Female Writing, and the Public Sphere." *Romanticism, History, and the Possibilities of Genre: Re-Forming Literature, 1789–1837.* Ed. Tilottama Rajan and Julia M. Wright. Cambridge: Cambridge UP, 1998. 86–106.

Gahan, Peter. "Colonial Locations of Contested Space and *John Bull's Other Island.*" *SHAW: The Annual of Bernard Shaw Studies* 26 (2006): 194–221.

Gainor, J. Ellen. *Shaw's Daughters: Dramatic and Narrative Constructions of Gender.* Ann Arbor: U of Michigan P, 1991.

Gregory, Lady Augusta. *Seventy Years: Being the Autobiography of Lady Gregory.* Ed. Colin Smythe. Gerrards Cross: Colin Smythe, 1974.

Grene, Nicholas. *The Politics of Irish Drama: Plays in Context from Boucicault to Friel.* Cambridge: Cambridge UP, 1999.

Harris, Susan Cannon. *Gender and Modern Irish Drama.* Bloomington: Indiana UP, 2002.

Hobsbawm, Eric. *Nations and Nationalism since 1780: Programme, Myth, Reality.* Cambridge: Cambridge UP, 1990.

Howes, Marjorie. *Yeats's Nations: Gender, Class, and Irishness.* Cambridge: Cambridge UP, 1996.

Innes, C. L. *Women and Nation in Irish Literature and Society.* Athens: U of Georgia P, 1993.

Jenckes, Norma. "The Political Function of Shaw's Destruction of Stage Irish Conventions in *John Bull's Other Island.*" *Essays in Theatre* 5 (1987): 115–26.

Johnson, Toni O'Brien, and David Cairns, eds. *Gender in Irish Writing.* Milton Keynes, UK: Open UP, 1991.

Kedourie, Elie. *Nationalism.* Oxford: Oxford UP, 1993.

Kent, Brad. "Shaw's Everyday Emergency: Commodification in and of *John Bull's Other Island.*" *SHAW: The Annual of Bernard Shaw Studies* 26 (2006): 162–79.

Kiberd, Declan. *Inventing Ireland.* Cambridge: Harvard UP, 1996.

Kohn, Hans. *The Idea of Nationalism: A Study in Its Origins and Background.* New York: Collier Books, 1967.

McCoole, Sinéad. *Hazel: A Life of Lady Lavery, 1880–1935.* Dublin: Lilliput P, 1996.

———. *No Ordinary Women: Irish Female Activists in the Revolutionary Years, 1900–1923.* Dublin: The O'Brien P, 2003.

Nairn, Tom. *The Break-Up of Britain: Crisis and Neo-Nationalism.* London: Verso, 1981.

O'Flaherty, Gearóid. "George Bernard Shaw and Ireland." *The Cambridge Companion to Twentieth-Century Irish Drama.* Ed. Shaun Richards. Cambridge: Cambridge UP, 2003.

Pethica, James. "'Our Kathleen': Yeats's Collaboration with Lady Gregory in the Writing of *Kathleen ni Houlihan.*" *Yeats Annual* 6 (1988): 3–31.

Plunkett, Sir Horace. *The United Irishwomen: Their Place, Work and Ideals.* Dublin: Maunsel, 1911.

Pomfret, John E. *The Struggle for Land in Ireland, 1800–1923.* New York: Russell and Russell, 1969.

Racioppi, Linda, and Katherine O'Sullivan See. "Engendering Nation and National Identity." *Women, States and Nationalism: At Home in the Nation?* Ed. Sita Ranchod-Nilsson and Mary Ann Tétreault. London: Routledge, 2000. 18–34.

Ranchod-Nilsson, Sita, and Mary Ann Tétreault. "Gender and Nationalism: Moving Beyond Fragmented Conversations." *Women, States and Nationalism: At Home in the Nation?* Ed. Sita Ranchod-Nilsson and Mary Ann Tétreault. London: Routledge, 2000. 1–17.

Ritschel, Nelson O'Ceallaigh. "Shaw and the Syngean Provocation." *SHAW: The Annual of Bernard Shaw Studies* 30 (2010): 75–94.

Ryan, Louise, and Margaret Ward. *Irish Women and Nationalism: Soldiers, New Women and Wicked Hags.* Dublin: Irish Academic P, 2004.

Saddlemyer, Ann. "*John Bull's Other Island*: 'Seething in the Brain.'" *Canadian Journal of Irish Studies* 25.1–2 (1999): 219–41.

Schrank, Bernice. "Staging John Bull: British Identity and Irish Drama," *Postcolonial Cul-*

tures and Literatures: Modernity and the (un)Commonwealth. Ed. Andrew Benjamin et al. New York: Lang, 2002. 128–60.

Shaw, Bernard. *John Bull's Other Island*. [1904]. In *John Bull's Other Island, How He Lied to Her Husband, and Major Barbara*. London: Constable, 1931.

———. *The Matter with Ireland*. Ed. Dan H. Laurence and David H. Greene. Gainesville: UP of Florida, 2001.

———. *O'Flaherty V.C.* [1915]. In *Heartbreak House, Great Catherine, and Playlets of the War*. London: Constable, 1929.

———. "Preface for Politicians," *John Bull's Other Island, How He Lied to Her Husband, and Major Barbara*. London: Constable, 1931. 13–70.

Sihra, Melissa, ed. *Women in Irish Drama: A Century of Authorship and Representation*. Houndsmills, Hampshire: Palgrave Macmillan, 2007.

Smith, Anthony D. *The Ethnic Origins of Nations*. Oxford: Basil Blackwell, 1989.

Smith, James M., ed. *Two National Tales*. Boston: Houghton Mifflin, 2005.

Solow, Barbara Lewis. *The Land Question and the Irish Economy, 1870–1903*. Cambridge: Harvard UP, 1971.

Steele, Karen. *Women, Press, and Politics during the Irish Revival*. Syracuse, NY: Syracuse UP, 2007.

Swift, Jonathan. "The Story of an Injured Lady, Being a True Picture of Scottish Perfidy and English Partiality." *Irish Tracts and Sermons*. Ed. Herbert Davis and Louis Landa. Oxford: Basil Blackwell, 1963. 1–12.

Synge, J. M. *In the Shadow of the Glen*. In *The Playboy of the Western World and Other Plays*. Ed. Ann Saddlemyer. Oxford: Oxford UP, 2008.

Trumpener, Katie. *Bardic Nationalism: The Romantic Novel and the British Empire*. Princeton, NJ: Princeton UP, 1997.

Ward, Margaret. *Unmanageable Revolutionaries: Women and Irish Nationalism*. London: Pluto P, 1983.

Weintraub, Rodelle, ed. *Fabian Feminist: Bernard Shaw and Woman*. University Park: Penn State P, 1977.

Werbner, Pnina, and Nira Yuval-Davis. "Introduction: Women and the New Discourse of Citizenship." *Women, Citizenship and Difference*. Ed. Nira Yuval-Davis and Pnina Werbner. London: Zed Books, 1999. 1–38.

Wilford, Rick. "Women, Ethnicity and Nationalism." *Women, Ethnicity and Nationalism: The Politics of Transition*. Ed. Rick Wilford. London: Routledge, 1998. 1–18.

Yeats, W. B. "Man and the Echo." [1939]. *W. B. Yeats: The Major Works*. Ed. Edward Larrissy. Oxford: Oxford UP, 2008. 178–80.

Yeats, W. B., and Lady Augusta Gregory, *Cathleen ni Houlihan*. [1902]. *W. B. Yeats: the Major Works*. Ed. Edward Larrissy. Oxford: Oxford University Press, 2008. 211–20.

Yuval-Davis, Nira. *Gender & Nation*. London: Sage, 1997.

———. "Gender and Nation." *Women, Ethnicity and Nationalism: The Politics of Transition*. Ed. Rick Wilford. London: Routledge, 1998. 24–37.

II

Shaw's Relationships with Women

5

Bernard Shaw and
the Archbishop's Daughter

• • • • • • • • • • • • • • • • • •

LEONARD W. CONOLLY

Shaw's relationships with various actresses have been discussed extensively in works such as Margot Peters's *Bernard Shaw and the Actresses*
(1980) and documented in collections of correspondence such as *Ellen
Terry and Bernard Shaw* (1932), *Bernard Shaw and Mrs Patrick Campbell*
(1952), and *To a Young Actress: The Letters of Bernard Shaw to Molly Tompkins* (1960).[1] Most of these relationships were disputatious in one way or
another and were usually initiated and sustained by professional and personal (sometimes sexual) imperatives on both sides. There is no doubting
the vibrancy of the correspondence sparked by Shaw's volatile engagement with actresses throughout most of his life, but one very low-profile
relationship with an actress, hitherto overlooked, suggests that even an
emotionally detached Shaw could write insightfully to actresses on a wide
range of personal and professional matters, particularly, in this case, the
challenges facing young women as they tried to establish a professional
career in the early years of the twentieth century.

The actress's name in this instance is Mary Hamilton, remembered, if at
all, in Shavian studies as the first Minnie Tinwell in *The Doctor's Dilemma*,
which opened at the Court Theatre on 20 November 1906. She also appeared as the Parlour Maid and Violet in early productions of *Man and
Superman* at the Court in 1906–7. The critics barely noticed her, but Shaw

did, recalling many years later in a letter (25 February 1942) to British director Irene Hentschel that as Minnie Tinwell "the way she managed to convey in two minutes that she was quite open to an adventure with any of the doctors was so delicious that Lewis (the original B.B.) slipped his card into her hand as she went out."[2]

The correspondence between Mary Hamilton and Shaw began during the Court seasons and went on, sporadically, for a dozen years or so. None of Mary Hamilton's letters to Shaw have survived, and only seven from Shaw to her are extant (recently acquired by Brown University, and here published for the first time),[3] but there is enough to piece together the nature of the relationship, a relationship that while never intimate prompted Shaw to write freely and engagingly not just about theater but also about the Life Force, religion, and personal philosophies. Like many other women in Shaw's life, Mary Hamilton seems to have had a knack of prompting or provoking him to make some memorable pronouncements in his letters to her. In the longest and most interesting letter he wrote to her (23 November 1918) he bolstered her professional ambitions by telling her, "Acting and playwriting would be the most senseless of tomfooleries if they were ends in themselves. But as attempts to make sense out of life they are among the most important of human activities." And as she apparently struggled to come to terms with personal issues—she never married—Shaw told her that "A life in which intellectual interests and practical activities do not take up fifteen times as much of the waking hours as the affections and sexual passions is a morbid and poor life." Kant, he said, "was certainly a much happier man than Don Juan as well as a nobler one."

Perhaps Shaw's interest in Mary Hamilton was piqued by her particular circumstances, circumstances that set her apart from other actresses in the Vedrenne-Barker seasons at the Court Theatre. She was born in Canada, probably in the Niagara region of Ontario, in 1885. Her Oxford-educated father, Charles, born in 1834 in Hawkesbury on the south side of the Ottawa River in what is now Ontario, was ordained in the Anglican Church in 1858 and served for many years in Quebec before being elected bishop of Niagara in 1885. In 1896 he moved to Ottawa as the city's first bishop, subsequently (1909) being appointed archbishop. He died in 1919.[4]

Known for his strong conservative views on church and religious issues, Charles Hamilton did not approve of his daughter's interest in the stage. Nonetheless, Mary Hamilton left Ottawa for New York in 1903 to attend the New York School of Dramatic Art, where she became the first Canadian to win the gold medal. That achievement led her to move to London in 1904, where she soon found stage work, her first appearance coming in a small role in *The Finishing School* by Max Pemberton, which ran at Wyndham's Theatre for thirty performances in June and July 1904. She then returned to New York, where efforts to find work appear to have been unsuccessful. An inquiry to David Belasco received a polite but curt reply: "Thank you for your note. I am very happy to know that you won the medal. I am sure you deserve it. You know you have my very best wishes for your future success. Some time soon, I shall hope to have the pleasure of meeting you."[5]

So back to London, where she joined the Vedrenne-Barker company at the Royal Court, first appearing there in *Man and Superman* in October 1906 as the Parlour Maid, a role she repeated at the Court when *Man and Superman* was revived in the spring of 1907.

Mary Hamilton was also an understudy for the much more substantial role of Violet Robinson in *Man and Superman*, and in November 1906 she appeared as Violet (for an unknown number of performances) at the same time as she was creating the role of Minnie Tinwell in *The Doctor's Dilemma*, which opened at the Court on 20 November 1906. It was then that Shaw started to write to her, initially in the professional and constructive (and in this case encouraging) tone that many actors who appeared in Shaw's plays were subjected to.

29 November 1906
Dear Miss Hamilton
Violet was all right: you did everything we planned to do very successfully except one line "Let us talk sense,"[6] which you perhaps thought inapplicable to my dialogue.

In Minnie you make only one little miscalculation. You have found out how to make a point; but, being still a young thing, you insist on making all the points. Now there are some points that make themselves. One of them is "*I'm* his wife, sir."[7] You make a little pause before this to show the audience that there is something good coming. Now that is the right thing to do when there is any chance of their being unprepared; but it is stagey when they *are* prepared. In this scene everybody is listening with all their ears; and you begin by saying "Don't believe him, sir: she cant be his wife." Go straight on, quite simply & spontaneously, and you will find it come[s] ever so much better. Perhaps you have found that out already: if so, do not bear malice against me for telling you.

Everything else was just *peu*-ee-fict (the peu is in French): you will do very well in your profession unless some millionaire snaps you up & marries you.

In great haste
Yours sincerely
G. Bernard Shaw

Appearances in *Man and Superman* and *The Doctor's Dilemma* and new—but still minor—parts in John Galsworthy's *The Silver Box* (the Unknown Lady) and Laurence Housman and Granville-Barker's musical comedy *Prunella* (Romp) kept Mary Hamilton on the Court stage regularly until the end of June 1907. Galsworthy was at the performance of *The Silver Box* on 8 April 1907 and wrote to Hamilton (Shaw-like) the next day with some advice. He wanted her to alter the timing and pacing of her entrance, to exercise more body and voice control ("don't try so hard"), keep the giggle ("just right"), but don't "overdo the wriggle of your back." Bear this advice in mind, Galsworthy urged, and you can "make the part a real gem."

But Hamilton's growing frustration with these small roles is evident from Shaw's next letter to her. She had clearly expressed to him the hope that her understudying Violet (apparently successfully) would lead to having the role on a permanent basis, and his reply must have disappointed her.

15 April 1907
Dear Miss Hamilton

I am afraid all the other Violets[8] are disengaged, and on the war-paths; and I must not throw them over. Perhaps they will better themselves presently; and in that case your chance will come.

I have been away in France and so have not seen *The Silver Box*. I hope to, next week.[9]

In haste
much overworked
G.B.S

In the meantime, Hamilton's father had been expressing concerns to friends in London about his daughter's chosen profession. One of them,

Neville Lytton, who had painted Shaw's portrait in April 1906, contacted Harley Granville-Barker, who wrote reassuringly to him on 6 February 1907, taking the opportunity to praise (with some reservations about the handicap of a Canadian accent) Hamilton's abilities. Hamilton herself, Granville-Barker told Lytton, had recently asked him about her professional prospects, and he had told her "she had an excellent fighting chance of achieving some distinction as an actress." "To anybody else," Granville-Barker continued, "I should have said, as I say to you now, that I think she has quite a considerable chance of doing so." Hamilton, Granville-Barker said, "is a hard worker, & beyond that she possesses just the one or two things which even hard work doesn't give." The accent, he stressed, is a problem, and "victory" over that "is essential if she is to do thoroughly well in England, but that could be gained." Lytton should let Hamilton's father know, Granville-Barker concluded, that "the girl has got steady, congenial &, as far as it goes in this profession [*sic!*], useful work to do. We certainly should be very sorry to lose her."[10]

Hamilton persevered, and appeared again in *Man and Superman* (still as the Parlour Maid) on 29 June 1907, but that performance marked her final appearance at the Court and in England. Obituaries spoke of her London performances having "won her fame," but in truth her work in five plays attracted little attention and signified promise rather than achievement.

What thwarted that promise, however, was not lack of talent or commitment, but parental intervention. Shaw's next letter to Mary Hamilton, dated 2 November 1908, shows that she had returned to Ottawa to nurse her sick mother, but the immediate pressure to return very likely came from her father, who, perhaps more to his daughter's dismay than delight, came to London in the summer of 1908 as one of 241 bishops who attended the fifth Pan-Anglican Conference, held at Lambeth Palace and presided over by the archbishop of Canterbury. The conference ran from 6 July to 5 August 1908. There is no record of any conversations that Bishop Hamilton had with his colleagues about his daughter's profession, and there is no record either of conversations that he had with his daughter about that profession. But the first must have been marked by embarrassment for him, and the second by pressure he put on his daughter to exchange frivolity and disrepute for respectability and responsibility. It is more probable than not that Mary Hamilton accompanied her father back to Ottawa at the end of the conference.

Mary Hamilton's dilemma was now as clear as it was painful: how to choose between family and professional priorities. She turned to Shaw for advice, and he gave it forthrightly.

2 November 1908
My dear Mary Hamilton

I really don't know what to say to you. An actress musnt have a mother or a father or anything else than her art; and as under existing circumstances the art is seldom as valuable as the parent, it is impossible to make a fixed rule as to which to choose. If your mother's ill health is not carefully nursed she will probably get well. If it is, she will go to bed for the next 20 years; and how old will you be by that time? Whether you return to the stage or not, your proper place is not in a sick room. One must be human and helpful; but there is a limit to self-sacrifice: no man sacrifices his career to nurse his father; nor does public opinion allow a father to demand or allow such a sacrifice. If you must nurse, nurse your own children.

However, this is only the cold drawn general morality of the situation: I don't know the personal circumstances. I only know that the aphorism in *Man & Superman* (the Revolutionist's Handbook part of it) is true—"If you begin by sacrificing yourself to those you love, you will end by hating those to whom you have sacrificed yourself."[11]

What does the bishop say?

Yours ever
G. Bernard Shaw

It's not hard to guess what the bishop said, but there is almost a ten-year gap until Shaw's next letter to Mary Hamilton, with not much to go on to determine what she was doing during that time. She did, however, spend more time in New York (perhaps after her mother died), playing multiple roles in an operetta called *Little Boy Blue* that ran for 184 performances first at the Lyric Theatre and then the Grand Opera House, closing there in April 1913. And according to one of her obituaries she also did some acting in Ottawa. Her "last stage appearance," says the obituary, was at the city's Russell Theatre on 3 May 1917 in a play called *The Mollusc* (by Hubert Henry Davies), which she may well have seen when it premiered at the Criterion Theatre in London on 15 October 1907. That she was tenaciously holding on to her acting ambitions is also evident from the next Shaw letter, even though by now she was a volunteer nurse for the Canadian army. Asking Shaw to write a play for her was a touch audacious—"cheek" is Shaw's word—especially since she laid down conditions about just what she needed (a comedy with four characters) as entertainment for the troops. Her cheek didn't get a new play out of Shaw, but it did prompt some thoughts from him about charity as well as a whimsical suggestion about how she might persuade her father (now an *arch*bishop) to think more favorably of her acting ambitions. Whatever acting she had been doing in Ottawa was in amateur theater—sharing the stage of the Russell Theatre, as the obituary puts it, with "well known Ottawa residents." And acting for the troops also came in the acceptable category of worthy theater. That might be all right for now, but Shaw—and Mary Hamilton—had higher ambitions.

4 September 1917

My dear Mary Hamilton

Of course I have not forgotten you, and am not likely to. But why must I write you a new play all to yourself? *How He Lied to Her Husband* has four characters. *Overruled* has four characters. *O'Flaherty V. C.*, just published in *Hearst's Magazine*,[12] has four characters. *The Man of Destiny* has four characters. *Passion, Poison & Petrifaction* has four characters. Is it reasonable to ask an elderly gentleman of 61 to try to throw off another youthful trifle for four characters? Just like your cheek to ask me! I am much too old; and the war has left us all too grim and bitter for lighthearted work. However, if I can think of a suitable plot, I will think of you.

If you add the nursing of the whole Canadian army to your domestic duties, you will not have too much time for acting. On principle I object to all gratuitous work for soldiers or anyone else: I think the Government should be made to pay for everything the soldiers need; for in the long run, where people get tired of war charities, there will be no provision for more than their barest necessities, and they will no longer be petted and hero-worshipped: they will be like faded beauties or cast-off mistresses, more wretched than if they had never been popular and adored. But as things are arranged that way for the present, you may as well give your talent for acting a chance: it will be less wasted on the soldiers than in complete disuse. It may even assert itself as imperatively as to insist on its rights, which would be a very good thing for the world. Has your father ever considered that there may be trouble when God asks you what you did with that talent? You can say that you created Minnie Tinwell; but the Almighty might only exclaim "Is that all?" (for he may not think much of my works) and then you will feel just awful.

ever

G. Bernard Shaw

A year goes by before the next extant letter from Shaw to Hamilton. And it seems to have been a momentous year for her. Her father's mental health collapsed, and she seems to have had some kind of less-than-honorable proposition from someone in Ottawa. She turned again to Shaw for guidance, and what he gave her (in a letter written while he was staying with Lady Gregory at her home in Coole Park, Ireland) was a combination of practical help (the name and address of his New York lawyer) and down-to-earth advice about what to expect if she persisted with her "incurable" determination to return to acting. It's not a pretty picture of the barriers facing someone of Mary Hamilton's age (she is now in her early thirties) and limited experience.

5 October 1918

My dear Mary Hamilton

What a ridiculous situation! There MUST be a legal remedy for such an accident: havent you a lawyer to consult? If people become *non compos mentis* the courts must appoint trustees or committees (with the accent on the first syllable)[13] or custodians and administrators of some sort. If a millionaire goes raving mad and leaves a baby to take care of itself, the baby doesnt go to the workhouse. You can get yourself appointed to administer your father's affairs. If you don't know a lawyer, mine is Benjamin H. Stern, 149 Broadway. I must have had some satisfactory introduction when I consulted him; and he has not since robbed or cheated me; and he seems to have a weakness for the theatre.

Your own weakness in that direction seems incurable, and is no doubt of divine origin. But oh, Mary, Mary, you cannot drop such a profession as acting for a dozen years and then pick it up like a ball of knitting wool. Vedrenne's attitude towards an applicant (not to say a suppliant) over thirty is not the same as towards one under thirty unless she has a continuous record of leading ladyhood[s] with no serious gaps in it. I infer from the disgraceful conduct of the gentleman who offered you $500 a week (and cheap enough too: *I'd give you that*) that your personal attractions have developed rather than faded; and in any case your cleverness as a character actress would keep you on the stage in good work at seventy; but you must not expect to get back *instantly*: the door will not open at the first tap. Indeed there never is a door: there is nothing but a stone wall round which you may wander for many months before you find an accidental hole in it to crawl through. Still, the accidents do happen. Every manager has a list of ten actresses for any part, just as he has a list of six authors who are in the swim. But when he has a production on, the ten actresses are engaged elsewhere, or abroad, or ill, or have offended him, or are having divorce cases or babies or what not, and the manager is reduced to saying "I wonder would that little Hamilton girl be any good. She's comparatively cheap, anyhow"; and so you tumble through the wall. It is the same with the young author. He is kept out by what he calls a Ring; but someday none of the Ring have plays ready for the manager; and the stopgap gets his chance. You will be a stopgap until you get yours. But when you get it you will make good.

Barker has married an American authoress (both parties had to get divorced first) and has retired from management into war work and authorship.[14]

I note what you say about the Coburns,[15] and shall for your sake accord them my most distinguished consideration. But the difficulty about *The Devil's Disciple* is that I have withdrawn it for the period of the war. Before the United States joined up it was in demand by the pro-Germans; and I refused to let them have it. Now that America is in the war it is only asked for by political ignoramuses, which includes most of the actors who long to figure as Dick Dudgeon. So there was nothing personal in my refusal of the play to the Coburns, who must, by the way, be great sillies to want to produce an anti-British play during the war.

When you have an idle moment let me know how you get on.

ever

G. Bernard Shaw

And then Mary Hamilton became seriously ill. The so-called Spanish flu of 1918 was an influenza pandemic that killed millions of people worldwide. Hamilton survived, but the near-death experience seems to have caused her to reflect deeply on a number of fundamental issues, and she shared her thoughts with Shaw. He returned her confidence in an extraordinarily revealing letter of his own, one in which he speaks openly and freely about the Life Force, playwriting, acting, morality, love, marriage, and happiness.

23 November 1918

My dear Mary Hamilton

That must have been just the most terrific attack of Spanish flu that has ever come to a mortal woman. However, it has made you write me an interesting letter.

When I talk of God (if I ever do) I am not thinking of the white bearded old gentleman with a frightfully short temper and vindictive nature who was the bogey of our childhood. As to all that I am a square toed mid-nineteenth-century atheist. But I am not in the least a materialist. There is a divine spark in you and me which drives us to do all sorts of things that have no sense as far as our own immediate personal interests are concerned, including the risk of death in terrible ways. There is nothing mysterious about it: it is visibly at work everywhere, and is the driving force that has made life evolve from a speck of live slime in a ditch to mankind, which seems to be its best so far. It makes all sorts of mistakes, from fleas to tigers, and from pain and fear to greed and pugnacity; but throughout it all it seems to be following a steady purpose, and that purpose is the increase of power and the increase of knowledge. We are only its organs: our hands are its hands and our brains its brains; and as it is never satisfied with the power and knowledge these give it, we are never satisfied either, and want continually to know more and be able to do more. The people who are conscious of this, and recognize that they are here for something far bigger than the satisfaction of their own appetites and the ease of their own bodies, and who find such interest and pleasure in those extra pursuits that their bodies and appetites are rather a nuisance to them than otherwise, are the really religious people. You will find it all in the third act of my *Man and Superman*, in Bergson's *Creative Evolution*, in Thomas Hardy's *Dynasts*,[16] and cropping up all over the place in modern thought.

Acting and playwriting would be the most senseless of tomfooleries if they were ends in themselves. But as attempts to make sense out of life they are among the most important of human activities. If you look out into the street you will see life as it actually happens, streaming and jostling along without any discoverable meaning or purpose, ugly, noisy, uninteresting, absurd. The spectacle has no comfort and no instruction for you: you simply ask what the devil all these people are doing and why they are doing it, where they are going to and why they don't stop where they are. To make it intelligible and helpful and instructive it must be taken out of its apparently haphazard happenings, and arranged so that its meaning comes out clearly; so that Minnie Tinwell or Dolly Clandon[17] no longer appear as two figures moving about in a crowd with no discoverable purpose, but as people with characters, histories, experience, the knowledge of which will help those who see them to understand their own characters and histories and purposes and experiences. And as this is part of the divine purpose of attaining to greater knowledge, it follows, dear Mary, that you and I find ourselves urged by the divine spark in us to rescue Minnie and Dolly from the crowd and hold them up to their fellow creatures as complete and intelligible examples of life. We are therefore not the victims of a craze, I for telling lies about people who never existed, and you for dressing up and painting your face and pretending to be somebody else, but instruments of a high purpose, and thus able to preserve our self-respect and even a sense of high importance whilst acting in a way your father thought positively wicked.

The mischief of teaching children to believe in the old God, whom William Blake called old Nobodaddy,[18] is that when the children grow up enough to find out that there is no such person, and that he is an old beast anyhow, they do what you say you did: that is, "pitch him overboard with the words duty, sacrifice, good woman, bad woman" &c. They empty the baby out with the bath [water]. When you are rid of Nobodaddy you still find that there are things that you will feel mean if you don't do; that you will still have to choose between two attractions and sacrifice the less valuable (often the more attractive); and that there are still amiable women and hateful [women?]. Nothing is altered except the application of the words. You perceive that it is your duty to God to go on the stage instead of its being your duty to your father to keep off it; that you should sacrifice your family affections to your vocation instead of the other way about; and that a respectable married lady may be in an advanced state of damnation and a woman with six children and no husband very eligible for Heaven.

Love and happiness are very tricky things. Many people thrive astonishingly on a diet of pure strong hatred. Very few people can stand much happiness. A life in which intellectual interests and practical activities do not take up fifteen times as much of the waking hours as the affections and sexual passions is a morbid and poor life. The philosopher Kant was certainly a much happier man than Don Juan as well as a nobler one. Napoleon said truly that woman is the occupation of the idle man; and he might have added that man is the occupation of the idle woman. Almost all the modern cant about Love is the cant of a class; and that class is the rich middle class in which the women are more idle and luxurious than any others: the main example being the rich American woman. Working women have no use for that gospel. It is part of that gospel that old maids and old bachelors must be very unhappy. As a matter of fact they are not a bit unhappier than other people if they have enough to do.

According to your own account of yourself, you have been a very unreasonable young woman. You have been looking for an ideal man without considering that if you found him, you could not very well have the cheek to ask him to marry a real young woman. How long do you suppose this unlimited and magnificent creature could have stood your limitations if you had found him and seduced him into idealizing you? And then as to your body being the temple of his children, would any woman have children if she reserved her body for dukes or demigods, knowing all the time that it was just an ordinary body like any other woman's body ? But there is a deeper error here than mere self-conceit. What you call your children and his children are neither yours nor his: they are, in the old terms, members of Christ, children of God, and inheritors of the kingdom of Heaven. In modern language they are the children of the Life

Force, of the Élan Vital, which will give to the same couple half a dozen children as different from one another as if they were not even seventeenth cousins, much less brothers and sisters. And that two little impudent animals like Molly Hamilton and Dicky Tompkins[19] should dare to set themselves up as respectively a temple and a priest and an almighty God into the bargain, and refuse to get married until these monstrous privileges should be conferred on them is enough to make me wonder whether you are not ten times as crazy as your father. You need not marry a drunkard or an epileptic or a man like the hero of Brieux's *Les Avariés*,[20] because you wouldnt enjoy the company of such a person; but short of that you can just go out into the street and marry the first reasonably decent fellow with an adequate income ($30 a week will be enough) that you find there. Then *you* will have done your best, anyhow. Surely, though you have played the fool with your chances so long, you can still lift your finger and get a husband as easily as call a cab.

This is the common sense of the case. But of course no case is quite a common case; and each individual must make the necessary adjustment to idiosyncrasy. There is such a thing as a virginity that must wait for the right man, even if it waits forever; but that is not the same thing as waiting for an impossible man under the spell of inhuman ideals. And beware of exaggerating the value of your present body. It will wear out, and the life in it will be remanufactured into fresh bodies. There will be a long string of Mary Hamiltons under different names (though some of them will be quite like the original—which by the way is only a quintillienth copy of the original in the Garden of Eden) who will be busy until the end of the world. One must take chances with one's body if one is to use it at all.

I havent time to write any more.

Ever

G. Bernard Shaw

Mary Hamilton survived the Spanish flu and then finally fulfilled her ambition to return to the stage. The "excellent news" that Shaw refers to in his next letter is her appearance as Minnie Tinwell in a production of *The Doctor's Dilemma* that opened in Henry Jewett's production at the Copley Theater, Boston, on the day that Shaw wrote the letter.

27 January 1919

That is excellent news; but do not let them spoil your Minnie Tin-well, which is exactly right, by telling you to *play out* at it, and try to give the play the hackneyed attraction of a loudly painted person whom the fastidious Dubedat would not have touched with a pair of tongs, and who would certainly not have let him spend her savings. Stick to your inimitable quite glad eye.

All that you say about the company is very interesting, and will be serviceable to Mr Jewett[21] with me. Many thanks for the list.

When you have an idle hour let me know how things march.

G. Bernard Shaw

P.S. I have heard from Mr Jewett himself, and hope to write to him presently, when the political turmoil[22] has quieted down somewhat.

There are just three more letters in the Hamilton-Shaw collection, none from Shaw. Perhaps encouraged by Shaw's support and by her Boston experience—and now free of domestic responsibilities—Mary Hamilton returned to London in 1920. She must have been in touch with Shaw, but the only extant letters are two from John Vedrenne and one from Algernon Blackwood, a writer of novels about the supernatural.

Vedrenne wrote to Hamilton at her London address (63 St. George's Road, SW1) on 9 December 1920, enclosing tickets for a production of J. M. Barrie's *Mary Rose* at the Haymarket Theatre, and complimenting her on "looking so well and charming" when they met. Almost a year later, on 21 November 1921, Vedrenne wrote again, this time in a letter sent to Hamilton at the Charlesgate Hotel in Boston. Vedrenne had been, he says, "surprised and a little hurt" that he hadn't seen her again in London, putting it down to the fact that "woman is fickle." But Hamilton's "long letter" to him had explained that she had again been ill, and so he apologized for his initial reaction. Vedrenne responded to her query about a play she has heard about (he was thinking of producing a play called *Adventure*, but never did), but he declined to answer her questions about Henry Arthur Jones and Shaw "because I would keep on dictating until my typist refused to go on." Vedrenne asked for a permanent address so that he might write again, but there is no record of any further correspondence between Hamilton and Vedrenne.

Nor is there any record of Hamilton's getting any acting engagements in England or the United States after the Minnie Tinwell role at the Copley

Theatre in 1919.[23] The final letter in the Hamilton-Shaw collection, from Algernon Blackwood, written from the Savile Club in London on 17 December 1926, suggests that Hamilton was now thinking in terms of writing rather than acting. Blackwood had previously encouraged dramatizations of his stories and novels (most recently with *Through the Crack*, adapted by Violet Pearn for production at he Apollo Theatre in December 1922), and he gladly gave Hamilton the permission she sought to adapt a story called "Wolves of God" (though "I cannot see how there is enough stuff to make a play out of").

It is not clear where Hamilton was living when she was corresponding with Blackwood, but it seems likely that she was back in Ottawa. Nothing seems to have come of her interest in Blackwood's work, and all indications are that the final twenty-five years of her life were spent in the upper echelons of Ottawa society, with no particular purpose or direction. Her funeral at Christ Church Cathedral on 7 February 1945 was a major social event. Shaw, living alone at Ayot, would not have known of Mary Hamilton's death, but had he been told he would have surely expressed regret that a promising and dedicated talent had been thwarted by a greater dedication to family and social position.

Notes

1. Margot Peters, *Bernard Shaw and the Actresses* (New York: Doubleday, 1980); Christopher St. John, ed., *Ellen Terry and Bernard Shaw: A Correspondence* (New York: Putnam, 1932); Alan Dent, ed., *Bernard Shaw and Mrs Patrick Campbell: Their Correspondence* (New York: Knopf, 1952); Peter Tompkins, ed., *To a Young Actress: The Letters of Bernard Shaw to Molly Tompkins* (New York: Clarkson N. Potter, 1960).

2. *Bernard Shaw Theatrics*, ed. Dan H. Laurence (Toronto: University of Toronto Press, 1995), 212. The "original B. B. [Bloomfield Bonnington]" in *The Doctor's Dilemma* was played by Eric Lewis. In the letter Shaw mistakenly identifies Mary Hamilton's father as an "American" bishop.

3. There are fourteen letters and postcards in the Hamilton-Shaw Collection. The seven Shaw items are all quoted in full in this essay. The other items from the collection referred to and quoted from here are letters to Mary Hamilton from David Belasco (22 March 1905), John Galsworthy (9 April 1907), John Vedrenne (9 December 1920 and 21 November 1921), and Algernon Blackwood (17 December 1926); an undated letter from Lena Ashwell to [Hugh] Ford; and a letter from Harley Granville-Barker to Neville Lytton (6 February 1907). The collection also contains a photograph of Shaw, dated and signed by Shaw on the back of the photograph, 2 November 1908, and presumably sent

to Hamilton with his letter of that date. Particular thanks are due to Don B. Wilmeth, Asa Messer Professor Emeritus at Brown, for drawing the Hamilton-Shaw materials to my attention, and to Stephen Thompson, Scholarly Resources Librarian at Brown, for providing me with copies of the materials.

4. Information on Charles Hamilton is drawn from two websites: http://chamilton.awardspace.com/niagara.htm and http://chamilton.awardspace.com/ottawa.htm, both accessed on 19 February 2009.

5. The Belasco letter is dated 22 March 1905.

6. In act 4 of *Man and Superman* Violet says to Malone, "Oh, well, let us talk sense, Mr Malone. You must feel that we havnt been talking sense so far" (*The Bodley Head Bernard Shaw: Collected Plays* with *Their Prefaces* [London: Reinhardt, The Bodley Head, 1970–74], 2: 705; hereafter cited as *BH*). Presumably, Mary Hamilton forgot the line.

7. The line comes toward the end of act 2 when Minnie asks for the address of "the young gentleman" (Dubedat), the one "that went to catch the train with the woman he brought with him." "Do you mean the lady who dined here? The gentleman's wife?" asks Ridgeon. "Don't believe them, sir," Minnie replies. "She cant be his wife. I'm his wife" (*BH* 3: 372).

8. The "other Violets" were Sarah Brooke (the first) and Grace Lane.

9. It is not clear exactly when Shaw saw *The Silver Box*, but he referred to the play's "penetrating social criticism" in a speech he gave at a dinner in honor of Vedrenne and Barker on 7 July 1907. (*Bernard Shaw: The Drama Observed*, ed. Bernard F. Dukore [University Park: Penn State P, 1993], 3: 1149.)

10. The letter is on Court Theatre letterhead and signed by Barker, but the letter itself is in another hand, presumably that of Barker's secretary.

11. The final maxim in "Maxims for Revolutionists" (*BH* 2: 797).

12. *Hearst's Magazine* (New York), August 1917.

13. Shaw is presumably alluding to the possibility of Hamilton having her father committed to a hospital. In the event, her father moved to La Jolla, California, where he died the following year. There is no record of her mother's death, though it looks as if she predeceased her husband.

14. The American "authoress" was Helen Huntington. Granville-Barker had divorced actress Lillah McCarthy in 1917.

15. Charles Coburn and his wife, Iva Wills, formed the Coburn Players in 1905 as a touring company, performing mostly on college and university campuses with a mostly Shakespearean repertoire. From 1917 the Coburns devoted themselves to full-time management and acting on Broadway (Durham 86–90).

16. French philosopher Henri Bergson's *L'Évolution créatrice* (1907) was published in English in 1911 as *Creative Evolution*. Bergson coined the phrase "élan vital," used later in this letter by Shaw. Thomas Hardy's epic verse drama of the Napoleonic Wars, *The Dynasts*, was published in three parts in 1904, 1906, and 1908. The action of the drama reflects Hardy's concept of an all-controlling "Immanent Will."

17. In Shaw's *You Never Can Tell*.

18. In Blake's poem "To Nobodaddy" ("Why art thou silent & invisible / Father of jealousy . . .").

19. Shaw uses the diminutive "Molly" for Mary, whose prospective husband was, presumably, named Richard Tompkins. The names here are an eerie foreshadowing of Shaw's later relationship—professional and sexual—with Molly Tompkins, whom he first met in 1921.

20. Eugène Brieux's 1901 play was published in England in 1912 (by A. C. Fifield) as *Damaged Goods* (with two other plays by Brieux, and a preface by Shaw).

21. Henry Jewett was an Australian-born theater manager who formed the Henry Jewett Players in Boston in 1914. In 1915 he leased the Copley Theatre in Boston, where he ran repertory seasons that included plays by Shaw (Durham 239–41).

22. Shaw probably had Ireland in mind. On 21 January 1919 the Dáil, or Irish Parliament, met for the first time and reaffirmed the 1916 Declaration of Independence. On the same day, members of the Irish Republican Army shot and killed two police officers in County Tipperary, an event that marked the beginning of the Irish War of Independence.

23. She may have tried again to find work in New York. Among the Shaw-Hamilton letters is an undated one from Canadian-born actress (and friend of Shaw) Lena Ashwell, written from the Algonquin Hotel, to a "Mr Ford," probably the director Hugh Ford, in which Ashwell commends Mary Hamilton as "a *very* clever actress—she did splendid work in London which I saw & admired very much." Ford was active as a director in New York in the 1920s.

Works Cited

Dent, Alan, Ed. *Bernard Shaw and Mrs Patrick Campbell: Their Correspondence.* New York: Knopf, 1952.

Durham, Weldon B., ed. *American Theatre Companies, 1888–1930.* Westport, CT: Greenwood, 1987.

Peters, Margot. *Bernard Shaw and the Actresses.* New York: Doubleday, 1980.

Shaw, George Bernard. *Bernard Shaw Theatrics.* Ed. Dan H. Laurence. Toronto: Toronto UP, 1995.

———. *Bernard Shaw: The Drama Observed.* Vol. 3. Ed. Bernard F. Dukore. University Park: Penn State P, 1993.

———. *Collected Plays with Their Prefaces.* 7 vols. London: Reinhardt, 1970–74.

———. *To a Young Actress: The Letters of Bernard Shaw to Molly Tompkins.* Ed. Peter Tompkins. New York: Clarkson N. Potter, 1960.

St. John, Christopher, ed. *Ellen Terry and Bernard Shaw: A Correspondence.* New York: Putnam, 1932.

6

Writing Women

Shaw and Feminism behind the Scenes

• • • • • • • • • • • • • • • • • •

D. A. HADFIELD

In the latter half of the nineteenth century, "writing women" presented significant anxiety and discomfort as both objects and agents of discourse. Throughout the last decade of that century, perhaps no one wrote more for and about women than George Bernard Shaw, whose advanced views on the "woman question" earned him significant notice as an ardent champion of early feminism. Casting himself as Ibsen's dramatic disciple, Shaw took up the cause of Nora Helmer and Hedda Gabler and wrote the female parts in his own plays with depth and complexity in motivation and thought, placing them squarely center stage to argue their case and earning himself a place alongside Ibsen as one of modernism's great feminist playwrights. However, while Shaw's dramatic writing has generally served to cast him in the role of feminism's champion onstage, a closer look at some of his offstage productions—especially in personal correspondence and relationships with some aspiring feminist playwrights—presents a slightly different vision of Shaw's commitment to women's emancipation: one that suggests that his efforts to liberate women from the bonds of convention may have largely served a desire to constrain and confine them instead within the ones he himself defined. These less-emancipatory impulses may help explain the fate of "Mrs. Daintree's Daughter," the first play attempted by the celebrated Ibsen actress Janet Achurch. Shaw's advice to a dear friend and aspiring playwright suggests that, no matter how advanced his writings *about* women, he was just as anxious as many of his contemporaries when it came to writing *by* women, particularly in the theater.

Throughout the century, rapidly increasing literacy rates, urban migration, and the economic stratification that facilitated the creation of a semi-leisured middle class created unprecedented demand for reading material of a more recreational nature.[1] The symbiotic relationship between developing literary forms and a changing social structure placed popular forms like periodicals and novels in an ideal position to help explain and contain anxieties around social, cultural, and economic upheaval. As Nancy Armstrong has pointed out, this explanation quickly assumed a distinctly gendered flavor, with women becoming the rhetorical figure onto whom a nation could project its anxieties. Citing examples as diverse as the Brontës, Dickens, Thackeray, Eliot, and Carroll, right up to the preeminently popular sensation novelists, Wilkie Collins, Mary Elizabeth Braddon, and Mrs. Humphry Wood, Armstrong argues that "once a novel relocated the cause of economic inequity and the exploitation of labor in the female body, it was a relatively simple matter to resolve those problems symbolically by bringing that body under control, whether through that woman's reform, her incarceration, or her banishment from the text" (100). Of course, in order to be effectively subjected to discursive recuperation, the narrative first had to objectify her as the embodiment of excessive disorder, unruliness, and transgression, a project these narratives undertook with sensational gusto and escalating vigor, because the more unchaste the woman, the more cathartic her chastening.

However, while the novels' plots tended to discipline or defeat the women who dared to defy the gendered terms of cultural control, the economics of the publishing institution contributed to a rather different story. There, the urgency of supplying the demand for print fiction provided vocational opportunities for literate middle- and upper-class women, giving them unprecedented access to a public sphere that otherwise took pains to exclude them. Authorship offered one of the few viable professions for respectable women, and not surprisingly, many enterprising females took up the pen and enjoyed popular success, celebrity, financial stability, and independence through their writing. As their possibilities for careers outside the domestic sphere increased, society had to realign its assumptions and expectations to accommodate these career women. In this way, the New Woman was literally writing herself into existence.

Indeed, women seemed so dominant in the print marketplace that toward the end of the century Grant Allen thought to blame the failure of his first New Woman novel on his identity as "a male author participating in a woman's book market" (Warne and Colligan 23), casting himself as the victim of discrimination against a male author by a female audience.[2] Like Allen, Bernard Shaw was unsuccessful in his early forays into the novel market, a failure all the more bewildering to him because "it is clear that a novel cannot be too bad to be worth publishing, providing it is a novel at all, and not merely an ineptitude" (*Plays Unpleasant* 8)—in other words, that this explicitly female-gendered industry is first and foremost characterized by a low qualitative threshold. When Shaw recuperates his "want of success" in fiction as, characteristically, evidence of his actual superiority—he "saw things differently from other people's eyes, and saw them better" (8)—he distinguishes himself from the feminized masses engaged in the production and consumption of novels to revel in his superior, flattering—and implicitly more masculine—"abnormal normality" (9). In turning to playwriting, Kerry Powell points out, Shaw eschewed the feminized field of fiction for a profession that would increasingly be characterized as "emphasiz[ing] certain qualities of mind—scientific, technical, intellectual—that Victorians rarely associated with women" (*Women* 79).

Nonetheless, in making this change, Shaw saw also himself as adopting an even more effective platform for preaching the gospel of female emancipation, because theater, unlike the glutted fiction market, was still largely untouched by serious debates on the "woman question." Moreover, Shaw located this lack firmly in the male-dominated actor-manager system that governed the theatrical institution. Recognizing that the stage would remain silent on the "woman question" as long as actor-managers had no investment in staging plays that didn't cater to their male egos, Shaw predicted victory for greater female control in the theater: "we cannot but see that the time is ripe for the advent of the actress-manageress, and that we are on the verge of something like a struggle between the sexes for the dominion of the London theaters, a struggle which . . . must in the long run end disastrously for the side which is furthest behind the times. And that side is at present the men's side" (Preface, *Theatrical World* xxix–xxx). Possibly displaying a keen sense of self-preservation, Shaw firmly aligned himself with the women's side, creating a dramatic universe—and a successful career—inhabited by an extraordinary cast of complex female characters.

Shaw's support for triumphant women in the theater, however, had very well defined limits. He was much in favor of the "actress-manageress" who might stage his plays, and adored the avant-garde actress who would play his parts, but he generally disapproved of women who attempted to take the stage by writing parts of their own. As Kerry Powell has pointed out (see, for example, "New Women, New Plays"), Shaw's response to successful women's plays was often to rewrite them according to his own "philosophy," in versions that subsequently eclipsed the originals in the narratives of theater history. However, Shaw didn't necessarily have to wait for a woman to produce a play before he overwrote it: as the next two essays in this volume demonstrate, Shaw's advice to female playwrights was often to quit before they could even get properly started.

Unlike George Egerton (whose attempted playwriting career Margaret Stetz discusses in the next essay), Janet Achurch is not known for her writing ability: she has left her mark on history as a pioneering "Ibsen actress," the woman whom Shaw claimed should be "envied" for the way she "made for herself the opportunity of 'creating' Nora Helmer in England by placing herself in the position virtually of actress-manageress" (Preface, *Theatrical World* xxix). In her role as enterprising actress-manageress, enthralling actress, or beguiling social presence, Shaw's admiration and devotion was almost unequivocal. However, when she tried her hand at playwriting she met with a much sterner and less supportive Bernard Shaw, one who mocked, criticized, and belittled her attempts.

Since Achurch's original play, "Mrs. Daintree's Daughter," was neither publicly performed nor published, we largely owe our knowledge of its existence to Shaw, who mentioned it in a letter published in the *Daily Chronicle* in 1898, at the outset of the furor surrounding the ban on *Mrs Warren's Profession*. He wrote: "As to 'Mrs. Warren's Profession,' it came about in this way. Miss Janet Achurch mentioned to me a novel by some French writer[3]. . . . she told me the story, which was ultra-romantic. I said, 'Oh, I will work out the real truth about that mother some day. . . . 'Mrs. Warren herself was my version of the heroine of the romance narrated by Miss Achurch. . . . I finally persuaded Miss Achurch, who is clever with her pen, to dramatise her story herself on its original romantic lines" (*Collected Letters* [hereafter *CL*] 1: 403–4). In this little vignette, Shaw presents himself as the encouraging mentor, persuading the apparently reluctant but "clever with her pen" Achurch to dramatize the story that had so intrigued her, even though her version was an implicitly inferior—"ultra-romantic"—one.

The faintness of Shaw's public praise for Achurch the playwright pales in comparison to his more damning, personal campaign against her writing endeavors—which coincidentally took place within the context of his increasingly frustrated attempts to find a stage for his second play, *The Philanderer*, a play that had not yet been performed when he began writing *Mrs Warren's Profession*. Encouraged by the modest critical success of his first play, *Widower's Houses*, Shaw was clearly frustrated that his "new theater" compatriots considered *The Philanderer* so detestable that none would touch it—including the celebrated and innovative actor-managers Janet Achurch and her husband, Charles Charrington.

In a long letter to Charrington, Shaw excused the inadequacies of *The Philanderer* as the product of inexperience: "I grant you the work is not so skilful as if I had been more years at it. . . . It is as good as I can get it at my present stage" (*CL* 1: 491). He compares writing and acting, explaining that excellence in both is merely a matter of practice: "she [Achurch] has been doing every day for years and years on the stage what I have been doing every day for years and years with my pen. It is astonishing what work she does with the pen under these circumstances" (*CL* 1: 491). Nonetheless, later in the same letter, Shaw completely reverses his position on Achurch as a promising playwright: "indeed I shall, I think, always disparage her writing, since at the bottom of my soul I dont believe in any mortal achieving excellence in two arts with unrelated techniques. I should like her to attain the possible limit of perfection as an actress, and then to write her own life. Writing plays is all very well as an amusement whilst she is disengaged; but I am not sure that if I were she, I would not spend my time in working over Shakespear and all the drama I could lay hands on" (*CL* 1: 492).

Among the drama that Shaw thought Achurch could lay her hands on was a collection of plays by Hermann Sudermann, which he suggested to publisher T. Fisher Unwin that Achurch could translate, as she "speaks German like a native, and writes capital English dialogue" (*CL* 1: 599). The following year, Shaw's response to the imminent publication of a short story by Achurch confirms that his real concern is a fear that writing might divert her from acting. He cautions her, "But do you really mean to take to literature? . . . It means . . . growing your brain into the shape and condition proper to the professional pursuit of literature. What is more, it means, unless you are careful, the growing of your body into the literary shape, which is not effective on the stage, especially for young parts" (*CL* 1: 552–53).

Marshaling a stereotype as common a century ago as it is today about the inverse relationship between women's brains and their bodies, Shaw aims straight at an actress's most vulnerable point, the attractiveness of the body that her clientele must want to pay to see. Shaw can see only one use for Achurch's writing: "it seems possible to me that if you were to write fiction and elaborate the stage business of it, so to speak, in some detail, it might even exercise your imagination & suggest new ideas to you for what is, after all, your real profession" (*CL* 1: 553). Achurch might adapt and translate the plays of others or sell stories with stage directions, but she could never actually write a play. Clearly, the source of Shaw's objection here is not that Achurch *can't* write but rather that she *can* act, and he doesn't want to admit the possibility that she could do both well, lest she follow the example of an actress like Clotilde Graves and enter the playwriting profession by the stage door.[4] Not surprisingly, the talent he insists she should pursue is the one that complements, rather than competes with, his own.

Although Shaw explicitly expresses his opinion about the incompatibility of acting and writing here in gender-neutral terms—"I dont believe in any *mortal* achieving excellence in two arts with unrelated techniques" (emphasis added)—the volte-face from his earlier position about achieving excellence in either skill through practice is symptomatic of a fairly consistent inconsistency in his position that suggests a more gender-specific understanding of the problem. Certainly, the distinction between writing fiction and drama that Shaw insists on for Achurch is inconsequential for the New Woman author Grant Allen: at the same time as Achurch was unsuccessfully trying to get "Mrs. Daintree's Daughter" produced, Shaw accepted an invitation from Allen to lunch at the Savile Club, offering, "I can then let you into the secrets of a London success in the theatrical line" (*CL* 1: 451). Undermining his position regarding the impossibility of acting and writing well, Shaw explains in another long letter to Charrington that he could have easily become a fine performer despite his "slow, clumsy fingers and a mongrel, worthless voice" but that he "did not care enough about my fancy to overcome these as I overcame the obstacles to my becoming a speaker & a writer. If I had cared enough I should have overcome them" (*CL* 1: 613). Similarly, years later Shaw will admire Granville-Barker for "being already, at 24, noticed considerably as an actor and dramatic author" (*CL* 2: 458), without expressing any undue astonishment at these ostensibly incompatible accomplishments. Shaw's Janet, on the other hand, does not have the freedom of these choices because "Acting is her destiny. It cannot be put aside in her case as I can put aside, for instance, my own fondness for music" (*CL* 1: 613). In the same letter, Shaw makes the distinction between stage and life in very gendered terms: "Why, except as a means of livelihood, a man should desire to act on the stage when he has the world to act in, is not clear to me save in the cases of men who are only effective under stage conditions" (*CL* 1: 612–13). For Achurch, the option of being able to act in the "real" world was apparently out of the question as long as he needed her to act in the theatrical one. If, as Mary Jean Corbett argues, "feminist consciousness is something made—or performed—both in and out of the theatre" (110), then Shaw was effectively aborting the full development of Achurch's feminist consciousness by discouraging her access to the theatrical page and confining her exclusively to his stage.

In fact, Shaw completely failed to recognize the larger feminist resonances of Achurch's foray into dramatic writing. In attempting to trade the stage for the page by scripting her own version of *Mrs Warren's Profession*, Achurch could be taking a lesson from Mrs. Warren's school: trying to maximize the economic value of her own reputation and connections, and profit from an intellectual labor that could circulate independently rather than tying her income exclusively to the display and use of her body—a body that was seriously fatigued from an extended theatrical tour in Australia, New Zealand, India, and Egypt, and which included a pregnancy and the birth of her daughter, Nora. The strain of performing through pregnancy and around a difficult childbirth (she had probably less than two months off to recuperate)[5] only increased her dependence "on the brandy bottle ever more frequently as a source of stamina" (Peters 80) and likely also enabled a debilitating morphia addiction (Peters 80–81). Even while Shaw fretted, cajoled, and berated her for succumbing physically and emotionally to the strain of continual performance, he maintained that her real calling was in acting the women that he wrote (the source of *his* professional income) rather than trying to circulate her own.

Shaw's first recorded response to an attempt by Achurch to interest a producer in "Mrs. Daintree's Daughter" expresses no surprise that Lewis Waller declined the play: "I am not surprised about Mrs. Daintry [*sic*]. Waller's perfectly right; the ending is not the sort of thing for his audience. . . . This makes the play one for a Bernhardt to star in, not for a West End manager to run for the amusement of a smart clientele, who begin (thank Heaven!) to look on stage poisonings much as they do on broadsword combats. . . . [Y]our one really original point—a genuinely tragic one, with a real last act in it—was the mother's discovery of the daughter's worthlessness; and that you cut out" (*CL* 1: 478–79). What Waller should want, according to that same letter, is one of Shaw's plays: Shaw describes his plans to pitch Waller with *Candida* or *The Philanderer* and continues to insist that his Julia in the latter play is "a part which I still think you could do yourself good by playing, as it would put you to the height of your cleverness and technical skill to play it; and these are the qualities for which you most need to gain credit" (*CL* 1: 478).[6]

While Shaw endorses Waller's rejection of "Mrs. Daintree's Daughter" because of a fatal flaw in the play's dramatic structure, he apparently deemed the play perfectly viable as a companion piece in his ongoing struggle to get *The Philanderer* produced. Later that same year, Yorke Stephens, Kate Rorke, and E. W. Gardiner had made "an excellent start" for their proposed new theatrical management according to Shaw, "by asking me whether I cannot give them a play. Naturally I reply that I have the very thing for them in the Philanderer. . . . But of course they want another play or two in hand before they plunge. . . . Shall I, in that case, mention that Mrs Daintry [*sic*] is in stock? Kate Rorke would play it very well; and as Y. S. is bent on finding a part for Gould, there is your middle aged sentimentalist fitted to the life" (*CL* 1: 489–90). No mention here of the play's dramatic deficiencies, nor any hint of concern about sabotaging this new theatrical venture with a play that only a month or so earlier Shaw had easily dismissed as beneath the artistic bar of a "smart clientele."

In his descriptions of the play as "ultra-romantic" and "one for a Bernhardt to star in," with its stage poisonings, Shaw characterizes the play as an old-fashioned melodrama, an implication echoed by Stanley Weintraub in his annotation to Shaw's diary entry for 2 December 1893, where he describes the play as a "mother-daughter conflict, ending with the mother's suicide" (*Diaries* 2: 992). Unproduced and unpublished, the play has never circulated publicly to speak for itself—and to demonstrate that this is not, in fact, the ending that Achurch wrote. While Leila Daintree does die by poison at the end of the play, she does not commit suicide, succumbing to guilt and social disapprobation à la Paula Tanqueray; instead, she is accidentally murdered by the daughter she has protected so obsessively that the child is too naive to know the difference between quinine and morphia, and how crucial that distinction might be. In fact,

Shaw's careless dismissal of the mother character's fate in Achurch's play is yet another way of affirming the superiority of his pen over hers, as the mother represents the most significant site of divergence between "Mrs. Daintree's Daughter" and *Mrs Warren's Profession*, with Shaw confident, of course, that his version is "the real truth about that mother."

Neither Leila Daintree nor Kitty Warren, in fact, follows the original mother character of "Yvette," the story on which both plays are based. In de Maupassant's version, Mme Obardi assumes that she will eventually introduce her daughter into her profession and is surprised to find Yvette naive and uncompliant, ready to attempt suicide rather than become a courtesan. Apparently neither Achurch nor Shaw could countenance *that* mother: virtually the only thing Mrs. Daintree and Mrs. Warren have in common is their determination to keep their daughters *out* of their disreputable professions. However, they diverge significantly in their motives for it, highlighting in their difference the nature of Shaw's maternal "truth."

Early into his composition of *Mrs Warren's Profession*, Shaw wrote Achurch, "The play progresses bravely; but it has left the original lines. I have made the daughter the heroine, and the mother a most deplorable old rip (saving your presence). The great scene will be the crushing of the mother by the daughter," he explains, then gleefully describes how well his play is coming before ending with the inquiry: "How does your version progress?" (*CL* 1: 404).

Having transferred his interest to the daughter, Shaw turns the mother into a mouthpiece for his economic thesis about prostitution, relieving her of any conventional sense of morality or guilt about her continued involvement in the professional exploitation of women, and emphasizing instead her fitness for the profession she has embraced. Kitty Warren may have entered her profession pragmatically for the money, but she will willingly stay because she derives satisfaction from the particular type of work: "I must have work and excitement, or I should go melancholy mad. . . . The life suits me: I'm fit for it and not for anything else" (283).

In "Mrs. Daintree's Daughter," on the other hand, Achurch maintains a stronger focus on the mother character, scripting a more complex woman who is profoundly conflicted about the morality and human cost of her profession (in this case, money lending) even as she enjoys the financial advantages it offers; a woman who is capable of making pragmatic decisions, but not completely ignoring or dismissing their effect on herself or others around her.

Like Pinero's dramatic sensation *The Second Mrs. Tanqueray*, "Mrs. Daintree's Daughter" emphasizes that Leila Daintree was born to the expectation of a different life, only to find her options dictated to her by the desires of the man who controlled her. Leila Daintree was, in fact, "sold out" as usurer's bait by her own husband as she was attempting, with perfect Victorian feminine idealism, to reform him:

> SOTHERN: Could you get no work of any kind to do? Nothing better than playing into Geoffrey Howarth's hands?
> LEILA: What sort of work? I was brought up to do nothing. I married, and for four years I'd been my husband's partner—known half through Europe as the decoy of Daintree's set. I should have made a good governess for instance, shouldn't I? I might have married again, but I couldn't do that. Even for Violet's sake I could put no one in her father's place.
> SOTHERN: You loved him in spite of what he was?
> LEILA: I loved him, being a woman, *because* of what he was. I steeped myself in his life because no other had any chance of holding him. And just—when I was feeling my way to winning him from it—just when I was beginning to be more to him than a pretty toy to trade in—he died—and I was left to face my own ruin and the child's. . . . Oh, I'm soon disposed of. A decent woman—spoilt.
> SOTHERN: *Not* spoilt. That's the miracle of it.
> LEILA: I wish I could believe you. It's one of my big temptations.
> (8–9)

While both Mrs. Warren and Mrs. Daintree claim that they are working only to provide a better life for their daughters, Mrs. Warren's absolute unwillingness to consider Vivie's request that they find alternate means of support clearly implies that her motives are, in fact, a little more self-serving.

Shaw downplays the maternal implications of her decision by making Vivie Warren an educated, adult career woman, easily able to live independently of her mother. Violet Meredith (Mrs. Daintree's daughter has been raised under this pseudonym) is in a much more vulnerable position and age, absolutely dependent on her mother, completely devoid of independent education or career skills. Mrs. Daintree's determination to quit "the business" demonstrates the sincerity of her stated motives: "I have lived in this slavery because it means peace and independence for me and the child, and now . . . I'll speak to Howarth tonight. He must wind up the business and he ought to be satisfied. He will have made a fortune, and I shall have enough for Violet" (11). Unlike Mrs. Warren, Mrs. Daintree doesn't justify herself with a unique "fitness" for the profession—later, she will insist to Howarth that she is eminently replaceable—but more closely resembles Crofts in being blatant about her mercenary motivations for sticking with this particular profession: she is in it for the money.

So, while she sometimes expresses regret about the human cost of her profession, she adamantly defends her involvement in it from Sothern's judgment of her in terms that resonate in interesting ways with Mrs. Warren's argument for recruiting more girls into prostitution. Early in act 1, Mrs. Daintree tells Sothern, "After all how am I such a dreadful person? All my dupes deserve to be duped, and would be, by someone else, if not by me. . . . I have my scruples—only they are my scruples, not other people's. They are—what life has left me. As I'm a woman society feels it due to itself to cut me—if I were a man I might be a gambler—a money lender fifty times over and society would probably black my boots" (12). Mrs. Daintree's defense of her position demonstrates that she has matured beyond the naive idealism that motivated her in marrying her husband to reform him, and she refuses to let her old friend Sothern (the "middle aged sentimentalist" of Shaw's earlier description) judge her according to the discriminatory, gender-based double standard that so many of Achurch's contemporaries were still comfortable wielding.

By transferring his attention to Vivie Warren, Shaw can project the more optimistic career prospects for future generations of women, while Achurch remains rooted in exploring more fully the position of her own contemporaries—she was almost the same age as Leila Daintree at the time she wrote the play; her own daughter, Nora, was somewhat younger than Violet. Specifically, in expanding on the position of a very contemporary "working woman," Achurch more fully explores some topics that Shaw barely mentions in passing, like the extreme imbalance of labor that disadvantages the female partner.[7] Dr. Edith Keighly, a female doctor recognizably made up as a stereotypical New Woman, suggests that, as a childhood friend of Leila's, Sothern should "see fair between her and Geoffrey Howarth. It's a great deal too bad. She does all the work and he takes two thirds of the profits and no risk. Of course it's an open secret among some of us who finds the money, but it isn't generally known. Twice the gambling here has made the police attentive, and she had to bear the whole brunt, and she's known as the most unscrupulous money lender in town" (21).

As the scene unfolds, Howarth demonstrates the familiar charade that allows him to appear gentlemanly and magnanimous while leaving Leila to consummate the financial ruin of a young man infatuated with her:

HOWARTH: (Pushing back his chair: to LORD KENTWOOD) My dear Kentwood, a man who will bluff three times running on such hands as yours, deserves to be shut up as a lunatic. No one with any self respect can go on winning his money.

DR. E[DITH]: (To SOTH[ERNE]) Listen to him—that means that he's won and won't risk a change of luck. What consummate impudence!

KENTWOOD: (brightly) Hang it, Howarth, give me a chance of revenge.

HOWARTH: Not tonight. Allow me to know when you've plunged deep enough. I was playing cards before you were thought of.

(to Leila as he comes down stage)

Get Kentwood to play you a hand at piquet and make the stakes high.

(LEILA stands a moment frowning—shrugs her shoulders)

LEILA: (To servant) John bring some wine for Lord Kentwood and Mr Howarth. (To Kentwood) If you're not tired of cards will you play me at piquet?

KENTWOOD: Just the thing. The old stakes—doubled.

LEILA: Very well, only don't count on my leaving off in that considerate manner. I'm not so scrupulous as Mr Howarth. (22)

Clearly, the business arrangement leaves the burden of the dirtiest work to Leila, who has learned to accept the cost as necessary to achieving her own goals for a life with her daughter, free from a (hypo)critical society and financial worry. Nonetheless, even her pragmatism has apparently had its limits, as Howarth intimates in their discussions about Leila's replacement, "Yes, yes, we know my dear Leila . . . your moral precepts are unimpeachable. . . . Rest assured of one thing—I will install no one in your place who is cursed with what has stood in your way—and consequently in mine—more than once in our business relations—a conscience" (34). In the meantime, while Geoffrey Howarth clearly moves about freely in town and country with no need to give up his unscrupulous financial and personal affairs, the play confines Leila Daintree to her house or the rural estate that she has specifically set up away from larger society: the only locations where she is free of the judgmental double standard that isolates her.

Despite accepting the moral and economic implications of her chosen profession without any regrets or moral qualms, Mrs. Warren is nonetheless adamant that Vivie would be "a fool" (250) to ply the sex trade, as her first-rate education and social position open enough other, less morally ambiguous options for her. Indeed, Vivie has already mapped out a career course in actuarial accounting, and shows a problematically priggish distaste for the actuality of the family business. While she accuses her mother of hypocritical conventionality, Vivie is not immune from the same quality when she insists on an absolute distinction between her chosen profession and her mother's, despite noting that they are otherwise identically implicated in the capitalist enterprise: "No: I am my mother's daughter. I am like you: I must have work, and must make more money than I spend. But my work is not your work, and my way not your way. We must part" (284). Recognizing in Vivie the "pious, canting, hard, selfish" attitude (285) of a middle-class moralizer, Mrs. Warren ultimately comes to regret the extent to which she shielded Vivie from seeing the reality of her world, but her anger is largely impotent: there is no real likelihood that Vivie will enter the world that has already bought her the independence through which she can reject her mother socially, morally, and economically.

Leila Daintree similarly desires to keep her daughter away from her own profession, partly because of the moral equivocality that she understands so well, but even more significantly, to save Violet from the ultimate emptiness of a life spent entirely in the pursuit of "grow[ing] rich for your own [sake] . . . the excitement—the success—one's own beauty—the power of it" (95–96). Leila's own experience has taught her that these pursuits are "only good for a little time—and power wrongly used—leaves—a bitter taste. . . . It—it isn't real somehow—when one is in trouble or ill—no beauty saves one from that—it's all no use—one clutches—and clutches at empty air—and it makes one so tired" (96–97).

Unlike Mrs. Warren, Mrs. Daintree hopes to keep Violet "innocent" through "ignorance"—a plan clearly doomed to failure even without the warning in act 1 from her friend Sothern ("Ignorance is not innocence, Leila, it isn't even bliss, except at Eton") that has been struck from the typescript of the play. Violet discovers the truth about her mother quite by accident, in a revelation that Shaw declares, "dramatically speaking, stops [the play]" (*CL* 2: 478). Geoffrey Howarth has stumbled across Violet Meredith in the country and befriended her, unaware of her real identity as Violet Daintree. Violet, charmed by the sophistication of the gentleman and the urbane lifestyle he represents, casts him as the fairy godmother in her Cinderella narrative, emplotting him to help her escape the boredom and drudgery of country life for the glamour and excitement of the ball. After Leila's ultimatum concluding their business partnership, Howarth introduces his young country Cinderella/kitten as Mrs. Daintree's successor in a moment that brings an abrupt end to Violet's fairy tale as surely as if the stroke of midnight had sounded, when mother and daughter unexpectedly meet face-to-face.

Upon learning the truth about her mother's lifestyle and activities, Violet Daintree angrily accuses her mother of being "selfish and cruel—living in this lovely house, all this time" (87) while she exiled her daughter from the glamour and excitement of high society. When she asserts her independence from her mother's values, Violet echoes Vivie Warren, telling Leila, "I must live in my own way, and it isn't yours" (95); unlike Vivie Warren, however, Violet's proclamation insists on her right to "do what I please—and sit up all night—and wear low-necked dresses cut with trains ever so long. . . . have carriages and horses and loads of jewels and a box at the opera and go to the races on a coach" (62–63). In rejecting Mrs. Daintree's insights into high society's greed and hypocrisy, Violet embraces all the meaningless frivolities that Vivie (and, most likely, Shaw) abhors as the trappings of a thoroughly "worthless and vicious" life (Shaw, *Plays Unpleasant* 283). Shaw claims that the play's "one really original point—a genuinely tragic one, with a real last act in it—was the mother's discovery of the daughter's worthlessness" but then accuses Achurch, "and that you cut out" (*CL* 2: 478). However, the typescript of the play filed with the Lord Chamberlain does, indeed, show Leila Daintree coming to terms with her daughter's disappointingly superficial nature—to the point of ultimately recognizing that she may have to accept her daughter's desire to enter the very profession she has devoted her life to keeping her from:

LEILA: (going towards VIOLET who remains immoveable) Violet, my daughter, what can I say to you. Ah, don't shrink from me. There's nothing in my heart for you but love. I suppose all this did look very splendid to you—these rooms—and the dancing—and the lights and—your own dress. Ah love you were prettier in your cotton frocks. I've been all wrong. I've worked to get you some of this without the stains, and now I see it's impossible. Sothern was right, it's not fit for you. Come away with me. See, look at me, do I look very happy—does this life content me. And oh! you don't know, you'd never stand the life. Come, and we'll leave it altogether—work together and love each other and begin life on a new plan.

(Pause, VIOLET looks from her mother to HOWARTH)

HOWARTH: Goodbye Miss Daintree.

VIOLET: No, no, I won't stay with her. It's all dreadful. I never was happy till you made me so—why should I stop with her to be poor and wretched and have nothing that I care for.

SOTHERN: Is her love for you nothing?

VIOLET: Love! love! Love. I'm tired of love, what's the use of it—I've been loved all my life and what's it ever done for me. (To HOW-ARTH) *You* never said you loved me.

HOWARTH: No, I said I understood you.

VIOLET: There! (to LEILA) So he does.

LEILA: (Quietly) I see. (touches bell twice, ENTER MARY L.I.E.) Mary, this young lady will stay with me to-night. Help her to take off her dress in my room. (VIOLET makes a movement to speak) Hush! She will come to you presently. (MARY goes out) You shall have your own way to-morrow, I promise, but you must stay with your mother to-night. . . .

HOWARTH: One moment Mrs Daintree, I'm not interested in this gentleman's views of my conduct—he is welcome to his pictur-esque opinions—but I don't choose to leave you with such a com-pletely false idea. If I had had the faintest notion that she was your daughter this would never have happened. She would have been safe from me—but make no mistake—if not I—another. There was no hunting down. The fruit was ready to be gathered, I had but to stretch out my hand. Violet is her father's daughter. You're a very clever woman Mrs Daintree—and since I've known you I've never seen you meet your match. Unless I'm very much mistaken—you have met it now. Never whilst you live will you bend that girl to your way of thinking. I regret that it is through me that this fact should be first brought home to you. Will you permit me to say goodbye. (88–89, 91)

Howarth exits with the ominous suggestion that "You won't get out of this difficulty by killing *me*" (91). The implication is clear: as long as she lives, Leila must be prepared at any time to replay this scene with any man ready to take advantage of Violet's "ripeness" for adventure. Leila turns with melodramatic predictability to thoughts of suicide, telling Sothern "dreamily" that she is thinking of "Death, and it's very beautiful" (92).

However, Leila Daintree doesn't actually commit suicide in the time-honored tradition of the chastened fallen woman: instead, she is accidentally murdered by the very unworldly innocence that she worked so hard to cultivate in Violet, and which Violet so precipitously tried to disavow. Just before the climactic confrontation between Mrs. Daintree and her daughter, Leila had introduced her reliance on an array of drugs—"Morphia . . . Quinine—camphor—antipyrine"—that she clearly uses regularly as part of her professional toilette. Sothern is disgusted by Leila's "drug-shop," but she insists they are "better than drink" and demonstrates a familiarity with their use that might have mimicked Achurch's own:

LEILA: (laughing) Rather a shabby exit, isn't it? To sneak away in the dark—like a thief—Well, so I am—a murderer—so I am—and what is it they always call me—a very clever woman—so I am—I like your plan, Sothern—it will do—with modifications. . . . I'm quite strong now—or shall be in a moment.
(goes to escritoire and opens case on top, taking out white bottle)
SOTH: What's that?
LEILA: Morphia. (filling syringe)
SOTH: Leila! (goes towards her)
LEILA: What!—Oh, don't be afraid. I shan't take an overdose—but I must pull myself together somehow.
SOTH: I thought morphia made one sleepy.
LEILA: So it does if you take enough—that's the one aspect of morphia the popular mind has grasped. I thought you better informed. Have you read no reports by the Opium Commission? (79–80)

Sothern and Leila here express opposing views about the value of self-administered drugs that were themselves part of the larger social concern about opiate use in the 1890s that led to the establishment of the Royal Commission on Opium in 1893.[8] The commission was established as the result of growing disquiet about recreational (i.e., non-medicinal) drug use, especially among the privileged classes; however, motivated as much on both sides by economic, professional, and political imperatives as by altruistic humanitarian concern, debates on the "opium question" readily yielded ample "proof" to support virtually any position in the controversy.

While the commission didn't submit its official report until 1895, the newspapers carried regular reports from the Opium Commission hearings taking place in England and India throughout 1893 and 1894, which frequently included versions of the opinions that Leila expresses here, as for example in this report filed by the *Times* correspondent on 25 December 1893: "There was a general impression, bordering on conviction, that the moderate use of opium was beneficial . . . and its abuse was much less harmful than the abuse of alcohol. . . . Miss Lillias Hamilton, M.D., had never seen any ill effects of opium in women of the upper classes, among whom she practised. . . . He [Inspector-General of Civil Hospitals] regarded opium as one of the greatest blessings to mankind. If it were prohibited men would take to other stimulants" ("Opium Commission" 5). As a worldly, upper-class woman of society, Leila could be seen as a knowledgeable, informed user of these "beneficial" substances, not a degenerate abuser, and explicitly not one contemplating a suicidal overdose.

With this distinction clearly established, the actual circumstances of Leila's death by morphine overdose do not play into the melodramatic conventions that Shaw implies. Even in her more overtly moralistic ending, Achurch again focuses on an aspect of the life of a woman forced to sell herself that Shaw prefers to gloss over. While Sothern expresses disgust for Leila's "drug-shop," the narcotics are nonetheless clearly a habitual necessity for Mrs. Daintree to anesthetize the moral ambiguity of her employment, just as the alcohol that flows freely at her parties helps to overcome moral and financial prudence among her clientele. In *Mrs Warren's Profession*, Kitty Warren presents a more benevolent vision of brothel life, from Mrs. Warren's first glimpse of Lizzie's "long fur cloak, elegant and comfortable, with a lot of sovereigns in her purse" (Shaw, *Plays Unpleasant* 248) to the "plenty of girls who have taken to me like daughters and cried at leaving me" (284). The girls may be forced to put up with "some drunken fool that thinks he's making himself agreeable when he's teasing and worrying and disgusting a woman so that hardly any money could pay her for putting up with it" (249–50), but it is a point of pride with Mrs. Warren that they don't rely on any substances to fortify themselves for the work, just as she credits her success to being better than a "good-for-nothing drunken waster of a woman that thinks her luck will last forever" (249). The girls in Mrs. Warren's profession don't need to flirt with the dubious non-medicinal use of stimulants, because apparently they see their work as "just like a nurse in a hospital or anyone else" (250).

For Leila Daintree, as for Janet Achurch herself, the cost of living was too high to face without some kind of chemical aids. Their presence and the easy accessibility of the drugs and all their paraphernalia in Mrs. Daintree's escritoire serve as a potent reminder of the lifestyle that her profession entails, a lifestyle that was equally strongly associated with Mrs. Warren's profession in the popular imagination, despite its general omission from Shaw's version of it. Having the fatal dose accidentally administered to her through Violet's carelessness serves instead to highlight Violet's own profound ignorance and indict the society that encourages young girls to aspire to a fairy tale of superficial leisured society while keeping them utterly sheltered from reality. With Violet as the exemplar of those social conventions, Leila's death by her daughter's hand can be read as her defeat by a society that rejected a "fallen" and self-redeeming mother, a woman who was completely willing to accept and live with the consequences of her actions.[9] For Violet, the ending clearly demonstrates the young girl's dangerously naive assumptions about the lifestyle that she so desperately craves and the "profession" that she will willingly enter to get it.

Shaw, like Sothern, made no secret about his disgust around his friend's use of drugs and alcohol, and his letters to her contain frequent references to Achurch's "shocking little vices" (CL 1: 492) and use of "poison after poison" (CL 1: 581). When Janet contracted typhoid fever (originally self-diagnosed as pleurisy), Shaw warned Charrington, "I snatch a moment to implore you to go easy with that accursed anti pyrine. It was recklessly used in the first influenza epidemic and there was a considerable row about it afterwards. . . . People recover from pleurisy: they dont recover from poison. I am in despair at the discovery of your medical mania" (CL 1: 568).[10] During her convalescence, Shaw warned Janet against "coming back to your weak wicked old self, your brandy and soda self, your fabling, pretending, promising, company promoting, heavy eyelidded, morphia injecting self" (CL 1: 582).

For Achurch, the use of drugs and alcohol went hand-in-hand with the lifestyle and demands of her own profession—a profession that was, after all, still closely identified with Mrs. Warren's because of the way it tied her earnings and status exclusively to the staging and use of her own body. Shaw's only remedy for her situation, however, was to insist that she should discipline herself to take (or make) even more opportunities to play the women's roles that he wrote, rather than attempt to create her own. Dependence on drugs was to be discouraged even as it was to be replaced with dependence on him. Achurch's acting and playwriting both succumbed to these influences, the addictions eroding her abilities on the stage and Shaw's exhortations undermining her confidence and abilities on the page.

Ultimately, Janet Achurch has left behind little in her own words either onstage or off. Shaw's letters to and about her have been published as part of the homage to his authorial greatness, while history records mainly silence where her corresponding voice should be. Her only play, her most concerted attempt to exert control over the representation and circulation of a woman's place onstage, has likewise been eclipsed by the more powerful voice of the male playwright, allowing Mrs. Warren's "real truth" about motherhood to circulate publicly while Leila Daintree's alternate version remains isolated and unnoticed in an unpublished archival version, allowing others to speak for her. The silence and misconception around "Mrs. Daintree's Daughter" can be read as symptomatic of the similar conditions that ground Shaw's status as a playwright. Looking at Shaw's oeuvre, it is easy to see how he built his success on writing women's parts. What is less obvious, but no less worth investigating, is the possibility that his success in writing women was built in no small part on his ability to keep them from writing themselves.

Notes

1. The cultural and demographic changes throughout the nineteenth-century, and their relationship to the development of reading audiences, has been the subject of numerous works, such as J. A. Sutherland, *Victorian Novelists and Publishers* (London: U of London, Athlone P, 1976); N. N. Feltes, *Modes of Production of Victorian Novels* (Chicago: U of Chicago P, 1986) and *Literary Capital and the Late Victorian Novel* (Madison: U of Wisconsin P, 1993); Gaye Tuchman, *Edging Women Out: Victorian Novelists, Publishers, and Social Change* (New Haven: Yale UP, 1989); and Kate Flint, "The Victorian Novel and Its Readers," *The Cambridge Companion to the Victorian Novel*, ed. Deirdre David (Cambridge: Cambridge UP, 2001, 17–36). For readers wanting a brief overview of this complex topic, I especially recommend Flint's "The Victorian Novel and Its Readers."

2. To combat what he saw as gender discrimination, Allen adopted the pseudonym Olive Rayner Pratt to publish some of his "New Woman" novels.

3. The work was *Yvette* by Guy de Maupassant.

4. See Powell's *Women and Victorian Theatre* (83–84, 141–43) for a brief introduction to Clotilde Graves and her career as a playwright.

5. According to notices of performance in the Australian newspapers, Achurch was still performing as late as 12 April 1890 (*Argus*) and was set to resume on 5 July 1890, although her opening was postponed until 12 July to accommodate an extended of the successful Brough/Bouciault production of *School* (*Sydney*). Even with this extra week, Achurch returned to the stage at most six weeks after childbirth.

6. Julia is one of the two main female characters in *The Philanderer*, both of whom are rivals for the affection of the philanderer, Leonard Charteris. Charteris uses the sexual emancipation of the "New Woman" entirely to his advantage, exploiting the naive Julia, who adopted a New Woman identity because it was fashionable, without understanding the full implications of it. When Julia expects their (possibly sexually intimate) relationship to lead to marriage, Charteris moves on to the other woman, asserting that their "advanced views" preclude any such obligation to Julia. Charteris ultimately connives Julia into a marriage with another man that she doesn't want so that he can continue to "philander" with her without fear of any further claims by her. The play ends with Julia swooning in profound grief as she realizes how she has been trapped, while Charteris (a semi-autobiographical character) looks on laughing.

7. Sir George Crofts merely tells Vivie, "Your mother has a genius for managing such things. . . . Of course there are others besides ourselves in it: but we hold most of the capital; and your mother's indispensable as managing director. Youve noticed, I dare say, that she travels a good deal" (Shaw, *Plays Unpleasant*, 263). A few lines later he emphasizes his "passive" role in the arrangement—"I take my interest on my capital like other people: I hope you dont think I dirty my own hands with the work" (264). But as Vivie is concerned only with the nature of the business, she doesn't follow up on the implications of this highly inequitable division of labor.

8. For an excellent general background on the changing social and medical conceptions about the value of opiates and the nature of addiction, see Virginia Berridge, "Victorian Opium Eating: Responses to Opiate use in Nineteenth-Century England" (*Victorian Studies* 21.4 [1978]: 437–61); Terry M. Parssinen and Karen Kerner, "Development of the Disease Model of Drug Addiction in Britain, 1870–1926" (*Medical History* 24.3 [1980]: 275–96); Berridge, "The Origins of the English Drug 'Scene,' 1890–1930" (*Medical History* 32.1 [1988]: 51–64); John F. Richards, "Opium and the British Indian Empire: The Royal Commission of 1895" (*Modern Asian Studies* 36.2 [2002]: 375–420); Susan Zeiger, "'How Far Am I Responsible?': Women and Morphinomania in Late-Nineteenth-Century Britain" (*Victorian Studies* 48.1 [2005]: 59–81). The commission's report would ultimately uphold the status quo in the production and consumption of opium and its derived substances.

9. Leila Daintree's fate contrasts significantly in this respect with that of Herminia Barton, the title character in Grant Allen's book *The Woman Who Did*, a work that finally helped him achieve significant status as a New Woman novelist. Adhering to her advanced principles, Herminia enters into a free-love union with her partner, who dies just before their child is born. When the daughter, Dolly, grows up to reject her mother's

radical views and see her as an impediment to her own happiness conceived along more conventional social lines, Herminia Barton commits suicide, willingly sacrificing her life to her daughter's future happiness. While Allen subsequently had to defend common misreadings of Herminia's suicide by arguing that "her failure was the result of the twisted values of Victorian society, not of her own deficiencies, and that society, not he, was punishing her for transgressing sexual taboos" (Ruddick 26), Leila Daintree's death is much less open to this type of misinterpretation, since it is clearly precipitated, ideologically and literally, by the hand of conventional society.

10. Shaw would give full vent to his despair over medical mania in his play *The Doctor's Dilemma*.

Works Cited

Achurch, Janet. "Mrs. Daintree's Daughter." TS. Lord Chamberlain's Plays, 1824–1968, British Library. Hand paginated.

The Argus (Melbourne) 12 Apr. 1890: 16. http://nla.gov.au/nla.news-article8600257, accessed 3 Mar. 2010.

Armstrong, Nancy. "Gender and the Victorian Novel." *The Cambridge Companion to the Victorian Novel*. Ed. Deirdre David. Cambridge: Cambridge UP, 2001. 97–124.

Corbett, Mary Jean. "Performing Identities: Actresses and Autobiography." *The Cambridge Companion to Victorian and Edwardian Theatre*. Ed. Kerry Powell. Cambridge: Cambridge UP, 2004. 109–26.

"The Opium Commission." *The Times* (London) 25 Dec. 1893: 5.

Peters, Margot. *Bernard Shaw and the Actresses*. Garden City, NY: Doubleday, 1980.

Powell, Kerry. "New Women, New Plays, and Shaw in the 1890s." *The Cambridge Companion to George Bernard Shaw*. Ed. Christopher Innes. Cambridge: Cambridge UP, 1998. 76–100.

———. *Women and Victorian Theatre*. Cambridge: Cambridge UP, 1997.

Ruddick, Nicholas. Introduction. *The Woman Who Did*. By Grant Allen. Peterborough: Broadview P, 2004. 11–43.

Shaw, Bernard. *Collected Letters*. Ed. Dan H. Laurence. 4 vols. London: Reinhardt, 1982–84.

———. *The Diaries*. Ed. Stanley Weintraub. 2 vols. University Park: Penn State P, 1986.

———. *Plays Unpleasant*. Harmondsworth: Penguin, 1985.

———. Preface. *The Theatrical World of 1894*. By William Archer. London: Walter Scott, 1895. xi–xxx.

Sydney Morning Herald 1 July 1890: 2. http://nla.gov.au/nla.news-article13792155, accessed 3 Mar. 2010.

Warne, Vanessa, and Colette Colligan. "The Man Who Wrote a New Woman Novel: Grant Allen's *The Woman Who Did* and the Gendering of New Woman Authorship." *Victorian Literature and Culture* 33 (2005): 21–46.

7

Feminist Politics and the Two Irish "Georges"

Egerton versus Shaw

• • • • • • • • • • • • • • • • • •

MARGARET D. STETZ

On receiving news in 1901 that one of his young acolytes, the fledgling critic and theatrical agent Reginald Golding Bright, had married, Shaw sent the bridegroom a tongue-in-cheek and less than wholly congratulatory note. "When I gave you that advice," he began, presumably alluding to some romantic advice, "what was in my mind was that you were as likely as not to marry your landlady's daughter in a fit of sentimentality. I did not foresee that you would rush so violently to the other extreme as to marry George Egerton. How do you like it?" (Shaw, *Advice* 91–92).

What did he mean by referring to this marriage as "the other extreme"? It was a phrase that many turn-of-the-century readers besides the recipient of this letter would have understood. Golding Bright's new bride, who used the pseudonym "George Egerton" throughout her literary career, had distinguished herself as the most radical and most pilloried of the so-called New Women writers of the 1890s. She was known for her short hair, her pince-nez, and her solemnly penetrating gaze, all of which appeared in numerous caricatures that circulated in *Punch* magazine and, most famously, in a theatrical poster by Albert Morrow for Sydney Grundy's 1894 satirical stage comedy, *The New Woman*. But she was chiefly notorious for *Keynotes*, a volume of short stories published in 1893 by the Bodley Head, which only a few reviewers praised as brave and original, but which most denounced as shockingly improper, artless, and even pornographic.

The year 2009 was the 150th anniversary of *The Origin of Species*; it was also the less-celebrated 150th anniversary of the birth of "George Egerton," whose real name was Mary Chavelita Dunne, a figure largely forgotten today, but infamous at the end of the nineteenth century. Shaw's disciple, Golding Bright, born in 1874, chose as his wife an outspoken feminist who was fifteen years older than himself and nearly a precise contemporary of Shaw. Like Shaw, she could be garrulous, combative, narcissistic, and highly idiosyncratic in her tastes and personal habits. It was perhaps the many connections and resemblances between himself and this other "George," divided though the two writers were by gender, that would encourage Shaw to treat her so harshly, when he found himself later in the powerful position of literary gatekeeper, blocking her access to the Court Theatre. To deal with her would have been, for him, an unwelcome exercise in self-reflection, for the qualities that he saw both in her and in her writings mirrored his own worst tendencies, especially those toward arrogance and self-aggrandizement. At the same time, he might well have felt himself competing with this female double for the loyalty of Golding Bright, whom he had so enjoyed lecturing, in a semi-paternal fashion, as a "guide, philosopher and friend," and whom he had warned, from the start of their acquaintance, "[D]on't for your life get married" (*Collected Letters*, vol. 1, 465). Then again, Shaw's antagonism toward Egerton may have been merely an example of his usual response when confronting, whether in person or in correspondence, the very thing he claimed to admire—the strong, bold, and ambitious New Woman (a patently contradictory response that he himself mocked through the behavior of his onstage alter-ego, Leonard Charteris, in *The Philanderer*). That she was an Irishwoman who refused to be looked down upon and who expected from men the same reverence that Shaw demanded from women would only have exacerbated the friction between them.

Her roots, like Shaw's, were in Dublin, and her feelings about her Irish compatriots were, like his, a mixture of affection, exasperation, and despair. In "Oony," a short story from her 1897 volume titled *Symphonies*, she used a fictional mouthpiece to describe the Irish as "a queer lot, these countrymen of mine, tender and cruel, flint and wax, ineradicable savages, with the old pagan beliefs in black magic and the devil" (138). After settling in London to promote her literary career, she, like Shaw, regarded her adopted home with an outsider's wariness, and she prided herself on defying its standards of propriety.

During the mid-1890s, Egerton moved in "advanced" circles, forging both literary and personal connections with the aesthetes and decadents of the *Yellow Book*, in which her own work appeared, at the same time that Shaw was writing for Arthur Symons's rival magazine of decadence, the *Savoy*. Shaw and Egerton held in common notions about sexuality that were aggressively anti-puritanical and distasteful to the English. Shaw's avowal that "I never associated sexual intercourse with delinquency, nor had any scruples or remorses or misgivings of conscience about it" ("Love Affairs" 169) was matched by her very public assertion that "Things were natural or unnatural, true or untrue; the latter was the only sin" (*Rosa* 14).

She shared with Shaw a sense of outrage over Oscar Wilde's prosecution, which seemed to her, as an Irishwoman, an act of political persecution. In May 1895 she wrote two letters (now housed at UCLA's William Andrews Clark Library) to John Lane, who was both her publisher and Wilde's, denouncing those who had convicted Wilde and protesting the whole proceedings as unjust treatment by the English, whom she dismissed as a nation of hypocrites—a view she would later echo in her 1898 story "The Well of Truth."

She also had in common with Shaw a strong literary connection to Norway. Shaw was the quintessence of an Ibsenite and a proselytizer for Ibsen's plays to British audiences. Through her translations from Norwegian, George Egerton introduced to British readers the works of Knut Hamsun and Ola Hansson. For her short story "Virgin Soil," moreover, which appeared in the 1894 volume *Discords*, Egerton borrowed from *A Doll's House* the final confrontation between Torvald and Nora, which ends with the latter leaving home and shutting the door, and transposed it to a battle between mother and daughter, doing so at the same moment when Shaw was pursuing a similar strategy in *Mrs Warren's Profession*.

It might seem, then, that Golding Bright, who looked up to Shaw with something like hero worship, had come as close as he could to marrying Shaw himself. Yet there were some important differences (I mean, besides the obvious ones) between the two Irish Georges. By 1901, Shaw was a theatrical insider through and through. He had long ago abandoned novels as a literary form, and his world centered upon the stage, whereas George Egerton had built her career solely on writing fiction (though as early as 1899, "The Cricket," a pseudonymous gossip columnist for the illustrated London weekly, *Hearth and Home*, reported that Egerton had "written a monologue entitled *Neighbours*" ["People, Places, and Things" 674]).

Her literary direction changed, however, in the first decade of the new century. With her marriage to Golding Bright, George Egerton suddenly gained access to the inner circles of London theater, for her new husband was pursuing a livelihood by moving from drama criticism for the newspapers to a career as a dramatic agent, as he followed in the footsteps of his older brother, Arthur Addison Bright. When his brother died—a suicide—in 1906, Golding replaced him as the London representative in partnership with the American agent, Elisabeth Marbury (West 10). Even before that, he had begun working on behalf of playwrights such as Shaw, Somerset Maugham, and J. M. Barrie. Egerton claimed always to have had ambitions to write plays, but her shift from one genre to the other, after 1901, was furthered by external prompts, including the decline of the reading public's interest in polemical New Woman fiction (a genre that flourished in the 1890s but was on the wane by 1900), and by the opportunities for getting her work produced on the stage that seemed to go along with marrying a well-connected and energetic young Londoner.

Thanks to her husband's intervention, Egerton was able, for instance, to arrange in 1903 for Elisabeth Marbury to forward the script of a play to no less a star than Ellen Terry. But not even Terry's friendly relationship of several years standing with Golding Bright could guarantee a favorable reception. Referring to the play, which bore the title "A Divided Duty," Terry sent an affectionate note to Egerton, emphasizing how busy she was—too pressed for time to read anything. Later, however, Terry wrote directly to Bright, letting him know as gently as she could that Egerton's debut effort was not for her: "Act I was fine—in fact all was clever as it could be—but *somehow as a play* the workmanship went wrong sometimes" (emphasis in original). Shaw noted that after he'd returned the play he couldn't remember the little mistakes he had noted earlier. But, he added, "it was very clever" (White 94).

It was time to resort to the heavy artillery, and there was no bigger gun in Golding Bright's arsenal than Bernard Shaw. He had become part of Shaw's circle of acquaintances, and then Shaw's business representative, despite their wildly inauspicious first encounter. At the opening night of *Arms and the Man* in 1894, one lone heckler had dared, at the end, to boo. Shaw famously quipped in response, "My dear fellow, I quite agree with you, but what are we two against so many?" That heckler was, according to Michael Holroyd, none other than the twenty-year-old Golding Bright

(Holroyd 367). In the world of Hollywood romantic comedies, this scene would probably be called "meeting cute" and would end in an embrace. In any case, it seems a tribute to the goodwill—or perhaps to the pragmatic sense of being able to make use of one another—of both of these figures that, after so public a contretemps, a close relationship could spring up between them.

So it was Shaw who received the manuscript of Egerton's first play. The correspondence about it that ensued, as reproduced later in the volume *A Leaf from the Yellow Book*, edited by Egerton's cousin Terence de Vere White, indicates that the Golding Brights pressed to have the play produced at the Court Theatre, while Shaw put up caution flags and delayed issuing a final verdict. In December 1904 he urged Egerton to undertake further revisions, even as he assured her that her previous revisions had improved it greatly, so that the play clamored for production (White 64). Evidently, though, it didn't clamor loudly enough. The performance records of the Incorporated Stage Society, published in 1909, as well as J. P. Wearing's *The London Stage, 1900–1909: A Calendar of Plays and Players*, show that nothing by Egerton made the leap from page to stage in England during the first decade of the century, and most certainly nothing of hers was produced at the Court Theatre, with a repertoire both dominated and greatly determined by Shaw.

It wasn't merely Egerton's first play that wound up in Shaw's hands, only to come back to hers, having been unsuccessful in its bid for production; this was also the fate of a second work, titled "His Wife's Family." This time, Shaw was neither encouraging in his message nor kind in his delivery of it. In a May 1907 letter to Egerton he wrote,

> I have read *His Wife's Family* . . . [and] it is of no commercial use. You have not got the proper quality of dramatic dialogue: and you will write a practicable commercial play as soon as you condescend to study the market and materials you have to work with.
>
> On the London stage at present there is no actor-manager with a turn for Irish parts: in fact, it is very hard to get Irish parts played at all with any sort of genuineness. . . . Yet in the face of this you deliberately go and write a comedy in which all the parts are Irish. How would you propose to cast it? . . . I ask you, what success can you expect when you deliberately start by making your play impossible? (White 65–66)

But that was not all that Shaw found to lambaste, for "Even if all these objections could be got over, the last act of the play would not be a success. It is really nothing but a happy ending spread over half an hour." Moreover, the characters seemed to him weakly drawn, with only "a ha'porth of reality to an intolerable deal of worn-out stage Irish." There was, of course, more than a little irony to this final criticism; in his 1904 play, *John Bull's Other Island*, Shaw himself had pushed the limits of "worn-out stage Irish" with the creation of his "Begorra"-spouting character, Tim Haffigan. He concluded by offering Egerton, a fellow countryman, what must have struck her as a most galling and patronizing bit of advice: "Try an English comedy" (67).

Shaw had treated Egerton's husband in an avuncular manner, but Golding Bright was a much younger man, and he was not a writer for the stage; thus, Shaw viewed him as neither a peer nor a rival. Although Shaw may have considered himself the political champion of the New Woman, that late-Victorian embodiment of feminist rebellion, both onstage and off, the gloves came off when he was faced with a representative of the type who was also a playwright. Had Egerton been a beautiful actress of twenty-one seeking his assistance, instead of a fairly plain-looking professional author, forty-seven years old, perhaps his tone of address might have been different. His pattern of dismissive, if not abusive, behavior toward women who expected to meet him on equal ground was already a longstanding one before Egerton came on the scene.

Writing in 1907 to Erica Cotterill, another would-be playwright, Shaw had justified his rudeness and domineering manner toward her by, in effect, blaming the victim. He was, he insisted, merely doing what anyone would, when dealing with someone too "childish" to stand up for herself. It was her responsibility to remove the temptation: "You are, in short, a naughty little girl, and everybody bullies you instinctively," he asserted, by way of vindicating his own conduct, "but do you suppose I dare bully a responsible, dignified, grown-up woman like that[?]" (*Collected Letters*, vol. 2, 700). In fact, as his correspondence with Egerton demonstrated, the answer to this rhetorical question was an emphatic yes. Any woman with literary aspirations was a target, and the more she impinged on his territory, the more he felt compelled to demolish her hopes of succeeding in his own theatrical sphere. Whether or not she answered him in kind proved irrelevant, for it did not abate one jot his almost sadistic pleasure in laying down the law as brutally as possible.

In the case of the actress-turned-playwright (and novelist), Elizabeth Robins (1862–1952), who was also Egerton's contemporary, he was often not merely unkind, but malicious. As Joanne E. Gates records, "toward Robins, however, Shaw was particularly antagonistic. The clever insults he circulated privately and in print did not assist her career . . . and did not improve her professional reputation in years to come" (Gates 95). Similarly, Angela V. John, in her own biography of Robins, maintains that from the mid-1890s onward, Shaw deliberately demeaned a fellow artist whom he could neither cow nor control: "Elizabeth has been represented by Shaw . . . as an aloof kill-joy, disparaging the male sex. Used to flirting via epistolary relationships and impressing actresses, Shaw found that his verbal gymnastics and comments on her attractiveness fell flat with 'Saint Elizabeth'" (John 80). Though he was, as Kerry Powell puts it, "unsympathetic to Robins in some respects," Shaw showed himself to a certain degree supportive of her efforts to reform the gender hierarchies of the London theatre world. Nonetheless, as Powell asserts, "Shaw was thinking only of actresses who would usurp the powers of actor-managers, not at all of women playwrights—indeed he had ridiculed the efforts of Janet Achurch and Robins herself when they had attempted to write plays of their own." The explanation for such conduct, according to Powell, had much to do with Shaw's sense of ownership over the materials and the perspectives that Robins and other New Women brought to this enterprise: "He saw his own plays, and Ibsen's, as providing all that was needed to address the gender crisis of the late Victorian theatre" (Powell 168). And Shaw's methods of ensuring that women playwrights left the field open to him were anything but gentle.

As it was, George Egerton felt she had been stung to the core by his treatment of her, no doubt expecting better from a fellow émigré from Dublin (White 67). She would declare years afterward in a letter to White that "Shaw has been . . . the worst influence" on the theater "in fifty years" (White 146), and, after seeing the 1932 production of *Too True to Be Good*, she would dismiss it as "Brilliant thumb-nail sermons or essays with spotlight illuminating them, superbly spoken by [Cedric] Hardwicke and others in long dull stretches of poor dialogue" (White 146–47).

It certainly did not soften Egerton's feelings toward Shaw when events proved him right about the dim commercial prospects of her Irish comedy. Arnold Daly (1875–1927), the American actor-manager who had brought Shaw's work to the United States with a successful production of

Candida in 1903 and a notorious one of *Mrs Warren's Profession* in 1905 that ended with police action against the cast, decided to take on Egerton's "His Wife's Family." But the results were disastrous. In October 1908 her play opened at Wallack's Theatre in New York City and closed almost immediately, after a mere fifteen performances. The anonymous reviewer for the *New York Times* damned it with the faintest of praise, allowing for its "many charming and appealing qualities," while bemoaning the absence of "any real dramatic quality" and concluding, "It must be viewed as a series of pleasant and amusing sketches rather than as a play" ("Humorous Types" 9).

Still, Egerton was not one to creep away quietly. She had survived a hardscrabble youth, then supported herself and various family members for decades through her ingenuity and stubbornness, before enjoying an international literary coup with the publication of *Keynotes* in 1893, which engendered mixed reviews but large sales and translations into several languages. She had also lived her sexual life boldly, in a highly un-Victorian fashion. When nearly thirty, she had run off with another woman's husband, married him in what was certainly a bigamous union, and settled with him in Norway. After his death, she had wed and later divorced a good-looking ne'er-do-well, Egerton Clairmonte, with whom she had a child before he abandoned her. And, while deciding whether to marry Golding Bright, who wished so ardently to be able to admire her, help her to live in comfort, and advance her career as a playwright, she had engaged in a romance with another man, a Norwegian, who was also fifteen years her junior. She was nothing if not an example of independence and willfulness. It must have pained her to have to turn to Shaw at all, when she sought his help in trying to get her plays produced by the Stage Society. Like Shaw himself, she preferred to be the one in control in any relationship, whether a romance, a friendship, or a business arrangement. Such a daring, tough, determined, and rather formidable Irish New Woman certainly would not have allowed Shaw to have the last word about her prospects as a playwright. And indeed she didn't.

Once again Egerton wrote a play, this time titled "The Backsliders." Did Shaw believe that, as a pro-suffrage man, he was a true friend to women and that he knew what they wanted and needed? She would set him right, returning to the theme she had explored repeatedly in her earlier works, from the 1893 short story "A Cross Line" to her 1901 prose meditation on affairs of the heart, *Rosa Amorosa*—the inability of men to speak truly either for or of women. As she had put the matter in "A Cross Line," all men attempt to solve "the riddle of the *ewig weibliche*," thinking that they are capable of mastering women, "and well it is that the workings of our hearts are closed to them. . . . They have all overlooked the eternal wildness, the untamed primitive savage temperament that lurks in the mildest, best woman. . . . an untameable quantity that may be concealed but is never eradicated by culture" (22). By the time she issued *Rosa Amorosa*, though, some eight years later, she had also become a mother and had added to her definition of women's nature the maternal impulse. To bear and raise a child, she would assert, was women's deepest longing and delight, and knowledge of this pleasure was inaccessible to men.

As we can see by reading the 1910 typescript of "The Backsliders," now in the New York Public Library for the Performing Arts at Lincoln Center in New York City, George Egerton had two major aims in writing this play. One was to create a mouthpiece for her own brand of feminism—that is, the character called Loreta Bosanquet, a successful playwright, who loses and then wins back her errant husband, who is also the father of her son. Loreta identifies herself as one of the "backsliders. We don't really care an atom about suffrage, and we simply loathe the idea of universal sisterhood" (act 3). Speaking out confidently on behalf of all womankind, she proclaims that "the woman who can't say *My man and my children*, and *my home*, has been cheated by fate out of the key to her kingdom, and she knows it" (emphasis in original) (act 2). Her chief interest is in her right to express and to claim what she desires, rather than to front any political movement—especially the suffrage movement, with which G. B. Shaw had publicly joined forces.

For Egerton's other aim in this comedy was to mock and discredit George Bernard Shaw. While separated from her husband and waiting for the profits from her plays to roll in, Loreta Bosanquet supplements her income as a writer by going to work for a socialist organization. Act 2 opens in the "Office of the International Social Alliance"—or, as Loreta calls this enterprise, "a regular playground for freaks." Among the many absurd enthusiasts who populate it is the editor of a vegetarian journal, titled *Fair Fruits of the Field, and Nuts for Nutriment*, as well as a representative from the "In Nudity Purity League." Lest the audience fail to understand, though, that Egerton wished above all to disparage Shaw, she included a stage direction at the start of act 2, describing the rooms of this risible "International Social Alliance" as decorated with "busts of G.

B. S., Ibsen and Tolstoi." Evidently, she did not trust the public to understand merely from her play's subtitle, "A Serious Comedy"—an imitation of a Shavian oxymoron—that she was determined to beat Shaw at his own game. Yet even in creating this detail involving props, to tip off the spectator as to her intentions, she was echoing Shaw's own stage directions for act 2 of his New Woman play, *The Philanderer* (first performed at the Royal Court Theatre in 1907), where the action opens in the Ibsen Club, which is graced with the looming presence of a bust of the author. Her satirical thrust could, in fact, be said merely to have reaffirmed the importance of Shaw's earlier play.

Did Egerton get the last laugh? Yes and no. The script of "The Backsliders," which this time she most assuredly did not send to Shaw for his opinion, was received with delight by the American producer George Tyler, who brought it to the stage in New York City and Chicago in 1911. Yet in neither city could it find an audience, even with Annie Russell as star (Russell was also, of course, the actress who had originated the title role of Shaw's *Major Barbara* in 1905). As George Egerton's playwriting career sputtered, Shaw's went from triumph to triumph. It would seem, therefore, that Shaw had been right about the business of theater and Egerton wrong.

But Egerton did succeed in one respect: she got under Shaw's skin. Some time after the death of his elderly cousin in 1945, Terence de Vere White wrote to Shaw and, as he recounts the story, received a postcard a few days later. Shaw's note read: "I remember G. E. (Mrs. G. B.) very well. She was so intolerably loquacious that she talked herself off the stage after she had won her way to the centre of it by her literary talent. It was incessant gabble, gabble, gabble, without any grace of address or charm of speech. Many sought to meet her once, but not twice. There was nothing else to complain of. She was quite good-natured and well-meaning. Her loquacity was meant for companionableness; but its excess undid her" (White 101–2). Shaw's charge against her was a telling one. Like many a male feminist, he was an advocate for the New Woman so long as *he* was the one giving voice to that character, and so long as she was merely a literary character, not a flesh-and-blood figure who refused to please, withholding the "grace of address" and "charm of speech" that he expected women to exercise around him—in other words, so long as she did not dare to resemble himself or behave as he did toward others.

By marrying "George Egerton" in 1901, Golding Bright had indeed, as

Shaw put it in his snide and ironic congratulatory note, gone to "the other extreme." That decision would also involve a commitment, over the coming years, to helping his author-wife bring her plays to the stage. The results would be disheartening for both of them. But in embracing both the New Woman and her words, rather than dismissing the latter as "gabble," it was he, not his mentor Shaw, who proved himself the New Man.

Works Cited

Egerton, George. "The Backsliders." TS 948711. Billy Rose Theatre Collection, New York Public Library.

———. "A Cross Line." *Keynotes*. London: Elkin Mathews and John Lane, 1893. 1–36.

———. "Oony." *Symphonies*. London: John Lane, The Bodley Head, 1897. 109–59.

———. *Rosa Amorosa: The Love-Letters of a Woman*. London: Grant Richards, 1901.

———. "The Well of Truth." *Fantasias*. London: John Lane, The Bodley Head, 1898. 123–56.

Gates, Joanne E. *Elizabeth Robins, 1862–1952: Actress, Novelist, Feminist*. Tuscaloosa: U of Alabama P, 1994.

Holroyd, Michael. *Bernard Shaw. Volume I: 1856–1898, The Search for Love*. London: Chatto and Windus, 1988.

"Humorous Types in 'His Wife's Family.'" *New York Times* 7 Oct. 1908: 9.

John, Angela V. *Elizabeth Robins: Staging a Life, 1862–1952*. London: Routledge, 1995.

"People, Places, and Things," by "The Cricket." *Hearth and Home: An Illustrated Weekly Journal for Gentlewomen* 7 Sept. 1899: 674.

Powell, Kerry. *Women and Victorian Theatre*. Cambridge: Cambridge U P, 1997.

Shaw, Bernard. *Advice to a Young Critic: Letters, 1894–1928*. London: Peter Owen, 1956.

———. *Collected Letters*. Vol. 1. Ed. Dan H. Laurence. London: Reinhardt, 1965.

———. *Collected Letters*. Vol. 2. Ed. Dan H. Laurence. London: Reinhardt, 1972.

———. "Love Affairs." *Shaw: An Autobiography, 1856–1898*. Ed. Stanley Weintraub. New York: Weybright and Talley, 1969. 163–71.

Ten Years, 1899 to 1909. By The Incorporated Stage Society. London: Chiswick P, 1909.

Wearing, J. P. *The London Stage, 1900–1909: A Calendar of Plays and Players. Volume I: 1900–1907. Volume II: 1908–1909*. Metuchen, NJ: Scarecrow P, 1981.

West, E. J. Introduction. *Advice to a Young Critic: Letters, 1894–1928*. London: Peter Owen, 1956. 5–12.

White, Terence de Vere, ed. *A Leaf from the Yellow Book: The Correspondence of George Egerton*. London: Richards P, 1958

8

The Passionate Anarchist and Her Idea Man

· · · · · · · · · · · · · · · · · ·

VIRGINIA COSTELLO

The absence of any discussion about Bernard Shaw and Emma Goldman's acquaintance is peculiar. While it would be an overstatement to say that Shaw dabbled in anarchism,[1] he and Goldman shared some similar political values—about birth control and prostitution, for example. Their similar concerns, as well as their affection for literature and Goldman's appreciation for Shaw's plays, would suggest that when they finally met they might have enjoyed a lively conversation. But this was not the case.

Goldman was born in Kovno, Lithuania, in 1869, immigrated to the United States in 1885, and soon became both active and notorious in American politics. She was imprisoned several times for such acts as inciting riots, agitating against the draft, and distributing information about birth control. She died in 1940 in Toronto, Canada. Not surprisingly, Shaw's growing fame and wide-ranging interests eventually brought him into contact with Goldman. The two exchanged a few letters, met once at Frank Harris's apartment (probably in 1928), and had a hand in editing Harris's unauthorized biography of Shaw. But Shaw, the prolific writer of drama and letters, never discussed his connections with Goldman, the "notorious" anarchist. And, at a time when Shaw had become a virtual cottage industry, Goldman wrote but never sold her story about meeting Shaw. Furthermore, neither Shaw's nor Goldman's biographers have explored the relationship.

In all likelihood, Goldman's anarchist politics, her frankness, and the sensationalized news reports of her advocating violence contributed to the tension between these writers. Her political message was much more radical than Shaw's, her approach more direct, and her delivery more aggressive. Shaw's plays inspired thought and reflection, while Goldman's lectures inspired awe and righteous indignation. "To the public she was America's arch revolutionary, both frightening and fascinating," writes Alice Wexler, one of Goldman's biographers. "She flaunted her lovers, talked back to the police, smoked in public, and marched off to prison carrying James Joyce's *Portrait of the Artist* under her arm" (1). Whether addressing modern drama, free love, or anarchism, Goldman's lectures attracted laborers, disgruntled socialists, budding anarchists, and curiosity seekers alike. If Shaw, the Nobel Laureate, was a force by virtue of his writing, Goldman impressed the public primarily by her impassioned speeches and complete commitment to her cause. She willingly went to prison for the ideas she considered important, and in doing so she challenged traditional notions of femininity and paved the way for other women, such as the suffragettes, to express publicly their commitment to their cause.

In contrast, Shaw supported women's rights, not by risking his freedom, but through his writing, essays, and drama. He asserted that *Mrs Warren's Profession*, for example, was a play for women because it portrayed prostitution as a systemic problem, rather than attributing it, as Victorian reformers did, to a lack of morals.[2] In general, he recognized how the nineteenth-century political and social systems obstructed women's progress. On 28 March 1913 the publication *Votes for Women* quotes him as saying that most women were "exceedingly well able to care for themselves" (367). Goldman clearly fits into this competent category. Aside from the odd absence of discussion about the two famous writers, their acquaintance itself is strange too, not so much because Goldman's competence but in spite of it.

The Shaw/Goldman relationship, both what it was and, equally important, what it wasn't, not only offers insight into the nature of Goldman's anarchist message but also enriches the biography of an important literary figure via his acquaintance with a radical and passionate woman that was unlike any of the relationships he had with other strong-willed, independent women. Aside from adding one more element to the complexity of Shaw's character, this hitherto unexplored acquaintance, offers a particular view of Shaw privileging aesthetics over politics, which results in aesthetics limiting his politics. While Shaw ostensibly blends art and politics, when he is analyzed through a feminist anarchist lens he lands firmly on the side of art. The latter part of this essay focuses on how Goldman's appreciation for and popularization of drama has been eclipsed by her radical politics. The narrowing of our focus to this one acquaintance allows us to look through Goldman's radical politics at how she employs Shaw's *Mrs Warren's Profession*, which does not have an anarchist agenda, as a driving force behind her anarchist message. Goldman's appreciation of *Mrs Warren's Profession* spilled over into curiosity about the man himself, but his socialist and her anarchist politics prevented comradeship between the two.

Although the Shaw-Goldman acquaintance is worth examining for what it can tell us about the differing conceptions of politics and gender in their relation to literature, their personal connection is rather slight, consisting of many indirect public and private references but a confirmed direct exchange of only two letters and one meeting. Shaw received two letters from Goldman; he wrote one to her, but it did not survive except by virtue of being embedded in Goldman's second letter.[3] Goldman's letters disclose a rather provocative and enduring tension, reaching back at least as far as their first meeting with their mutual friend Frank Harris, and referenced in the letters by means of a series of subtle and not-so-subtle insults.

Furthermore, Goldman's second letter—a reply to the missing Shaw-Goldman letter—enables an indirect examination of Shaw's missing letter. The tense relationship that can be teased out of these letters and other archival fragments, including correspondence from Frank Harris and attorney Arthur Ross, might serve as an analogy for examining two different views of the tension between poetic and political activity. Neither Shaw nor Goldman was particularly a fan of the other, but art, politics, curiosity, and friendship with Harris brought them together briefly.

In her book *The Social Significance of Modern Drama*, which grew out of her lectures, Goldman openly recognizes that Shaw finds anarchy more than simply offensive: "Shaw the Fabian would be the first to repudiate such utterances as rank Anarchy, 'impractical, brain cracked and criminal'" (107). But she also admires the revolutionary spirit embodied in his plays. She continues, "But Shaw the dramatist is closer to life—closer to reality, closer to the historic truth that the people wrest only as much liberty as they have the intelligence to want and the courage to take" (107).

For Goldman, Shaw's personal politics and the politics embodied in his characters do not coincide; in his private life, Shaw didn't take as many liberties (or risk as much) as his characters do. She thought his works were thoughtful, original, and suggestive of anarchistic principles, but the man himself, an excellent writer, provocateur, and even propagandist, misunderstood anarchy and the breadth and depth of the messages in his own work. Goldman "believed the originality of art is tied to revolutionary politics" (Clark 49) and could not comprehend the disparity between Shaw's drama, his rudeness when they met, and, as she saw it, his conservative politics. And yet in her letters to him, written twenty-three years after she published her book on modern drama, she is trying to convince him to connect the revolutionary spirit in his plays to his personal life.

On 2 March 1937, Goldman wrote one of only two letters that she would pen to Shaw. The ostensible occasion was to invite Shaw to lend his name to a proposed memorial celebration of the most influential public political event in both of their lives: the death of the Chicago anarchists of 1887. But while the event disturbed Shaw at the time, it did not redirect his life as it did Goldman's. Goldman's misunderstanding aside, her invitation to Shaw must be read more broadly as a provocation.

At the time of the writing of the letter, Goldman and Shaw lived in London, just a few miles from each other. Shaw's reputation as a dramatist, social critic, and promoter of women's rights was well established in England and abroad. He was a celebrity. While Goldman was not unknown in England, few people supported her humanitarian aid fund for the women and children in war-torn Spain. She thought that if she gained the support of popular writers, then the public was likely to follow. So she wrote to Shaw, H. G. Wells, Theodore Dreiser, and others to ask them to endorse her efforts. While none of these writers were anarchists, Goldman expected to find a sympathetic audience because their published texts demonstrate a revolutionary spirit. In the end, Dreiser agreed wholeheartedly, but both Shaw and Wells rejected her request.

In her first letter to Shaw, Goldman referred to meeting Shaw at Frank and Nellie Harris's house in the south of France. The experience, Goldman wrote, "was no doubt as unsatisfactory to you as it was to me" (Falk,

Zboray, and Cornford, *Emma Goldman Papers*, 2 March 1937, reel 39; hereafter cited by date and reel only). But neither Shaw nor Goldman ever publicly admitted they had met, let alone discussed whatever made the meeting "unsatisfactory." Neither do their biographers offer much information. However, Frank Harris, notorious philanderer and sensationalist, described the meeting in his book *Bernard Shaw: An Unauthorized Biography*. As the accuracy of the text is questionable—due to Harris's tendency to embellish descriptions of events—I point to primary sources that refute, confirm, or leave open for question Harris's interpretations. In the end, Harris's story offers one possible explanation of the Shaw/Goldman meeting in 1928.

Another layer of controversy around Harris's text stems from its production: while the book notes Harris as the only author, it was actually written and edited by Harris, Shaw, Frank Scully, Goldman, and Alexander Berkman. It is difficult to discern who wrote what. When Harris first contacted Shaw about the biography, Shaw threatened legal action (Weintraub, *Pirate* 441). However, a few months before Harris's death, Shaw changed his mind. In a generous effort to provide for Nellie Harris, Shaw agreed not only to edit the book but also to write a postscript. By the time Shaw saw the manuscript, Frank Scully, Harris's friend and collaborator, had already been revising the text. Goldman too had contributed, although it is not clear exactly what she did.

While Shaw's nine-page postscript lent the text credibility and encouraged sales, his hand in editing the text is more controversial. In a letter to Alfred Douglas years after the book was published, Shaw wrote, "As the man [Harris] was dying, the book fell to pieces at the end; and at the beginning it was full of stupendous inventions, as he knew nothing about my early life. Consequently a good deal of it is autobiography on my part, with the advantage of making Harris say one or two things that I could not decently say myself" (*Collected Letters* [hereafter *CL*] 24–25).

In his letter to Nellie shortly after he finished the manuscript, Shaw made similar, if less dramatic, claims: "I have had to fill in the prosaic facts in Frank's best style, and fit them to his comments as best I could; of all I have most scrupulously preserved all his sallies at my expense" (*CL* 261–63). In addition, Shaw doctored parts of the text and eliminated five libels that he suggests Scully added. Finally, the book included quite a few letters that Shaw had written to Harris years before, and Shaw changed a few of his own words in those letters. The word changes, such as "gallantries" for "copulations" and "mistress" for "whore" (Weintraub, *Pirate* 253), show Shaw censoring himself. The changes indicate that Shaw wanted to publish a more genteel version of himself. He privileges mainstream aesthetics over direct self-presentation.

Before Shaw stepped in to revise the book and gave his permission for Harris to publish his letters, Harris wrote to the editor of the *London Times Literary Supplement* asking the public for postcards, letters, or other materials about Shaw (Weintraub, *Pirate* 244). At this time, Harris or Scully may have also solicited a story from Goldman. A story written by Goldman was originally included in the manuscript of Harris's biography on Shaw. While it is probable that the story was her own version of the meeting with Shaw, the content is unknown.

By fall—shortly before the Shaw book was published—Shaw removed Goldman's story. In a letter to Scully, Goldman claimed she felt relieved because her story did not really belong in the Shaw book: "I am . . . glad to know that Shaw has thrown out my story. I cannot for the life of me see why I should have been dragged into Shaw's book and I am greatly relieved that I am no longer gracing its pages" (18 November 1931, reel 25).

Shaw eliminated Goldman's story for unknown reasons. It could be simply because, as Goldman says, it did not belong, or because he did not wish to be associated with her or her politics, or because the story offended his aesthetic sensibilities. In the end, while the story she wrote doesn't appear in the book, Goldman graces the pages through Harris's version of the Shaw/Goldman meeting.

Finally published on 27 November, the book sold well, much to the relief of Nellie Harris. But Goldman was disappointed. In a December letter to Berkman she complained about Scully. The letter suggests that she had had a hand in editing the book and was not getting a percentage of the sales: "He [Scully] knew what he was doing when he offered me a percentage on the Taylor book, but NONE on the Shaw book" (12 December 1931, reel 25). Goldman's complaint suggests that she contributed to the text and that had she negotiated aggressively with Scully, she would have received a percentage of the sales. It also implies that she has been given a one-time payment for her work. While she may have simply contributed the story that was expunged by Shaw, if that were the case it seems unlikely that she would complain about the lack of percentage later.

To further complicate the matter, in a letter to Max Nettlau, Berkman too claims authorship:

[T]he book on Shaw, published by Frank Harris after his death last year, also had my hand in it. It was the secretary of Harris, Frank Scully, an American journalist, who was to help Harris write the book. Harris wrote some 40,000 words and could not go on. His memory failed and he repeated himself. So Frank Scully took the book in hand and invited me to help him, as he himself is not author, just a journalist. Some of the chapters in the book have been written by me from beginning to end. Later on Bernard Shaw read the proofs of the book and made some changes. (21 December 1932)

Why would Goldman complain to Berkman about not receiving a percentage if Berkman was the one who rewrote some of the chapters? Or if they had collaboratively worked on the book? There are no concrete answers to these questions; however, each of these letters suggests that Shaw had the final say on what was printed in the book.

This rather complex history of creating and editing the book by the five writers/contributors—Shaw, Harris, Scully, Goldman, and Berkman—allows the reader to understand the published text primarily as Harris's interpretation of events but also as edited and revised by those involved. If Shaw or Goldman found something particularly offensive or inaccurate in Harris's portrayal of their meeting, one might assume they would have removed or rewritten it.

The story of the Shaw/Goldman meeting published in Harris's unauthorized biography begins by noting that neither Harris nor Shaw felt comfortable at the beginning of Shaw's visit, because Charlotte, Shaw's wife, had burned Harris's book *My Life and Loves*. Because it contained photographs of naked women and described Harris's many sexual conquests, she did not want the servants to read it. The implication is that Shaw had not objected to his wife's actions and did not rescue Harris's book. Shaw's letters bear out these claims. On 31 July 1928, Shaw wrote that Charlotte did, in fact, burn Harris's book (*CL* 105–6), and Shaw admits that he only read the first volume of *My Life and Loves*, because Frank "was much too disgusted with me for not leaving it on the drawing room table to send me the others" (*CL* 263). Shaw was unwilling to risk his wife's or a visitor's disapproval in order to support Harris by displaying his book. A fighter for free speech in public life, Shaw adhered to conventional standards, aesthetic as well as those of decorum, in his private life.

Soon, however, both Harris's and Shaw's discomfort diminished, and they "got on together famously" (Harris 33). Almost as an afterthought, Harris mentions that Goldman was present. Then he writes, "Shaw and I talk a lot, but she has lived her convictions more than most of us and has been punished for them. Of course, I too have been in gaol—even as Shakespeare, Cervantes, Wilde, and nearly all the courageous writers (all seemingly but Shaw); but we went to gaol for our trumpery sins, and she for her deepest convictions" (34).

Here Harris set the stage for his interpretation of the events. He placed himself parallel to Shaw in "talking a lot" and in the same ring as venerates canonical writers, but Goldman, who is not a writer of plays or poetry, he elevates above everyone. In distinguishing between going to jail for "sins" and going to jail because of one's convictions, Harris differentiates between these canonical writers and Goldman, a political agitator who becomes a dramatic artist in living out her deepest convictions. Shaw is relegated to the parenthesis because he has not managed to be sent to jail for his convictions or his personal debauchery. Harris's preference here is already quite obvious; Goldman is his hero because she takes her politics literally.

While Shaw's plays, such as *Mrs Warren's Profession*, are often political in that they criticize social and political systems, Shaw himself is not at risk of being thrown in jail for disseminating his art. His greatest danger is that his art will be, and in fact is, censored.[4] Goldman, on the other hand, is so committed to her beliefs—political, social, and even poetic—that she risks and loses her freedom: she herself as the living drama is censored. The risks Shaw took to convey his politics, on the other hand, did not endanger his physical being.

Finally, Harris summarized the vast political differences between Shaw and Goldman:

Between Emma the Anarchist and Shaw the Fabian Marxist there could be no genuine *rapprochement*. In 1921, when Lenin was busy shooting Anarchists as Trotsky shooting White Tsarists, Shaw sent Lenin a book with a laudatory inscription which is now lithographed and circulated through Soviet Russia. Emma Goldman took to the revolution for the establishment of liberty. Shaw, who agrees with Mussolini that liberty is putrescent corpse, looks to the revolution for the scientific organization of slavery, which he declares to be the sole business of governments and an inexorable law of nature. (Harris 34)

Their differences and the possibility of a heated political debate excited Harris even as he wrote this, but when Shaw and Goldman were in the same room they did not discuss politics or, it seems, even literature. Shaw, Harris explained, "thought discretion the better part of valour, and talked at great length" about how Mussolini's first talking picture should have been produced (Harris 34–35).[5] Much to Goldman's disappointment, Shaw's sense of gallantry or aesthetics caused him to steer the conversation to innocuous topics instead of politics. If this part of Harris's story is to be believed, the lack of engaging conversation might be one reason Goldman calls the meeting unsatisfactory.

A more convincing reason appears in another description of the Shaw/Goldman meeting. Harris recounted this particular scenario during an interview with his own biographers Tobin and Gertz.[6] Harris's story gains credibility through a letter Goldman wrote to her attorney, Arthur Ross. The letter confirms that the meeting took place and describes her disappointment and annoyance with Shaw, although it does not offer details. Harris explained the situation to Tobin, clarifying what else was said that day: "Miss Goldman, you know, never met Shaw and always expressed a desire to meet him. A few weeks ago, Shaw called on me when Miss Goldman happened to be staying with us. Of course, I introduced them" (Tobin and Gertz 11). Goldman's letters support this much of Harris's story, but the rest, although plausible, has yet to be substantiated. Harris continues: "Shaw asked about Berkman and Miss Goldman told him he was living in a suburb of Paris. Emma then became reminiscent as the three of us talked, and told what appeared to me the greatest story I've heard in a long while" (Tobin and Gertz 11).

Goldman told the story of her involvement with Berkman's attempt to kill industrialist Henry Clay Frick. Her involvement, which she fully described in her autobiography *Living My Life*, amounts to her attempt to prostitute herself in order to earn some money to buy her lover, Berkman, a gun. She dressed the part but lost her nerve; a potential customer saw her nervousness, gave her money, and told her to go home (1: 93). It seems odd that Goldman would tell Shaw such an intimate story the first time they met, but she may have thought her story would constitute a point of connection between them, since she had been summarizing and analyzing Shaw's *Mrs Warren's Profession* in her lectures and in print since it was first published. The play, after all, is a social critique of a system that offers women no respectable way to earn enough to care for themselves. It centers around the connection between prostitution and economics, as did Goldman's life experience.

Harris seems to delight in this memory of events. He continues: "It was a great scene to me: Emma trying to become a street-walker, mind you, for the man she loved, and at the crucial moment losing her nerve" (12). But then Tobin, the interviewer, notes that Harris suddenly sneered and continued, "but when she finished her story, Shaw, without a word of comment, began talking to me about something else. I cut off his talk immediately, and turning to her I said: 'Miss Goldman, you've just told a great story, and I thank you for it!'" (13). Harris portrayed himself valiantly attempting to compensate for Shaw's snub. If Harris's version of the conversation is accurate, Shaw's snub suggests a more emotional and personal reason why Goldman might call the meeting with Shaw unsatisfactory. Further, it suggests that the topic was far too direct for the genteel Shaw.

Shaw, a feminist in his own right and a man who, after all, understood the economic issues that lay behind prostitution, didn't respond with sympathy to Goldman's story. Perhaps he simply didn't approve of Goldman's reasons for her attempt to prostitute herself: she wanted to buy a gun to kill someone. And yet that explanation is also unsatisfactory, because Shaw seemed interested in Berkman, the man who actually served time for the attempted murder. Perhaps Goldman's comfort with discussing such sexual vulnerability disgusted Shaw. In her refusal to focus on polite conversation, Goldman violated both class and gender norms and Shaw's aesthetic sensibility.

Goldman's letter to Ross supports Harris's story only in that Shaw offended her. Goldman didn't provide Ross with details, promising to explain everything in full in her autobiography, which she never did. However, she did give Ross this bit of information: "I can only say that with all of the fame of GB Shaw, Frank has more humanity, more warm interest in the life and struggles of his fellows than Shaw. That merely illuminates my contention of years that Shaw's characters in all his works are mere puppets that have no independent being; they merely move and

talk according to the turn of their creator—Bernard Shaw" (7 September 1928, reel 20).

Clearly, the conversation was a charged and uncomfortable one in which Goldman found herself disappointed that the private man was not as interesting, liberated, or dedicated to the common person as his work suggested. When Goldman criticized Shaw as not being particularly sympathetic to his fellow human beings, and said his characters do not have an "independent being," she accused Shaw of being just an artist, of mimicking life without grasping it. A humanitarian artist cannot create independent beings without fully being involved in the world, she contends, and her own writing—letters, essays, and autobiography—was inseparable from her compassion for others who struggle under the weight of oppressive authority. Shaw didn't meet the standards she expected of all true humanitarians. The artist was not as committed to politics as she had hoped. Yet despite publicly criticizing him for his lack of revolutionary commitment, she continued to integrate his plays into her revolutionary lectures.

Ten years later, Goldman's tone was quite different. In her original letter to Shaw, Goldman had suggested that the meeting at the Harris's might not even be memorable to Shaw. She wrote, "Perhaps it left no impression at all on you, you may therefore not remember it at all" (2 March 1937, reel 39). Her words seem both humble and salacious. Her self-deprecation might have been a result of his literary success and popularity. At this point she must have recognized that while she and her causes are not popular in England, Shaw has won the Nobel Prize (1925) and become a household name in many countries. The English public's fascination with Goldman was never as intense as America's, and by 1937 even it had waned.

Goldman found the meeting important enough to write her attorney and claim that she would include it in her autobiography; perhaps she would also send it to Scully for publication in the Shaw biography. Here she established an uneven relationship, remembering and valuing what she thinks he would not.

In the next line she built on the differing power relationship, complimenting him on the "generous part" he played in defending the Chicago anarchists in 1887, who were sentenced to death after the Haymarket bombing. Goldman reminded him that he "had been the Initiator in collecting signatures of outstanding men and women for a protest against the judicial crime in Chicago" (2 March 1937, reel 39). Her underlying message: While we may not agree on many issues, we once agreed on this political and controversial issue.

Most of her information is accurate. In 1886 Shaw, in fact, did more and less than collecting signatures. He did more in that he published the text of a resolution to protest the treatment of the anarchists in *Commonweal*, October 1887 (Laurence, *Bibliography* C364).[7] Along with Kropotkin and William Morris, Shaw sponsored a mass rally in London against the Haymarket death sentence as well. On the other hand, Shaw also did less because he didn't actually collect many signatures. In his essay "My Memories of Oscar Wilde," first published in Harris's *Oscar Wilde: His Life and His Confessions*, Shaw wrote that Wilde was the only literary figure in London whom he could convince to sign the petition for the reprieve of the Chicago anarchists, sentenced to death after a travesty of a trial. In a later letter to Harris, Shaw commented:

I was in no way predisposed to like [Wilde]. . . . What first established a friendly feeling in me was, unexpectedly enough the affair of the Chicago anarchists, whose Home you constituted yourself by *The Bomb* [Harris's novel]. I tried to get some literary men in London, all heroic rebels and skeptics on paper, to sign a memorial asking for the reprieve of these unfortunate men. The only signature I got was Oscar's. It was a completely disinterested act on his part; and it secured my distinguished consideration for him for the rest of his life. (*CL* 403)

The disappointed Shaw recognized that the literary London men, despite their reputations as rebel, heroes, and skeptics, were not willing to sign an unpopular petition. In effect, just as Shaw asked literary men for their signatures on his petition asking for reprieve in 1887, Goldman, in 1937, asked Shaw for his support in commemorating the anniversary of the Haymarket event. Surprisingly, Shaw's response was similar to the one that the literary men of London had given him. Although he had once protested the treatment of the Haymarket anarchists, he was unwilling to support the commemoration.

Goldman's letter continues, "Whatever objections I have entertained through all the years, to your interpretation of anarchism, I have never ceased to be grateful to you for the sympathy you had expressed during the Haymarket Tragedy" (2 March 1937, reel 39). Here Shaw's political act received personal gratitude. She reminded him that while he might not have agreed with her anarchist views, he did not think the innocent anarchists should be killed, and he was willing to assert it publicly, despite popular opinion.

In the fourth and longest paragraph, Goldman made her final and personal request for Shaw's public support. She explains that she wants to present to the British public the "antifascist struggle in Spain" but needs to raise funds. At this point she was not directly asking Shaw for money, but rather for his sponsorship, which, she explained, did not entail any financial responsibility. She used to be able to rouse crowds, but she complained that she could no longer attract the public unless titled people, "those with money or men and women known in the creative world," support her (2 March 1937, reel 39). The larger English public had dismissed her.

If Shaw recognized the Haymarket injustice in 1887, Goldman might have reasoned, then he would support the commemoration of the Haymarket martyrs and humanitarian efforts in Spain. But he did not. In fact, when he wrote to Goldman two days later, he asked her why she wanted "to resurrect those poor Chicago Anarchists" and didn't mention the poor Spanish women and children.

In the second, longer and more detailed, letter from Goldman to Shaw, dated 7 May 1937, Goldman quoted Shaw's missing letter seven times and attempted to systematically dismiss each assertion. Through these quotations, piecing together the content and tone of Shaw's letter is possible.

While Shaw responded to Goldman's letter within a week, she did not respond to him for two months. When she did write, she began politely and generously: "[Your letter] contains more than one surprise. But then your great function in life has been to give the world all sorts of surprises" (7 May 1937, reel 40). In the next line she tells him how she considers his work worthy of consideration: "It may interest you to know that I have years ago brought your works to the attention of the broad masses in the United States and other countries. I have actually talked to miners and longshoremen about G. Bernard Shaw, the man, his plays and many funny contradictions of his characters." In fact, she had been addressing audiences and "regularly featuring [Shaw] in her lectures" for nearly forty years in the United States, Canada, and England (Falk et al., *History* 542). This passage implies that Shaw did not know she popularized his work and that when he met her at the Harrises' years before they did not discuss literature. Again, that seems particularly odd in the light of Goldman's references to and analysis of Shaw's plays in her lectures and her writing.

Evidence of Goldman's appreciation of Shaw's work abounds. Goldman lectured on anarchism and literature throughout the United States from early 1890 until 1919, when she was deported, and then again for a three-month tour in 1934, when she was granted a temporary visa. For example, in May 1904 she gave a lecture called "The Unpleasant Side of George Bernard Shaw" at Etris Hall in New York (Falk et al., *History* 473). In September 1908 she lectured on "The Revolutionary Spirit in the Modern Drama" as a part of her Yiddish Language Series (Falk et al., *History* 495). She gave a similar lecture with the same title but addressed a few different plays later the same year at Cullis Hall in London, Ontario. Both lectures included a discussion of *Mrs Warren's Profession* (Falk et al., *History* 488). These were just a few of the many stops on Goldman's lecture circuit.

By 1914 Goldman had published *The Social Significance of Modern Drama*, which includes two chapters on Shaw's plays. And finally, although they were not published and it is unclear if they were ever completed, Goldman wrote two undated manuscripts about Shaw, titled simply "The Life and Works of George Bernard Shaw" and "George Bernard Shaw: A Biographical Sketch."[8] It is not clear if she, like so many other people, wrote about Shaw's life in order "to capitalize" on his celebrity or if, less ironically, she was gathering information for Harris's biography on Shaw, or if after years of lecturing on his work she simply decided to write about the man himself. The manuscripts, like her lectures, are full of quotes from Shaw and other reliable sources. But unlike the lectures, the manuscripts seem removed in that they show no signs of dramatic passion or propaganda.

Although Shaw was the sole force behind the Haymarket petition in 1887, he questioned Goldman's desire to remember the martyrs publicly, and in a rebuttal to Shaw's dismissal of the Chicago anarchists Goldman called attention to Shaw's hypocrisy. She compared Shaw's resurrection of Joan of Arc in *Saint Joan* (1924) to her "resurrection" of the Chicago anarchists. She asked, incredulously, "Have you not rattled her long decayed bones and turned her into living form?" (7 May 1937, reel 40). She reminded him that he also memorializes a martyr. Then she quoted him:

> If my "digging up those who died and making foolish speeches are a waste of time and energy" what is one to say of you, having done the same with your heroine and the long and foolish speeches delivered over her, her time and her contemporaries. No doubt you consider your effort in "digging up the dead" of greater value to the future than mine in digging up the Chicago Anarchists. In all due respect and appreciation of your great dramatic craftsmanship I must say that your waste of time and energy merely served to amuse your large audiences. (reel 40)

Shaw objected to her commemorating the dead not, it seems, for the controversies surrounding their deaths, but because, as he saw it, they were dead and their story died with them. More importantly, he also objected to how she would commemorate them—artlessly, in long, boring speeches as a politician might. Goldman, for her part, knew that Shaw wrote his plays for reasons greater than simple audience amusement: to abuse him for his popularity amounted to an insult.

In the following paragraph she was again dismissive. In his letter, Shaw must have mentioned the lack of signatures on the 1887 petition and the lack of public interest in fate of the Chicago anarchists. But Goldman, who was not privy to the story behind the petition, didn't believe him. She responded, "Since I wrote you I have learned from very dependable sources that scores of Englishman have also been moved to appeal for the lives of the Chicago Anarchists, among them William Morris, [and] Walter Crane . . . to mention only a few" (reel 40). Goldman reminded Shaw of others who were involved as if he didn't know them, but she knew he did. Shaw had listened to Morris speak several times in the 1880s and even shared the stage with Morris when they defended the Chicago anarchists.

As for Shaw's relationship with Crane, Shaw's review "Last Lecture at the Craneries: Walter Crane as a 'Lightning Sketcher'—The Exhibition Has Paid Its Way" (1888) provides evidence of their relationship (Weintraub, *Art*). And, ironically enough, five days before Goldman wrote her letter to Shaw, Shaw published a pamphlet in which he wrote an article called "Bernard Shaw's Appreciation [of Walter Crane] May Day Demonstration, Sunday, 2nd May, 1937" (Laurence, *Bibliography* B265). In all likelihood, Goldman knew of Shaw's connection to Morris and Crane, and she provoked him one more time. She reminded him of his old days when commitment to politics came before propriety or popularity. She also reminded him of his dead friends and demanded that he be loyal to their memory.

This needling tone continues throughout the letter. At one point the letter implies that Shaw had quoted the Bible. Goldman humorously wrote, "While I am not versed in scripture as you are I do remember a passage where it says that the Lord will save a city if but one just man can be found in it. With you and Oscar Wilde to have demonstrated a sense of Justice England will surely be saved even if you two happen to be Irish" (reel 40). Dripping with sarcasm, Goldman played the nationality card. While she attacked him for his lack of compassion, his hypocrisy, and his nationality, she never criticized his skill as a writer or his fairly traditional style. By the end of the letter, she seemed to find satisfaction, not with Shaw, but with her own understanding of him.

Instead of looking directly to the common folk as she did in her early years as lecturer and writer, by 1937 Goldman was forced to write to literary figures like Shaw who had become respected by the common folk as well as the elite and those whose endorsement would bring a positive response from the public. This fact alone may finally explain the antagonism of the second letter. That she should have to appeal to Shaw as a public figure of sufficient reputation to provoke public support could only have been seen by Goldman as a recognition of the failure of any true substantial social revolutionary consciousness in the people. And, perhaps, Shaw too must have recognized that a committed political activist was addressing him as merely a public figure, a celebrity. More importantly, Shaw's aesthetic sensibilities prevented him from lending his name to a cause that he originally supported.

In contrast to Shaw and Goldman's acquaintance revealed through their letters, Goldman's use of Shaw's plays is more rational and more consistent. She based many of the radical ideas she espoused on his plays and on other texts of canonical literature. In her lectures she referred to anarchists' writings, but she built her call for revolution on tradition by invoking writers such as Emerson, Whitman, Ibsen, and Nietzsche. As both Goldman and Shaw worked to make their audiences self-conscious, it is not surprising that Goldman emphasized Shaw's *Mrs Warren's Profession*. Here, art, politics, and notions of femininity intersect—both for Emma Goldman and, by proxy, for Bernard Shaw.

Some of Goldman's contemporaries, including Rebecca West and Van Wyck Brooks, declared that through her lectures Goldman was instrumental in popularizing Shaw's plays in the United States (Drinnon 156, 164). She sold his books next to her own, lectured on his plays, referred to him in her famous primary essay on anarchism, and published several chapters on his plays in *The Social Significance of Modern Drama*. In her publication *Mother Earth*, a "Monthly Magazine Devoted to Social Science and Literature" that ran without interruption from 1906 to 1917, she published poetry, essays, and art that showed a revolutionary spirit. The magazine also routinely published a full-page advertisement called "Anarchist Literature" that lists Shaw's plays for forty cents (plus five cents postage). A 1904 advertisement for a Goldman lecture on *Mrs Warren's Profession* also appeared in *Mother Earth*. She was already lecturing on the play a year before it was produced in the United States. In 1934, when she was granted a temporary visa to return to the United States, Goldman was still lecturing on Shaw and his drama.

When Goldman ventured into a coal mine in 1898 and summarized *Mrs Warren's Profession* to an appreciative group of miners, she recognized the power of literary narrative over anarchist doctrine, the provocative effect of discussing prostitution, and, more importantly, a way to state her truth that would make people listen, laugh, and, she hoped, rebel. The play itself is not particularly anarchistic (Mrs. Warren is, after all, a capitalist), but Goldman used it to point in that direction.

What is it about the play that lends itself, at least according to Goldman, to an anarchistic interpretation? Were she a literary critic, she might have focused on the gentleman artist, Praed. In the beginning of the play, he has a few inviting lines. Impressed by Vivie's unconventionality—her hearty handshake and direct answers—he feels comfortable showing his own. He declares, "I am an anarchist. I hate authority. It spoils the relations between parent and child: even between mother and daughter" (*Warren* 89–90). But Goldman's goal, like Shaw's, was to make her audience uncomfortable. Analyzing one pseudo-anarchist character who represented art more than anarchy, reason rather than revolution, would not do. In fact, she didn't mention him in her lectures or her books. She was a political, not a literary, reader, and her readings were interpreted by a political audience.

Goldman appreciated *Mrs Warren's Profession* for its social critique and, more importantly, for the portrayal of the distorted relationship between the sexes. This distortion, namely prostitution, goes to the heart of Goldman's critique of capitalism: prostitution capitalizes on humans' natural sexual instinct and as such represents the distortion of our most basic selves, before any authority-imposed morals. *Mrs Warren's Profession* shows "how capitalism has corrupted the relations between the sexes," Margot Peters explains in the introduction to the facsimile (Garland xxi). But for Goldman, capitalism is an expression of all sorts of prostitution. More concretely, *Mrs Warren's Profession* and anarchism share a similar approach to prostitution. Peter Glassgold writes, "Anarchism approached prostitution not as a moral question but as a social wrong rooted (as was conventional marriage) in economic exploitation and the lack of education for women, conditions aided and abetted by the hypocrisy of organized religion and the state" (113). And *Mrs Warren's Profession* does just that. The play radically criticizes society when it implies that sex is women's only commodity. Everyone, according to Goldman, is to blame.

If Shaw is the gentleman scholar writing social critiques about prostitution—properly—without actually mentioning the word or the act, then Goldman is the commoner or vulgarian not only announcing the words but spelling out the implications. The art of the play includes what is left unsaid, but everyone is meant to understand. But in her lectures, Goldman frequently disallowed this moment. For her, the art lay in content of the story, not in her retelling of it.

Because most of Goldman's lectures were not recorded or transcribed, her exact analysis of *Mrs Warren's Profession* is open for interpretation. But three varied sources provide some information: a summary of her lecture by Louis J. Domas, German interpreter and informant; an overall analysis of Goldman's drama lectures in Chicago by Margaret Anderson, editor of the popular *Modernist* literary magazine, *The Little Review*; and finally, as mentioned previously, a chapter in *The Social Significance of Modern Drama*. Goldman's critiques do not offer much in-depth analysis; however, they do suggest why she used this play to present her anarchist message.

Domas's report is only one document from a rather sizable government file that includes FBI reports, confiscated personal papers, and other written "observations" of Goldman.[9] Domas was assigned to attend Goldman's lecture "The Revolutionary Spirit of Modern Drama" and write a report for the Bureau of Immigration, Department of Commerce and Labor, who were looking for a way to revoke Goldman's citizenship. This was his third report filed on Goldman in 1907.

Domas provided a few basic facts: Goldman gave her lecture in

German to a packed hall on Leverette Street in Boston. His five-page report includes two paragraphs on *Mrs Warren's Profession* and one on each of six other plays. Goldman discussed plays by Gorki, Ibsen, Shaw, and others—all within an hour or so. Her intention in her drama lectures was not to move from revolutionary to literary critic but instead to expose the audience to revolutionary ideas that already exist in modern drama, and in this way to show her audience what, on some level, they already know.

When Goldman discussed Shaw's *Mrs Warren's Profession*, either she or Domas, the interpreter spy, or both did not have their facts straight. First, Domas quotes Goldman as saying, "Of American Drama, I will just mention *Mrs Warren's Profession* by Bernard M. Shaw." American drama? Bernard M. Shaw? Perhaps Domas was not paying attention. But the inexactness continues.

Domas includes what appears to be Goldman quoting the play, but she is not quoting the standard version. A "friend" is talking to Vivie. Domas writes: "Your mother's money is not any more tainted than all the money there is in the world. There is a mill owner employing 600 girls paying them $3 a week. Do you mean to say that these girls are able to live on this miserly salary? They are forced to prostitution" (Domas 5). Leaving Domas out of the equation for the moment, Goldman may be simply adapting the quote as a director might, but more likely she is adapting to suit her audience. While the inclusion of dollars instead of pounds can be attributed to Americanizing the play, the inclusion of the word *prostitution* makes the implicit explicit and is particularly out of sync with Shaw's style.

A comparable quotation in the original version occurs when, in defense of owning brothels, Crofts points to respectable men who also exploit women. In the facsimile of *Mrs Warren's Profession*, Crofts, who, contrary to the Goldman/Domas statement, is not Vivie's friend, says: "He [Crofts's brother] gets his 22 percent out of a factory with six hundred girls in it, and not one of them getting wages enough to live on. How do you suppose they manage? Ask your mother" (Garland 189). Both this and the previous statement from Goldman/Domas asked a similar rhetorical question about how poor women survive, but while Shaw left the answer clear but unsaid, Goldman bluntly stated what Shaw implied. In this way she simplified his message.

Although it is clear that the following Goldman/Domas lines look like they were supposed to be taken from the play, they do not exist in Shaw's original text:

The owner of the Department Stores is doing the same. Carnegie with all his libraries he gave to the people who have not the time to read the books in those libraries, produced more prostitution than your mother did. And finally, whose money was it that enriched your mother, and paid for your education? Your mothers numerous establishments were patronized by canons of the Church, by Pillars of Society, by representatives of the Army and by representatives of every walk in the life. (Domas 5)

If we assume that Domas, while he may have a few facts wrong, probably did not simply invent the lines about department stores, or Carnegie, and that Goldman, rather than using an unknown director's adaptation, was doing her own adapting, then we can see how she moved from Shaw's general social critique to a very specific anarchistic one. The only lines that Shaw himself wrote that have some of the same meaning occur here: "You wouldn't refuse the Duke of Belgravia because some of the rents he gets are earned in queer ways. You wouldn't cut the Archbishop of Canterbury, I suppose, because the Ecclesiastical Commissioners have a few publicans and sinners among their tenants" (Garland 139). Shaw's lines focus on the people who profit through renting to, we assume, prostitutes, although the word is not used. Goldman not only used the word but named the type of men who visited these women—the common man as well as the most respected men in the church, society, or army.

Shaw, the gentleman scholar, critiqued society for its acceptance of and responsibility for prostitution, but this critique is once removed. He only ventured to assert that respectable men receive rent, not sex, from prostitutes. Goldman, ever aware of her audience, spelled out what Shaw only implies—and then she added a few details. And while even she shied away from more fully developing the literal participation of men, she did mention them and name their occupations. Here Goldman reminded the listener that the distortion of the relationships between the sexes was not one-sided. On the whole, both Goldman and Shaw recognized that the cause of prostitution was much greater than any immorality in the prostitute herself.

One might generously claim that Goldman Americanized Shaw's play (and even Shaw) by adding details familiar to laborers. More critically, one might claim she added details that more directly fit her agenda. For example, she named industrialist Andrew Carnegie as one of the producers of prostitutes. While not diverging from the play's main message, Goldman adds Carnegie and other familiar images that attach actual faces and physical places to Shaw's implications.

Although the Domas report is a summary of Goldman's lecture as heard through the ears of one assigned to attend, it is remarkably uncritical and seemingly unbiased. The fact that the commissioner of immigration sent an infiltrator to Goldman's lecture on drama speaks volumes about his expectation that she would make radical statements that would help him build a case against her and eventually lead to her deportation. However, the Domas report does not offer evidence of blasphemy, plans to overthrow the government, or any other treachery. It summarizes Goldman summarizing Shaw's *Mrs Warren's Profession*, a play that criticizes a society that exploits women and then blames them for their condition. The play exposes hypocrisy and a deeply flawed system. While the Domas report does not suggest Goldman made direct connections between the play and anarchism, implications abound. The reasoning might look like this: If the present system is as flawed as the play suggests, the system should be eliminated and a new social order in which each individual adheres to his or her own authority created. In short, Goldman uses *Mrs Warren's Profession* as evidence of the need for a fundamental change— through anarchy.

Goldman's lectures on modern drama evolved over the years, and in 1914, seven years after the Domas report, Margaret Anderson sought out Goldman. As editor of *The Little Review*, Anderson read and published works by Ezra Pound, T. S. Eliot, and James Joyce. She also published a few of Goldman's letters and essays—not for their literary quality, although they were well written, but for the revolutionary spirit embodied in them. Anderson attended a number of Goldman's lectures in Chicago and wrote a critique, which was later published in *Mother Earth*. Anderson's attention says something about Goldman's reputation not simply for lectures on anarchist propaganda but on drama as well.

Early in the year, some of Goldman's organizers decided they wanted, in Anderson's words, "to enlighten a certain type of benighted human being—the type that will go to anything which happens to be featured in the Fine Arts Building but that shudders at the mere thought of Emma Goldman in Labor hall" (320). So Goldman addressed the Chicago Press Club. Her lecture, titled "The Relationship of Anarchism to Literature," included references to literature, but instead of summarizing plays for the audience, she directly addressed them. "You are mental prostitutes!" she hurled at them. "You sell yourselves and your work to your editors or your publishers. . . . You say what you are told to say—whether it's the truth or not; you must not have an opinion of your own; you dare not have any ideas; you'd die of indigestion if you had" (Anderson 321). The mental prostitute and Mrs. Warren were one and the same for Goldman; selling one's body or selling out amounted to the same thing. In the larger picture, Goldman objected to the way capitalism relies on a selling of the self. Prostitution of all kinds, she would assert, stems from the capitalist system, and anarchy, with its demand for "a new social order based on liberty unrestricted by man-made law," would set everyone free ("Anarchism" 50). After berating the reporters, explaining the philosophy of anarchism, and making connections to literature, Goldman ended by recognizing what these reporters were thinking—that she was an optimist and a dreamer, to which she agreed. She then accused them of forsaking their own dreams.

Anderson was impressed with Goldman's passion, but she was critical as well; she wrote that the drama lectures were not particularly interesting because Goldman covered too many plays and had only enough time to summarize and point out the play's social value. And at the same time, Anderson wrote that Goldman, "instead of being indiscriminate and uncritical . . . proved how creatively critical she is: she understands what the authors were trying to do and she doesn't distort and misinterpret in a effort to say something clever on her own account" (323). Anderson encouraged Goldman to be more than simply the dramatists' mouthpiece. But Goldman never claimed to be a literary critic. She was instead a disseminator of art, interpreter of the implied.

In *The Social Significance of Modern Drama*, published the same year as Anderson's review, Goldman quotes Shaw exactly and appropriately. She summarizes the plot of *Mrs Warren's Profession* and then asserts how Kitty and women like her make sensible choices in order to survive. She also asserts that most people dismiss prostitutes as simply immoral. To support her point, Goldman presents the scene when Mrs. Warren explains her choice to Vivie. Mrs. Warren asks, "Do you think I did what I did because I liked it, or thought it right, or wouldn't rather have gone to college and been a lady if I'd had the chance?" (*Warren* 121). According to Goldman, Mrs. Warren is a "superior sort of mother" because she has provided her daughter with what her own parents could not: choices. Vivie will not be forced to marry, work in a factory for a non-living wage, or prostitute herself in any manner.

In the end, Goldman's summary of *Mrs Warren's Profession*, while relatively true to Shaw's intentions, was used to further her own anarchistic agenda. By exposing the hypocrisy of the present social and political system, the play was for Goldman a step in the direction of anarchism and revolution. The fault in the system that Shaw critiqued and Goldman emphasized leaves women (and, she would add, men) few alternatives to literal and figurative prostitution. Shaw's solution was reform, while Goldman's was revolution and the creation of a new social order. Through Goldman's feminist anarchist view, Shaw's *Mrs Warren's Profession* takes on meaning personal to Goldman through her own experience and is made explicit to her audience through adaptation. One of her goals in invoking this and other plays, such as Ibsen's *A Doll's House*, was to show the depth and breadth with which international modern drama is imbued with a revolutionary spirit. In doing so, Goldman reminded her audience that the spirit was not new and was, if they dared to find it, within themselves.

Shaw, privileging aesthetics over politics, chose to remain in the mainstream, critical but still accepted and accepting. His emphasis on the aesthetics of form and manners prevented him from living out his politics in his everyday life. While he strongly believed that the social and political system needed reform, his primary method of criticism was through his plays, not direct action. Following his own politics to their fullest extent and perhaps risking his freedom and being imprisoned for his beliefs was not part of his agenda. But Goldman thought she had found a fatal flaw in Shaw's unwillingness to translate the criticism implicit in his plays into radical political action and take profound risks. She found his social critiques right on the mark—funny, poignant, and sexual (without explicitly being so)—but her disappointment with the man himself haunted her. Long after their uncomfortable meeting, she still wrote him in an effort to move him beyond writing plays—out into the world of suffering people.[10] She came just short of accusing him of prostituting his art through his lack of social commitment.

Notes

1. In 1885 there was some confusion about Shaw's political leanings that stemmed from his article "What's in a Name? How an Anarchist Might Put It." Appearing in *The Anarchist* (London) two months before the Haymarket bombing occurred, it was an ironic piece written to show Charlotte Wilson the proper way to write such an article (Gibbs, *Chronology* 392). However, anarchists took it seriously and Benjamin Tucker quickly reprinted it (without permission) in his New York publication *Liberty* ("Not the Daughter but the Mother of Order"). It was the first work of Shaw's to appear in the United States, and both the publication of the article in the anarchist journal and the article itself led "many to believe mistakenly that Shaw is an anarchist" (Gibbs, *Life* 57).

2. For an overview of the play and historical influences, see Leonard Conolly's introduction to *Mrs Warren's Profession* (Orchard Park, N.Y.: Broadview Editions, 2005).

3. The original Shaw-Goldman letters can be found in the International Institute of Social History, Emma Goldman Archives, Amsterdam, The Netherlands. They have been published in *The Emma Goldman Papers: A Microfilm Edition* (Chadwyck-Healey Inc., 1991), reels 39 and 40.

4. For an excellent analysis of censorship in Shaw, see Celia Marshik's "Bernard Shaw's Defensive Laughter" in *British Modernism and Censorship* (Cambridge: Cambridge University Press, 2006).

5. Goldman's text *My Disillusionment of Russia* describes her slow realization that the anarchist spirit was being quelled, not expanded, in Russia. In effect, for Goldman, the revolution failed, but Shaw saw success. In fact, when he visited Russia in 1931 he was impressed with what he found.

6. For biographies on Frank Harris, see Samuel Roth, *The Private Life of Frank Harris* (New York: W. Faro, 1931); Edward Merrill Root, *Frank Harris* (New York: Odyssey, 1947); Linda Morgan Bain, *Evergreen Adventurer: The Real Frank Harris* (London: Research Pub., 1975); Robert Brainard Pearshall, *Frank Harris* (New York: Twayne, 1970) (this text contains criticism and interpretation); Philippa Pullar, *Frank Harris: A Biography* (New York: Simon & Schuster, 1976).

7. Shaw published the text of a resolution he successfully proposed at a meeting to protest the treatment of the anarchists. The meeting took place on 14 October 1887, and the resolution was published in *Commonweal* (15 October 1887: 333).

8. These manuscripts can be found in *The Emma Goldman Papers*, reel 54.

9. The entire government file can be found in *The Emma Goldman Papers*, reels 56–67.

10. Evidence of their acquaintance not addressed or analyzed in this paper includes a letter from Shaw to Harris mentioning a meeting with Goldman (Aug. 27, 1930), numerous references to Shaw in Goldman's private correspondence, and connections through mutual friends and acquaintances like H. G. Wells. See my dissertation, "Revolutionizing Literature: Anarchism in the Lives of Emma Goldman, Dorothy Day, and Bernard Shaw," 2010.

Works Cited

Anderson, Margaret. "Emma Goldman in Chicago." *Mother Earth* 9.10 (1914): 320–24.

Berkman, Alexander. Letter to Max Nettlau. 21 Dec. 1932. Ed. Dana Ward. *Anarchy Archives*. http://dwardmac*f*.pitzer.edu/Anarchist_Archives/bright/berkman/iishberkman/berkMNcorr/ABtoMN12-21-32/abtomn12-21-32.html, accessed 15 Oct. 2009.

Clark, Suzanne. *Sentimental Modernism: Women Writers and the Revolution of the Word.* Bloomington: Indiana UP, 1991.

Domas, Louis J. "Letter to Georg B. Billings." 14 December 1907: 1–5. Falk, Zboray, and Cornford, *The Emma Goldman Papers.*

Drinnon, Richard. *Rebel in Paradise: A Biography of Emma Goldman.* Chicago: U of Chicago P, 1961.

Falk, Candace, Ronald J. Zboray, and Daniel Cornford, eds. *The Emma Goldman Papers: A Microfilm Edition.* 69 reels. Chadwyck-Healey Inc., 1991.

Falk, Candace, Barry Pateman, et al., eds. *Emma Goldman: A Documentary History of the American Years Making Speech Free, 1902–1909.* Vol. 2. Chicago: Illinois UP, 2008.

Gibbs, A. M. *Bernard Shaw: A Life.* Gainesville: UP of Florida, 2005.

———. *A Bernard Shaw Chronology.* New York: Palgrave, 2001.

Glassgold, Peter, ed. *Anarchy: An Anthology of Emma Goldman's* Mother Earth. Washington, DC: Counterpoint, 2001.

Goldman, Emma. "Anarchism: What It Really Stands For." *Anarchism and Other Essays.* New York: Dover, 1969. 47–67.

———. *Living My Life.* 2 vols. 1931. New York: Dover, 1970.

———. *The Social Significance of Modern Drama.* Boston: R. G. Badger, 1914.

———. "Victims of Morality." *Red Emma Speaks: Selected Writings and Speeches by Emma Goldman.* Ed. Alix Kates Shulman. Random House: New York, 1972. 126–32.

Harris, Frank. *Bernard Shaw: An Unauthorized Biography Based on First Hand Information.* New York: Simon & Schuster, 1931.

Laurence, Dan. H. *Bernard Shaw: A Bibliography.* New York: Oxford UP, 1983.

Shaw, George Bernard. *Bernard Shaw and Alfred Douglas: A Correspondence.* Ed. Mary Hyde. New York: Ticknor and Fields, 1982.

———. *Collected Letters.* Ed. Dan H. Laurence. Vol. 4. New York: Dodd, Mead, 1965.

———. *Mrs Warren's Profession: A Facsimile of the Holograph Manuscript.* Intro. Margot Peters. New York: Garland, 1981.

———. *Mrs Warren's Profession.* Ed. Leonard Conolly. Orchard Park, NY: Broadview Editions, 2005.

Tobin, A. I., and Elmer Gertz. *Frank Harris: A Study in Black and White.* Chicago: Madeleine Mendelssohn, 1931.

Weintraub, Stanley, ed. *Bernard Shaw on the London Art Scene, 1885–1950.* University Park: Penn State P, 1990.

———, ed. *The Playwright and the Pirate: Bernard Shaw and Frank Harris: A Correspondence.* University Park: Penn State P, 1982.

Wexler, Alice. *Emma Goldman in Exile: From the Russian Revolution to the Spanish Civil War.* Boston: Beacon, 1989.

III

Shavian Feminism in the Larger World

9

Mrs Warren's Profession and the Development of Transnational Chinese Feminism

•••••••••••••••••••

KAY LI

The premiere of *Mrs Warren's Profession* in China on 16 and 17 October 1920, during the Chinese intellectual revolution of 1919–23, exemplified the development of transnational Chinese feminism.[1] *Mrs Warren's Profession* had been translated by Pun Jia-sheng and appeared exactly one year earlier, in October 1919, in volume 2, issue 2, of *Xin Chao* (New tide), and it was the first Shaw play performed in China. Surprisingly, the Shanghai production preceded the first British public performance: *Mrs Warren's Profession* was banned in England until 1925.

With the overthrow of the Qing Dynasty in 1911, progressive thinkers politicized the woman question, using the equality of the sexes and feminism as a symbol of modern civilization, in contrast to traditional Chinese Confucianism, which subjugated women to men. The first production of *Mrs Warren's Profession* represented a climax of this movement toward equality in the early twentieth century. As Wendy Chen has shown, *Mrs Warren's Profession* played an important role in the development of modern Chinese spoken drama, which completely broke with traditional Chinese stage practices (99).

Advertisements for the performances of *Mrs Warren's Profession* in the *Shenbao*, Shanghai's most influential newspaper, emphasized their revolutionary character:

The first Western play on the Chinese stage
- Is *Mrs Warren's Profession*
- Is the most famous play in the new century
- Is the play that must be watched by women in the whole world

According to the advertisement, "the aim of the play is to topple women's lives in old society. The play shows the evil in women's lives, so that all women know the importance of their character and will not be the entertainment of men. This play is important to the dirty society of modern China, and must be seen by women and those concerned with the problems of women" (14, 16, and 17 October 1920).

Early Chinese Feminism

Feminist ideas had already begun to circulate in China before this historic performance of *Mrs Warren's Profession*. A year earlier, Kang You-wei, famous for his abortive "Hundred Days Reform" censored by the Empress Dowager, had published his *Datong-Shu* (Book of universality). Kang advocated the equality of the sexes and marriage hegemony (*Datong-Shu*). Believing in women's independence and the freedom of marriage, he thought that the contemporary marriage system trapped women for a lifetime. Instead, he advocated replacing lifetime marriage with one-year contracts between men and women. Chinese translations of important Western feminist works had already appeared, including John Stuart Mill's "The Subjection of Women" (1869) and Herbert Spencer's "The Rights of Women" (1902). And China had recently been ruled by one of the most powerful women on earth, the Empress Dowager Cixi (1835–1908), who handpicked child emperors so that she could remain in power.

Chinese feminist publications soon appeared, such as Chen Kit-fang's *Nu Bao* (Women's newspaper), which later became *Nu Xue Bao* (Women's education newspaper). Kit-fang railed against footbinding and supported such revolutionary ideas as female education, women's rights, female independence, and equality of the sexes.

In 1920, for the first time, Peking University accepted female students (Lee). Educated women began to promote female entrepreneurship to achieve economic independence. Various female factories with solely female workers and management and female corporations were set up by these educated women, and some of these advocated the link between feminism and nationalism. For example, the Xing Yeh Company advocated that consumers

"Buy Home Goods and Promote Female Entrepreneurship." After the May Fourth Movement in 1919 there were increasing concerns about female economic independence. There were a few female doctors and educators, and boys' schools and institutes of higher education began to employ female teachers. In cities like Guangzhou, Beijing, and Shanghai there were female custom officers, operators, policewomen, and shop girls. But most of these female enterprises were unsuccessful, not only because the women were inexperienced in business but also because the idea of female enterprises was not widely accepted and understood by the general public.

As I have shown in *Bernard Shaw and China: Cross-Cultural Encounters*, the Chinese translation of *Mrs Warren's Profession* was intended to manipulate culture for social and political ends, including a more Western attitude toward women (Li 54). Pun Jia-sheng's Chinese translation appeared in the October 1919 in volume 2, issue 2, of the progressive magazine *Xin Chao* (New tide). The groundwork had already been laid by a Chinese production of Ibsen's *A Doll's House* in June 1918, with a concession to Chinese propriety: Nora was played by a man, Wang Chung-hsien, who went on to produce *Mrs Warren's Profession* and play the role of Vivie.

Soong Ching-ling and Bernard Shaw

Some of Vivie's achievements would have been familiar to Chinese audiences because of the accomplishments of Soong Ching-ling, the daughter of a rich Chinese businessman and missionary, who became the third wife of Dr. Sun Yat-Sen in 1915. Ching-ling entered Wesleyan College in the United States in 1908, a rare privilege for Chinese women at that time. And like Vivie, Soong insisted on setting her own life course. Despite her father's disapproval (he literally locked her up at home), she went to Japan, married Dr. Sun, and became an outspoken advocate for women's rights.

Soong's life exemplified the freedom from family control that young Chinese intellectuals admired—and that Vivie Warren sought in *Mrs Warren's Profession*, defying her mother's attempt "to dictate her way of life, and to force on [her] the acquaintance of a brute [Sir George Crofts] whom anyone can see to be the most vicious sort of London man about town."[2] Shaw and Soong Ching-ling eventually met in Shanghai in 1933. Soong greeted Shaw on board the *Empress of Britain*, famously persuaded him to set foot in China, and invited him to a lunch with prominent Chinese scholars and intellectuals.

The First Performances of *Mrs Warren's Profession*

Despite high hopes for success, the first two Chinese performances of *Mrs Warren's Profession* did not go well; in fact, much of the audience left early. According to a contemporary report, "A quarter of the audience left before the production was over, some of them using obscenities on their way out" (Hu 19). The producer, Wang Chung-hsien, recalled that the latter were those from the second- and third-class seats (Chao). Obviously, this part of the audience was not familiar with the drama of ideas. Coming for an exciting plot, they found the actors engaged in endless stage talk instead. As Song Chun-fang, a scholar of Western drama who understood the difference between Chinese and Western drama, reported: "Just imagine there were just six persons on stage talking flatly for four and a half hours—Act I started with Vivie and Praed heedlessly talking for nearly half an hour. In Act III, Mrs Warren and Vivie talked for an hour. How can New Drama like this make people who are used to watching New Drama with a running plot stay in their seats?" (qtd. in Hong 36–37).

There was also a moral concern. In England the cause for the censorship was the suggestion of incest, but Chinese audiences censured the play because a prostitute was featured onstage. According to Hsiao Ch'ien, "In the second act, when Mrs. Warren began to tell Vivie about her prostitution business, several [three to five according to the producer] fashionable ladies in the front stalls rose to leave—and not without grumbling" (Hsiao 19). The failure of this first production of *Mrs Warren's Profession* showed progressive Chinese thinkers that the nation was not yet ready for transnational feminism. Rather than claiming sisterhood with women around the world, there was a need to focus on home ground first.

Realizing that imported Western plays might not suit the Chinese situation perfectly, many young Chinese intellectuals began to write their own plays advocating new attitudes toward women. This New Drama, spoken rather than sung, as was customary in China, soon paved the way for a new medium, film, which could capture a much larger audience. Many of these films, which became big hits featuring famous female stars, served a social agenda and aimed to arouse social conscience. In 1927, for example, Hong Shen and Zhang Zhi-chuan produced *Wai Nu Si De Zhi Ye* (Miss Wai's profession), loosely based on Shaw's play. The voices of feminists became louder in films like *Zi Mei Hua* (Twin sisters, 1933) and *Xin Nu Xing* (New women, 1935), both of which echoed themes in *Mrs Warren's Profession*.

A Chinese version of Vivie Warren came to life in Zhang Zhi-chuan's *Nu Chuan* (Rights for women, 1936), which explored a woman's quest for personal fulfillment. To find the answer, the female protagonist willfully relinquished both her family and her prospects for love, in the same way that Vivie Warren rejected her mother and Frank Gardner.

After the founding of the People's Republic of China in 1949, *Mrs Warren's Profession* was again put to social use. China celebrated the Shaw Centenary in 1956, during which acts 2 and 3 of *Mrs Warren's Profession* were staged. This was an obvious attempt to mimic the West, with the use of wigs and the whitewashed faces, which are commonly used in the depiction of westerners. Rubeigh Minney, who was invited there as a featured speaker, thought that the Chinese's acquaintance with Shaw's plays was confined almost entirely to *Mrs Warren's Profession* (65). Tien Han spoke from the social, realistic, and national levels in his major Chinese address, titled "Let Us Learn from the Great Masters of Realist Drama." Tien Han, chairman of the Chinese Union of Stage Artists, highlighted *Mrs Warren's Profession*: "Shaw suggests a different solution for Vivie, the new woman, in her determined and uncompromising struggle to leave her brothel-keeper mother and that rotten parasite who lived on the income derived from capital invested in houses of prostitution, Sir George Crofts; and that was an independent existence working at a profession. This is a development on *A Doll's House*. . . . even though in capitalist society, the problem of the professional woman is not an easy one to solve" (Minney 65).

These Chinese readings of *Mrs Warren's Profession* were quite different from what Shaw had originally intended. Shaw himself admitted in his preface to the play: "None of our plays rouse sympathy of the audience by an exhibition of the pains of maternity as Chinese plays constantly do. Each nation has its particular set of tapus [*sic*] in addition to the common human stock, and though each of these tapus limits the scope of the dramatist, it does not make drama impossible" (1: 240).

Despite these differences, Chinese intellectuals were able to make good use of *Mrs Warren's Profession* in their slow march toward equality for women. Despite a theater tradition that kept women offstage, and a subject so controversial that *Mrs Warren's Profession* could not even be publicly performed in England, Shaw's drama played an important role in the social history of China—more evidence, if such is needed, of Shaw's importance to the opening of new opportunities and rights for the women of the world.

Notes

1. I am grateful to Professor Melba Cuddy-Keane and Professor Robert Fothergill for reading various drafts of this essay.

2. George Bernard Shaw, *Collected Plays with Their Prefaces*, ed. Dan H. Laurence, 7 vols. (London: Reinhardt, 1970–74), 1: 307. Subsequent quotations are from this edition.

Works Cited

Chao, Chia-pi, ed. *Chung-kuo hsin-wen-hsueh-ta-hsi* [A comprehensive anthology of modern Chinese literature: 1917–27]. 10 vols. Shanghai: Shanghai liang-yu t'u-shu yin-shua kung-shih, 1935–36.

Chen, Wendy. "The First Shaw Play on the Chinese Stage: The Production of *Mrs Warren's Profession* in 1921." *SHAW: The Annual of Bernard Shaw Studies* 19 (1999): 99–118.

Hong, Shen. "Dao Yan" [Introduction]. *Chung-kuo hsin-wen-hsueh-ta-hsi* [A comprehensive anthology of modern Chinese literature, 1917–27]. Chia-pi Chao, ed. Vol. 9. Shanghai: Shanghai liang-yu t'u-shu yin-shua kung-shih, 1935–36. 1–100.

Hsiao, Ch'ien. *The Dragon Beards versus the Blueprints*. London: Pilot Press, 1944.

Hu, Gen-xi, *Lao Shanghai* [Old Shanghai]. Shanghai: Xue Lin, 2003.

Kang, You-wei. *Datong-Shu* [Book of universality]. Beijing: Renmin chubanshe, 2010.

Lee, Yuen-Ting. *Active or Passive Initiator: Cai Yuanpei's Admission of Women to Beijing University (1919–1920)*. http://www.sino.uni-heidelberg.de/eacs2004/content/abstracts/section-f.php?section=6&subsection=67#SunH.

Li, Kay. *Bernard Shaw and China: Cross-Cultural Encounters*. Gainesville: UP of Florida, 2007.

Mill, John Stuart. "The Subjection of Women." http://www.constitution.org/jsm/women.htm, accessed 2 July 2008.

Minney, Rubeigh. *Next Stop, Peking: Record of a 16,000-Mile Journey through Russia, Siberia and China*. London: George Newnes, 1957.

Shaw, Bernard. *Collected Plays with Their Prefaces*. Ed. Dan H. Laurence. Vol. 1. London: Reinhardt, 1970–74.

"Soong Ching-ling's Speech at Sun Wu and Its Meaning." http://www.ndcnc.gov.cn/datalib/2004/Opus/DL/DL-192/, accessed 3 July 2008.

Spencer, Herbert. *Social Statics: or, The Conditions Essential to Happiness Specified, and the First of Them Developed*. London: John Chapman, 1851. http://oll.libertyfund.org/?option=com_staticxt&staticfile=show.php%3Ftitle=273, accessed 2 July 2008.

10

Shaw's Women in the World

•••••••••••••••••

JOHN M. MCINERNEY

> Man's love is of man's life a thing apart,
> 'Tis woman's whole existence; man may range
> The court, camp, church, the vessel, and the mart;
>   Sword, gown, gain, glory, offer in exchange
> Pride, fame, ambition, to fill up his heart,
> And few there are whom these cannot estrange;
> Men have all these resources, we but one,
> To love again, and be again undone.
>
>   Byron, "Don Juan Canto I"

These lines, spoken by Julia, young Juan's first "conquest" in Byron's *Don Juan*, express what was unfortunately true, not only for most women of his time, but in Shaw's time (at least at the start of his career) as well. Even in literature and drama, women characters, unless they belonged to the lower classes, were typically defined, and therefore confined, solely by their relationships with men. They were viewed only as wives, would-be wives, mothers, daughters, sisters, or sometimes as mistresses, and nothing else.

However, Shaw created a gallery of women characters who do not fit into the velvet prison Byron described. They include women whose careers range as freely as men's do through the political, military, business, and professional worlds, and the phrase "Shaw's public women" is a kind of verbal umbrella that covers them all.

These characters are important to anyone studying his plays, and relevant for today's women, for a number of reasons. First, when they step out of the private, domestic, socially constructed role that effectively contained most women, they become points of reference and emblematic figures for a great many women today. Second, they exhibit the strength, confidence, and independent minds public women still require, and what Shaw postulates about the sources of such unique qualities can help us understand women leaders today and even predict where they will come from in the future. Third, and very significantly, many of the challenges these characters—and public women in our world—face stem from the ways they are perceived; indeed, when Hillary Clinton described her public career as a Rorschach test for the public (Kakutani), she could cite the sharply divergent reactions Shaw's Vivie Warren, Major Barbara, Saint Joan, the Millionairess, and others all evoked in his plays as illuminating precedents. Fourth, Shaw's public women exercise the freedom to *define* their interests, their standards of behavior, and their lifestyles in a way that anticipates the course many women follow today, and these characters navigate that course through social obstacles, storms of opposition, and conflicting currents that contemporary women will find familiar.

Indeed, although it should also be noted that Shaw's public women anticipate what we have seen about recent, real public women with regard to the importance of family tradition, faith, and even the confidence that comes from physical training in their development, this essay will focus on the kaleidoscopic perceptions of women leaders, in Shaw's plays and in our history, and on the challenges these virtual and many actual women face as they "perform their gender" their own way.

As such, it will follow in the path forged by scholars such as Kathleen Hall Jamieson, who has carefully studied what she calls the "double bind" women leaders face. The double bind refers to the traps society has always set for women who try to assume a role or take on a task heretofore reserved for men. Women are told that they are incapable of doing whatever it is they seek to do, because they are women, and if they succeed in doing it anyway, they are scorned for being "unwomanly." Jamieson adds: "The double bind is a strategy perennially used by those with power against those without. The overwhelming evidence shows that, historically, women are usually the quarry" (4–5).

Let us begin, then, by looking closely at the reactions to Epifania Fitz-fassenden, the imposing heroine of *The Millionairess*. At various times in the play, other characters describe her as "an acquisitive woman" (254), "a man" (283), "a psychologist" (285), someone who can reduce adults to the status of children (287), "a bank account" (312), "Niagara Falls" (297), a "tornado," "an earthquake," and "an avalanche" (312). Every character in the play regards her differently. To Sagamore, the solicitor, she is an amusing phenomenon; to Alastair, her estranged husband, she is a frustrating challenge; to Polly Seedystockings she is a noisy, unreasonable obstacle in the way of her happiness with Alastair; to the old couple at the sweatshop, she is an overwhelming force that takes over their livelihood before they can grasp what's happening; to the manager of the seaside inn she is an almost magical guide to business success; and to the Egyptian doctor she is a fascinating, irresistibly dynamic pulse. These reactions, which might better be called projections of the other characters' fears and wishes, are generated by her personality, her power, and her public activism, and they remove her from the categories or roles into which women ordinarily fit.

In contrast, Patricia Smith (alias Polly Seedystockings) is very astute, articulate, and in her own way as willful and successful as Epifania, but she has confined herself to familiar territory for a woman: the soothing helpmeet for a man. Even if she were able to do so, she would never dream of throwing a man down a set of stairs, as Eppy does to Adrian Blenderbland. In consequence, she is "read" in the same way by everyone, except for Eppy, and even she, who scorns Polly, sees her in domestic terms, as Alastair's doormat.

But Eppy, who is direct and confrontational, not diplomatic and polite, active, not reactive, and controlling, not submissive, is not readily classifiable to the people around her. Therefore, they must describe her, even to themselves, in terms of their individual impressions, which spring from their unique memories and culturally induced associations, as well as their direct experiences of her. This accounts for the variety of the "tags" applied to her.

Of course, all of those terms are extravagant or outsized, reminding us that Shaw calls this play a "Jonsonian comedy," which means that the characters might be described as "humours," dominated by exaggerated traits, in the tradition of Ben Jonson's plays. Can we infer then that if the play were titled *The Millionaire*, and the plot remained relatively the same, that the protagonist would be similarly outrageous and imperious? Yes, but the other characters' reactions to the millionaire would probably be much different. For instance, Adrian would not likely be so bold as to criticize the beloved father of a vigorous male companion known to have a hot temper. However, like most men (and most people, for that matter), he just does not expect a *woman* to resort to physical violence. So, when an attractive, even heterosexually desirable woman suddenly acts the way we would expect a man to behave, it causes sensation and confusion— among the other characters in the play, among people in the audience, and among people in general.

Nowhere is this phenomenon more evident than in Shaw's *Saint Joan*. Most of the male characters in the play are to varying degrees disturbed by the "masculine" role Joan adopts when she leads the French army against the English invaders. She is, first of all, described as variously as Eppie is. She is called a "slut" because she talks to soldiers (51–52), "an angel dressed as a soldier" (64), a "crazy wench," a woman of great faith, blessed by God" (74), and a "witch" or "sorceress" (88–89). Also, at her trial for heresy, one of the arguments that seems to appeal most strongly to the men in charge is that she must be evil because she refuses to wear women's clothes and dresses like a man (131–32). She gives a common sense explanation: "I was a soldier living among soldiers. I am a prisoner guarded by soldiers. If I were to dress as a woman they would think of me as a woman, and then what would become of me?" (132). That reasoning might well strike us as simply prudent today, but it fell on deaf masculine ears in the fifteenth century. A woman who put on the clothes or did the job of a man was wicked; there was no doubt in their minds. It was true then, as it was true for most of the twentieth century, what Song, the transvestite Chinese spy from David Hwang's play *M. Butterfly*, observes, in attempting to explain why women's roles in Chinese opera were always played by men: "Only a man knows how a woman is supposed to act" (1395).

In reality and in the play, Joan did capture the imagination and inspire the loyalty of French soldiers; she did lead them to an improbable victory over the English. And yet, after the Dauphin was crowned king of France, or in other words, after the objectives of the French leaders were achieved, they didn't want Joan to continue in what they saw as an abnormal role. They wanted her to give way once more to their judgment, their author- ity. Later, church authorities conducting her trial for heresy are willing to save Joan from the fire being prepared for her by the English forces, but they insist that she give up her trust in her individual conscience, submit to their demands, and accept permanent imprisonment for what they see as her sin of heretical defiance. One way to read their demands, therefore, is that they want to force Joan to settle back into the role imposed on all other women in that era. Joan's ghost acknowledges as much in the epilogue when she says: "I might almost as well have been a man. Pity I wasn't: I should not have bothered you all so much then" (148).

However, in the same speech Joan adds: "But my head was in the skies; and the glory of God was upon me; and, man or woman, I should have bothered you as long as your noses were in the mud" (148). This is her way of acknowledging the substantial military, political, and doctrinal issues generated by her spectacular career. As Dunois tries to explain to her in scene 5, there were plausible military reasons for rejecting Joan's plan for new battles. Earlier, in scene 4, Warwick, representing the medieval political structure, and Cauchon, representing the Catholic Church, explain very cogently why Joan's ascendancy and her views were dangerous to the status quo they honestly believed should be preserved. Her gender, then, is not the only reason why Joan suffered death and defeat (at least temporarily).

Shaw understood as well as anyone did that great leaders, whether men or women, have strong convictions as well as strong personalities, and that those convictions are bound to be opposed by people who hold equally strong (and often reasonable) convictions. (Indeed, dialectical patterns of arguments and counter-arguments can be found throughout Shaw's plays, with *Major Barbara* and *Man and Superman* being just two notable examples.)

We can also maintain that in the thrust and parry of public debate, in the struggle for support and supremacy that leadership requires, the kaleidoscope of perceptions attached to women leaders are, for Shaw's public women, both obstacles and stepping stones. For one thing, those perceptions seem to come in binary sets, one positive and one negative. Joan, for example, is a both "crazy wench" and "an angel," a "witch" and a "little saint" (101). Another Shavian public woman, Barbara in *Major Barbara*, is an intimidating, even emasculating force to the bully, Bill Walker, in act 2; to Jenny Hill, a young co-worker at the Salvation Army shelter, she is a sweet protector and inspiration.

Both women are helped and hindered by those contrasting perceptions. Joan's negative, gender-based images first complicate her work and then help to bring about her death. On the other hand, the fact that she was a young woman taking on a striking, unimaginable role as a soldier/ leader made her a magnet, first for curious soldiers and officials, then for the allegiance of an army starved for charismatic leadership. Though not as dramatic, Barbara's case is equally interesting. The fact that she is a young, attractive woman (and the granddaughter of the Earl of Steve-nage) helps her maintain an easy authority over her co-workers at the shelter and allows her to be quite boldly but charmingly persistent in her efforts to convert souls for the Lord. Yet her good looks and hearty charm make Adolphus Cusins fall in love with her, not with God or the Salvation Army; both Barbara's mother and her father tartly observe that Cusins beats the drum for the Army under false pretenses (54, 92).

If we look at the careers of real public women in the twentieth and twenty-first centuries we find that Shaw's characters are remarkably predic-tive, especially with regard to the way women leaders are perceived. They tend to be viewed as variously as Shaw's public women are in his plays, and in similar binary patterns. Jamieson, for instance, points out that political women like former Canadian prime minister Kim Campbell and California senator Barbara Boxer were attacked in the press for being shrill or mean-spirited, while Supreme Court justice Ruth Bader Ginsburg, and Texas senator Kay Bailey Hutchison received dubious "praise" for their past occu-pations as a baton twirler and a cheerleader, respectively (172–74). Former Speaker of the House Nancy Pelosi, likewise, has been criticized for being a shrill San Francisco liberal, and praised for being a grandmother. Let us consider Margaret Thatcher, England's first woman prime minister, to chart the process in detail.

The grocer's daughter, as she famously described herself, Margaret Rob-erts Thatcher rose steadily in the ranks of the Tory (Conservative) Party, beginning in 1959 when she was elected to the House of Commons for the first time. In those early years, she impressed people by her capacity for hard work, careful research, and forceful, arrestingly phrased speeches. However, her initial press coverage stressed her gender, her relative youth and blonde good looks, and the fact that, although she was married to a very successful businessman, Denis Thatcher, she could be portrayed as a rather typical, middle-class housewife and the mother of twins (Campbell 122–40).

As her career progressed, however, her image changed. She was un-apologetically a right-wing Tory, and she was not afraid to be blunt, even strident in her speeches and in her dealings with peers and subordinates (Campbell 243). This toughness, which was emphasized in the press because she was a woman, eventually became part of her national public image; it was sealed, some would say seared, into the public consciousness by the furor that was stirred up when, as education minister, she backed a bill decreeing that free milk would no longer be distributed to children in the public schools. Although she was actually just continuing a policy of such cutbacks begun by the previous Labour government, opponents in Parliament and the press launched a storm of protest and personal abuse at her. She was described as "Mrs. Scrooge" and "The Most Unpopular Woman in Britain." The cruelest and the most persistent label was "Thatcher–Milk Snatcher," and it seemed to stick. What might have been treated as just an unnecessarily strict policy if it had been introduced by a man was treated as an unnatural, disturbing aberration for a woman (Campbell 231–32).

After she became the leader of her party in opposition, then, Thatcher knew she needed somehow to change the public perception of her before the next general election. She turned, appropriately enough, to an image expert, Gordon Reece, who had been a very successful television producer. He soon began an elaborate Maggie Thatcher makeover. Some of his advice dealt with external factors; he told her to drop the South of England, upper-middle-class Tory matron look: no more hats, pearls, and stiff hair; he also worked with her to lower her voice to avoid the shrill registers, and coached her on how to appear more natural and comfortable for television cameras (Campbell 400–410).

Reece also dealt with a problem at once subtler and more profound: how to present a woman as a national leader to a public that had been trained by experience to think only of men in that role. Ironically, Thatcher's image problem had already done part of the job; no one doubted that this particular woman would be tough enough as prime minister. Next, Reece and Thatcher began to take advantage of her gender by highlighting and exploiting the variety of familiar, acceptable roles women played in British life. Sometimes, for example, she could present herself as a kind of teacher, explaining issues and problems in ways that everyone could understand. At other times she could seem like a nurse, reminding the nation to take its medicine, even if it didn't taste good. She could also be seen as Nanny Thatcher, briskly but kindly instructing voters to tidy up the nation's affairs. Campbell offers an interesting insight into why this strategy would be effective: "As Leo Abse noted, not entirely fancifully, there is a streak of masochism in the British male which responds to the idea of a woman in authority" (410).

Although it is true that Thatcher benefited from a variety of issues in the election that brought her to power, and she and her government were part of the widespread conservative revival in the 1980s, there is little doubt that Reece's strategy of stressing Thatcher's gender in multiple guises contributed to her victory. At the very least, it helped to ease if not erase the negative images, also gender based, that had earlier sharply limited her appeal.

Once in office, Campbell says, Mrs. Thatcher continued to play to, and finally embody, several other feminine-based images. Early on, her un-abashed strength and patriotism led to her being called, admiringly, "the iron lady," and after she enthusiastically led the country through the Falk-lands war she became "the full-blown Warrior Queen, the combination of Britannia, Boadicea, and Elizabeth I" (410). We might also say that, during the Falklands conflict, Thatcher's "charge forward" appeal to her public mirrored that of Shaw's Saint Joan, except that Joan tried to mini-mize or deemphasize her gender, while Thatcher used it to her advantage.

Throughout her decade-plus in office, Mrs. Thatcher was a contro-versial, divisive figure, and the opposition to her continued to focus on negative gender images. The "iron lady" tag, for instance, was as often used unfavorably as favorably, and the same was true of the "Nanny" epithet. Thus, the dual and dueling patterns of binary images applied to such Shavian characters as Joan and Major Barbara held true for Margaret Thatcher too, another mark of Shaw's prescience.

Of course, not every public woman has been as skillful (or as lucky) as Mrs. Thatcher in managing the perceptions that get attached to any woman who steps into the limelight and into the arena of public dispute. Hillary Clinton has always attracted more than her share of clashing per-ceptions. She first burst into national attention when she was chosen to give a student address at the 1969 Wellesley graduation ceremony. There she was, the former conservative Goldwater girl from Park Ridge, Illinois, stepping confidently up to the podium to speak scolding words for the "don't trust anyone over thirty" generation: "We feel that for too long our leaders have used politics as the art of the possible, and the challenge now is to practice politics as the art of making what appears to be impossible, possible" (qtd. in Sheehy 58–59). This brash declaration is reminiscent of Shaw's Joan telling Dunois that he and the other older, experienced military leaders are "fat-heads" and that they don't know how to use their artillery (82–83).

Clinton next surfaced to public view in 1979 in Arkansas as the wife of the nation's youngest governor and as a vital part of the ambitious, reform-minded Clinton administration. However, they were voted out of office two years later, and one of the reasons, according to a number of surveys, was that Arkansans didn't like his Yankee wife: she was a mother (of daughter Chelsea) by this time, but she was still very visible in state politics; she was working for a prestigious law firm; she wore baggy, "hippy" clothes, no makeup, thick glasses, and, worst of all, she still called herself Hillary Rodham. She wasn't even using her husband's name! (Sheehy 134–40). Like Saint Joan, Hillary was being punished for not conforming to the image expected of a woman.

The gubernatorial election in 1982 resulted in a restoration of the Clintons to the governor's mansion, and one contributing factor was the makeover Hillary gave herself; she lightened and styled her hair, replaced the glasses with contact lenses, chose more fashionable clothes, and stopped using her maiden name. She had, in short, made a strategic decision to soften her feminist stance and bow to conventional expectations regarding the way women were supposed to present themselves. The strategy certainly worked. She discovered she could still do what she had been doing—working as a lawyer, chairing state commissions, and so forth—without antagonizing the voters much, as long as she looked "nice" and called herself Mrs. Clinton (Sheehy 145, 151–53).

Nevertheless, she ran afoul of those conventional expectations again when her husband ran for president, and in the first years of his administration. During the campaign, she turned out to be a "mixed" asset for the candidate. He promoted her intelligence, articulateness, and excellent legal reputation by telling voters they would get "two for one" if they elected him, and the fact that she didn't even flinch when allegations about his past affairs surfaced probably saved his prospects. On the other hand, she alienated traditional women when she tried to explain why she didn't just stay home and "bake cookies and have teas" (Sheehy 210). Early in the administration, she was appointed to lead a commission that was supposed to develop a plan to reform health care for the nation. She controlled the commission's process so tightly and imposed such secrecy that potential supporters among key lawmakers and other opinion makers were turned off before the complicated plan ever emerged. She presented it ably then, and won some praise for her skill in doing so, but her refusal to compromise was one of the reasons the reform package failed to become law.

Indeed, press pundits, influential members of Congress, and some officials inside the administration fixed much of the blame for the defeat on the First Lady. For much of the public, too, she became the dragon lady, the witch who had to have her own way.

Interestingly, there were times when the militant Hillary, the stalwart feminist champion, did earn nearly universal praise. At the Fourth World Conference on Women in Beijing in 1995, she made a bold speech excoriating the host Chinese government and other regimes around the world for crimes against the dignity and the persons of women. She finished with a ringing declaration: "Human rights are women's rights. And women's rights are human rights, once and for all." The applause from delegates around the world was overwhelming. Despite her many enemies at home, many women abroad began to regard her, like Eleanor Roosevelt before her, as "the first Woman of the World" (Sheehy 276–78).

Ironically, however, her poll numbers did not go up substantially and consistently until her husband became embroiled in the Monica Lewinsky scandal. Suddenly, the woman who to many people had seemed brittle, if not cold, steely and domineering, became a wronged wife. And when she behaved with dignity and restraint in this crisis, eventually agreeing to work with her husband to repair the damage to their marriage, many Americans, men and women, seemed at last ready to embrace her with sympathy and respect. The American public very evidently preferred Hillary the vulnerable woman, the victim, to Hillary the feminist political power player.

As her husband's administration was drawing to a close, a reenergized Hillary Clinton struck out on her own as a candidate for the U.S. Senate in New York. After she won the hard-fought contest, she also faced a new challenge: many Washington observers wondered how the imperious First Lady (or so they thought of her) would get on in the men's-club milieu of the Senate. To most people's surprise, Hillary adapted quickly and smoothly. Her fellow senators noted approvingly that she was a "workhorse," not a "showhorse," and she proved she could be a team player in the legislative process, teaming up with Republicans as well as Democrats to get bills passed.

She therefore had a new image, a new confidence, and a new record of success, at the polls (she was reelected overwhelmingly in 2006) and in the Senate, when she entered the race for the Democratic nomination for president in 2007 as the universally recognized, seemingly inevitable front-runner. That privileged position gradually eroded, due in part to some strategic mistakes and tactical errors made by the Clinton campaign and the candidate herself, but mostly due to her main rival, Senator Barack Obama, the most instantly, powerfully charismatic political figure to emerge on the political scene in many years. His iconic status as the first African American candidate for president with crossover appeal and serious prospects trumped her status as the first serious woman candidate.

Indeed, as the long primary campaign wore on into the first half of 2008, Hillary's old problem with multiple, conflicting public perceptions reappeared and mushroomed, echoing Eppy's problem in *The Millionairess*. Some men viewed her as a kind of dominatrix, or as an emasculating, fire-breathing "feminazi." They were the ones who sold or bought nutcrackers labeled Hillary. Other men, however, including, surprisingly enough, many "blue collar" workers, admired her determination to keep running all-out in the face of increasingly long odds and storms of criticism; they thought she would be their champion in the Oval Office. Polls and voting patterns also showed that older, less educated women, particularly those who were born before women were allowed to vote, regarded Hillary's candidacy as a cherished dream that at last might come true. Younger, more educated women tended to dismiss Mrs. Clinton as a flawed candidate, because she seemed to be "trying too hard," because they didn't like her stand on some issues, because they thought she was just piggy-backing on her husband's career, or because they were appalled that she stayed married to a serial philanderer. The reactions became so numerous and so split that one observer declared: "she's in danger of being turned into one of those indeterminate semiotic texts academics love to dissect, made to signify everything from the aging of boomer dreams to the future of feminism, even as her every gesture and inflection is sifted, measured, and weighed, and her actual resume and record are increasingly shoved to the side" (Kakutani).

The truth of this observation can be verified from the way some observers often tried to solve the puzzle, the chameleon that the public made of Hillary Clinton, by comparing her to fictional characters. The *Seinfeld* character who would not recognize George's breakup, the Terminator, Jason or Freddy from the horror movies, even Glenn Close's rabbit-boiling villain in *Fatal Attraction*, Norma Rae, Norma Desmond—these are just a few of the similes floated in the primary season. After Clinton's final concession speech, Rebecca Traister, writing on *Salon.com*, came up with one of the most striking of these comparisons:

[I]n these last two months, when loss was so close at her heels but she was still out there, ripping up the stage, her name in lights, unapologetic in her self-celebration, she reminded me of no one more than Mama Rose (from the musical *Gypsy*), performing her grand finale, "Rose's Turn": *Here she is boys! Here she is, world! Ready or not, here comes Hillary!* It makes me happy to think of her this way, creating a gut-bustingly awful, memorably wonderful spectacle, training a spotlight on the end of a crucial chapter in American history.

After Senator Clinton suspended her campaign and endorsed Senator Obama in an impressive, passionate speech before thousands of ardent supporters, politicians and commentators, many of whom had been criticizing her unrelentingly a few days earlier, began to weigh in with tributes to her graciousness, her indomitable personality, the significance of her gritty campaign for women in the future, and so forth.

Perhaps the best way to put this phenomenon in context is to make yet another comparison to a fictional character: Shaw's Saint Joan. In the play's epilogue, Joan comes back from the dead in a dream the King is having to confront him and all the men who figured prominently in her rise and fall, and to greet a visitor from the far future, a Vatican official who announces that the Maid has been proclaimed a saint by the church. One by one, they all fall to their knees, praising her in extravagant language. In response, Joan says: "Woe unto me when all men praise me! I bid you remember that I am a saint, and that saints can work miracles. And now tell me: shall I rise from the dead, and come back to you a living woman?" They all jump up and retreat into the darkness, begging her not to do any such thing (157–58). I imagine that Secretary of State Clinton could appreciate the irony of that moment more intensely than most of us.

I can also argue confidently, then, that Shaw's public women, characters like his Saint Joan, Epifania, Major Barbara, and the others, help us understand what happens to contemporary public women like Hillary Clinton and Margaret Thatcher, what it must feel like to stand in an increasingly pitiless spotlight, and what their experience reveals about us. More specifically, we can conclude that all leaders—especially strong, change-minded leaders—will face opposition, and women leaders will not be exceptions to that rule. In fact, women who want to lead will face heightened opposition, much of which will follow the "double bind" pattern Jamieson describes. And yet, we see from Shaw's characters, and from real-life counterparts, that reactions generated by the double-bind prejudice are only part of the blizzard of impressions public women evoke. Also, since, as we saw, those reactions and impressions can often be sorted into binary pairs of unfavorable and favorable descriptors, women leaders can sometimes make strategic use of favorable impressions deriving from their gender. Further, the careers of Shaw's characters and of actual leaders demonstrate that negative images as well as positive ones are likely to fluctuate in intensity over time.

Let us now turn to the unique ways in which many of Shaw's public women perform their gender, to the nontraditional lifestyles they adopt, and the consequences they must face and negotiate. Viewed as a group, they are certainly nonconformist. We have already considered Barbara, the Earl's granddaughter in *Major Barbara*, who works at the Salvation Army center in London's rough East End; Epifania, the millionairess from the play by the same name, who discards her husband, physically punishes an offending suitor, applies her managing magic to businesses, and seduces an Egyptian doctor with her pulse; and Joan, the French village girl who becomes a soldier and a leader of the army while rejecting marriage and even women's clothes.

We can add Mrs. George Collins, the Mayoress from *Getting Married*, who is married to her coal merchant but who pursues temporary romantic liaisons with other men; Aloysia Brollikins, the alderwoman and political protestor from the Isle of Cats in *On the Rocks*, who selects her own husband-to-be, the son of the British prime minister; Begonia Brown, the bright-eyed typist from *Geneva*, who blithely launches a process that brings Europe's circa-1930s dictators into a Hague Courtroom in Switzerland, while simultaneously arranging her own astonishing social and political ascent to the rank of Dame of the British Empire; and Lina Szczepanowska, the trapeze circus performer from *Misalliance*, who risks her life regularly to maintain a family tradition, and first dazzles, then deserts all the men in the play except Bentley. They are a strong-minded, determinedly independent group, and Lina expresses the spirit they all share when she says: "I am an honest woman: I earn my own living. I am a free woman: I live in my own house. I am a woman of the world: I have thousands of friends . . . I am strong: I am skilful: I am brave: I am independent: I am unbought: I am all that a woman ought to be" (201).

Of course, there is a price they have to pay for this kind of freedom, this chance to be and do what they choose. Elsewhere in the speech just quoted, for example, we see the price Lina has to pay: everywhere she goes, she must put up with or fend off the advances of men who are entranced by her looks and her style, who regard her as a sexual challenge they cannot resist. In *Misalliance*, the airplane in which she is a passenger has crashed into the greenhouse of a country home filled with strangers, and within an hour, three of the men present, including the millionaire owner, the fiancé of his daughter, and his son, have propositioned her. She is at this stage of her life quite used to fending off such impromptu, unwelcome attentions with good humor, but the rationale offered to her by Johnny, the son, outrages her:

> He (says he) will do the straight thing by me. He will give me a home, a position. He tells me I must know that my present position is not one for a nice woman. This to me, Lina Szczepanowska! . . . And this Englishman! This linendraper! he dares to ask me to come and live with him in this rrrrrrabbit hutch, and take my bread from his hand, and ask him for pocket money, and wear soft clothes, and be his woman! his wife! Sooner than that, I would stoop to the lowest depths of my profession. I would stuff lions with food and pretend to tame them. I would deceive honest people's eyes with conjuring tricks instead of real feats of strength and skill. I would be a clown and set bad examples of conduct to little children. I would sink yet lower and be an actress or an opera singer, imperiling my soul by the wicked lie of pretending to be somebody else. (201)

Her vehemence reflects her (and Shaw's) disdain for conventional marriage, which was for too many women the only career option open to them, and often seen, especially by proto-feminists of the period, as a kind of servitude, giving women sustenance in return for their dutiful subjugation. So, Lina takes a tolerant view of invitations to short-term sexual dalliance; she only becomes really angry when the cheerfully chauvinistic Johnny offers to make her a respectable, complaisant wife.

Not all of Shaw's public women are against marriage, of course. Mrs. George, Aloysia Brollikins, and Begonia Brown are all for it—on their terms. Consider the case of Mayoress George. She is married to a man for whom she has affection, loyalty, and respect. Yet, with his approval, she has followed her heart into emotional relationships with a series of men who have, at least temporarily, fascinated her. Early in her marriage, according to Bill Collins, her brother-in-law, she would leave home to "throw herself" at these men, only to return very shortly to husband George in tears, because they usually fled from her passion. He finally coached her to stay at home and let them come to her, which Bill says many did. This life of passionate excess has taken its toll on the beauty of her face, but it has not, despite what conventional morality declares, corrupted her intelligence or her soul.

In fact, as Collins says: "it certainly made her interesting, and gave her a lot of sense" (399). She is indeed a prestigious woman in the community, not only an officeholder but also a sought-after consultant on all sorts of matters. She has lived her life her way, accepted the penalties for doing so, which include the unwelcome attentions of disruptive, possessive men like Hotchkiss in the play, and even emerged in middle age as a kind of seer, particularly when she periodically slips into a kind of hypnotic state. In that convulsive condition, she says: "I have not withered in the fire: I have come out at last beyond, to the back of Godspeed." Asked what she sees there, she speaks on behalf of all women about their relationships with men:

When you loved me I gave you the whole sun and stars to play with. I gave you eternity in a single moment . . . A moment only; but was it not enough? Were you not paid then for all the rest of your struggle on earth? Must I mend your clothes and sweep your floors as well? Was it not enough? I paid the price without bargaining: I bore the children without flinching: was that a reason for heaping fresh burdens on me? I carried the child in my arms: must I carry the father too? When I opened the gates of paradise, were you blind? Was it nothing to you? When all the stars sang in your ears and all the winds swept you into the heart of heaven, were you deaf? . . . We spent eternity together: and you ask me for a little lifetime more. (477)

This reproach becomes a response, from the other side of the gender divide, to Don Juan's famous complaint about marriage in the Dream Scene in *Man and Superman*: "Marriage is the most licentious of human institutions . . . that is the secret of its popularity. And a woman seeking a husband is the most unscrupulous of all the beasts of prey. . . . Come, Ana! do not look shocked: you know better than any of us that marriage is a mantrap baited with simulated accomplishments and delusive idealizations" (156–57).

It seems obvious to Shaw that conventional marriage is not fair or satisfying to either sex, and that the only way a marriage can be happy is if the partners are bound to each other, not by legal or religious obligations, but by a kind of durable, freely chosen friendship. Mayoress Collins says she isn't sure she loves her George, but she knows nevertheless that "George and I are good friends. George belongs to me. Other men may come and go; but George goes on forever" (464).

Shaw's public women tend to take that kind of free and forward approach to marriage, relationships, and all of life's opportunities. Take the case of Begonia Brown of *Geneva*. At the beginning of the play she is just an attractive, energetic girl stuck for financial/survival reasons (remember that the whole western world was sunk in the depths of the Great Depression in the mid-1930s) in a dead-end clerical position, working for The International Committee for Intellectual Co-operation, a neglected, minor appendage of the League of Nations. She is fairly bright and has always done very well in school, although her opinions are essentially unexamined, being based on the simplistic, Tory, imperialist notions she absorbed from her middle-class upbringing. (Indeed, she seems like a caricatured forerunner of the young Margaret Thatcher.)

Then one day chance brings her opportunities: petitioners for international justice stumble by mistake into her office and demand that action be taken by the League of Nations. She could have done the safe thing: declared that she had no authority and sent them all away. But she decides to write to the International Court at the Hague, asking for a warrant to bring the offending parties to justice. A young American journalist friend publicizes her actions, and a chain of events begins which, although it ends inconclusively, attracts the whole world's attention, and makes Begonia famous.

Once that chain begins, Begonia takes full, shrewd advantage of the publicity, her attractiveness, and her nerve. The next time we meet her, she tells the secretary of the League of Nations not to mind what the "silly clever" people think, because "If you want to know what real English public opinion is, keep your eye on me" (686). Before long, she is planning to stand for a seat in the House of Commons. Later, she makes a considerable fortune suing newspapers for libel, and is named a Dame of the British Empire. This seems to mark the summit of her luck and her abilities, because, although she is present for most of the rest of the action of the play, she takes very little part in the discussions.

Begonia is not presented as a character to be admired. She is certainly a caricature of the pluck and the limitations of the ordinary British public in the 1930s. It is significant, however, that their representative here is a woman, not a standard John Bull type, and that she rises as far as she does by taking chances and by refusing to settle for the status or the prospects set in place for women of her class.

Of course, anyone who lived through the American election cycle in 2008 cannot think of what happens to Begonia in *Geneva*, and what she says and does, without realizing the almost eerie parallels with the adventures of Sarah Palin. They seem to share the same sunny, imperturbable confidence, confidence that permits them to charge forward, in the midst of suddenly changed circumstances, without a moment's hesitation or doubt; the same belief that they represent the views and the feelings of ordinary citizens; and the shrewd ability to make the most of mass-media attention, whether favorable or unfavorable. Indeed, one can regard the careers of Begonia and Sarah as cautionary tales—about the ability of modern media and politics to hurtle unvetted individuals into instant celebrity and positions of potential power.

Finally, let us consider Aloysia Brollikins of *On the Rocks*. We first meet her as part of a delegation speaking for the unemployed workers on the Isle of Cats. She is described as "an unladylike but brilliant and very confident young woman in smart factory-made clothes after the latest Parisian models" (542). Later, we learn that she has been a teacher who left that profession when teachers' wages were slashed, and worked in a factory. There, she organized the other factory girls and wound up being the trade union secretary (614). In her first exchanges with Sir Arthur, the harassed Prime Minister, she is smooth and in control of her emotions and her language. However, by the end of their brief session, the Isle of Cats delegation feel more ignored and hopeless than ever, and when Sir Arthur hopefully asks Aloysia if she too feels nothing has been accomplished, her reply is curt: "I feel what they feel. And I don't believe you feel anything at all" (548).

At her next encounter with the Prime Minister and another of his visitors, the Duke, when the argument turns to a proposal to nationalize land, with compensation to the landowners, she unleashes a brutal, powerful speech about the past savagery of the landlords, including the Duke's ancestors, to their poor tenants, climaxing with: "I am only one of thousands of young women who have . . . sworn to ourselves that never, if we can help it, will it again be possible for one wicked rich man to say to a whole population 'Get off the earth'" (565).

The old Duke seems not to pay much heed to the content of Aloysia's attack, but he is bowled over by her eloquence and her looks, and clearly hopes to win her over, if not seduce her. Like several of Shaw's public women, she seems to have that kind of effect on men, especially on the Prime Minister's son. Offstage they discover their mutual attraction, and Aloysia, without young David's knowledge, consults the Prime Minister and his wife about a match. She explains that she is a "reading thinking modern woman," (610) and knows that the strong sexual attraction she feels for David means that "Evolution is telling me to marry this youth. . . . The evolutionary appetite. The thing that wants to develop the race. If I marry David we shall develop the race. And that's the great thing in marriage, isn't it?" (611–12). She admits that David doesn't agree with this analysis, and isn't sure about marrying her, but she's very confident that she can bring him around.

People who know Shaw's plays even moderately well will quickly recognize the link between Aloysia and Ann Whitefield of *Man and Superman.* They are both acting as agents of the Life Force in search of the mate who will help them fulfill their biological, evolutionary destiny as progenitors of better human beings. They are both intelligent, strong-willed, purposeful women. However, Ann feels constrained by the mores of her time, by the passive, dependent role imposed on women then, to hide her will and purpose, and to use guile and trickery to achieve her goal. Aloysia, who comes from a lower class, and a very different, post–World War I world, feels no need or inclination to be a siren. She says very clearly what she wants and marches straight toward it. Clearly, Shaw, who was seventy-seven at the time he composed *Geneva,* was not stuck in a late-Victorian or even Edwardian mind-set; he understood what was happening around him, and could even look ahead to see the shape of the future.

What he saw, among other things, was a world in which women could, if they were smart and strong and brave, proceed by trial and error, in the manner of creative evolution, after all, to construct their own ways of being women, to script their lives according to their individual inclinations and convictions, quite apart from the socially approved patterns. This freedom for development would apply to their personal and professional lives; they could pursue serial relationships as well as serial careers. Their way forward would not be easy; there would be large obstacles and fierce opposition; they might have to make temporary compromises, and some might fail, finally. But it would, he assumed, be possible to succeed.

We can find plenty of evidence in our world to show that Shaw was right and that his public women characters were prophetic. Sherry Lansing, the recently retired and longtime successful head of the Paramount Motion Pictures Corporation, is one prominent example. First, her career arc echoes that of Aloysia Brollikins. After graduating from Northwestern University, she first tried her hand at some typically "feminine" career options: she became a teacher, then an actress and a model. She decided, however, that those career paths didn't suit her, so she went to work in MGM's story department. At age thirty she was head of that department. A few years later she became head of production at Fox Studio, and then, in 1992, she was named chairman of Paramount Pictures. Her twelve-year tenure in that job saw the studio reap huge profits from the production of *Titanic*, and considerable artistic prestige, as well as profit, from films like *Forrest Gump* (Cagle). After she resigned from that position, she became a distinguished philanthropist, as a regent of the University of California, and as a member of the boards of the Carter Center and Teach for America, as well as others. She received the Jean Hersholt Humanitarian Award during the 2007 Academy Awards for her work in cancer research, particularly for establishing the Sherry Lansing Foundation, which promotes public awareness and raises funds for research ("Sherry Lansing," *Lansing Foundation*).

Ms. Lansing also resembles Mrs. George in the scope and variety of her relationships. After an early marriage and divorce, she was involved in a series of romances with some high-profile men, including movie executive James Aubrey, the architect Richard Meier, and Count Giovanni Volpi, before settling into a long marriage to director William Friedkin ("Sherry Lansing," lukeford.net/profiles). Although her exercise of this particular freedom inevitably led to unfair charges that she slept her way to the top, her unquestioned success and her good citizenship have allowed her to ignore the backbiters while she continues to flourish.

Of course, it's easy to argue that the most successful example of a woman living large and on her own terms is Oprah Winfrey. I doubt that there is a person in North America who doesn't know of her by her first name alone, and isn't aware that she has long ago moved beyond the status of successful entertainer into the rarefied realm of cultural force and national icon. No one was surprised, for example, that she was asked to host the nationally televised "Prayer for America" ceremony at Yankee Stadium in the immediate aftermath of the September 11, 2001, terrorist attacks, an event in which she presided over a gathering of celebrities that included Mayor Giuliani, the Clintons, Senator Ted Kennedy, and New York governor Pataki. Everyone knew that Oprah was a symbol of reassurance and optimism (Peck 1).

By now, everyone also knows the outlines at least of her personal story, of how the neglected, abused little black girl from Mississippi grew into a determined woman, and started very young in the broadcast television business, of how she parlayed a gift for gab, an amiable personality, and striking self-confidence into an enviable position as the host of the most popular syndicated television talk show in the country. What they might not recall, however, is that in the early 1990s Winfrey's show was lumped in with the "Trash Talk" programs and condemned as a corrupting, demeaning influence on American culture. These shows filled the airwaves with the dregs of our society and competed with the lurid tabloids to wallow in the excesses of the most dysfunctional people to be found within our borders (Peck 1–2).

In early 1994, however, Oprah herself expressed concern about the effect of such "talk rot" and made a 180-degree turn for her own program. She decided to be a positive force, to showcase strategies people could use to better their lives, in all dimensions: physical, spiritual, financial, and so forth. That decision marked the beginning of a transformation and a remarkable expansion of her influence (Peck 4–5). In the following decade, Oprah launched her wildly successful book club, her own popular monthly magazine, and a much visited website; she also produced movies and a Broadway show, founded a school for girls in Africa, and funded and publicized many other charitable ventures. Along the way, her show became a forum for a spectrum of national political figures, and before the 2008 presidential election she chose to apply her unrivaled media impact more directly in the political arena by endorsing and campaigning for presidential candidate Barack Obama (Peck 3).

Of course, Oprah the phenomenon has attracted some skeptics as well as millions of adoring fans. Professor Janice Peck, for instance, in her book *The Age of Oprah: Cultural Icon for the Neoliberal Era*, criticizes Winfrey's approach to the nation's ills for actually being a "synthesis of capitalism, religion, and the therapeutic enterprise" and for unrealistically prescribing only "self-help and empowerment as cures for poverty" (110, 167).

Nevertheless, however one regards her politics or the efficacy of her causes, there is no doubt that Oprah Winfrey has carved out a unique, and uniquely independent position in American popular culture. She is one of the richest women in the world, with a fortune estimated at $1.5 billion, and yet she comes across as everyone's girlfriend: approachable, and tuned into the tastes and feelings of blacks and whites, old and young, rich, poor, and everything in between (Peck 3). She balances a life of conspicuous consumption featuring multiple homes and elegant parties among the beautiful people, with dedicated, hands-on, grand-scale philanthropy. She is a widely accepted moral arbiter who has never married or borne children, and lives with a longtime fiancé. Indeed, Oprah's life makes it clear that the independence exhibited by Lina Szczepanowska, Aloysia Brollikins, Mrs. George Collins, and the others turned out not to be a totally implausible fantasy.

There are other interesting and powerful women in other Shaw plays, and they will reward scrutiny too. However, we should not overestimate the importance of such often minor, functional characters, and we need not push the parallels between any of Shaw's public women and women leaders today too far. Many of the characters, after all, reflect the contours of a long-vanished world.

Still, what these characters say, what they do, and what happens to them can have resonance and relevance. Shaw was always interested in the future, always worrying about what it would be like, always trying to peer into it. And when he tried to imagine women who would fit into the future, he was surprisingly insightful and accurate. Therefore, as long as people reach for analogies with fictional characters to give clarity and context to their readings of public women, Shaw's characters will answer a need.

Perhaps the most heartening insight for women leaders trying to cope with their status as floating signifiers for an often bemused public, and to design their own lives, is that they can just forge ahead, just do what they feel they should or must do, in public and in private. Shaw's characters and the lives of many real women suggest strongly that the attitudes they face, including the negative ones, will wax and wane. Therefore, ambitious women need not be paralyzed by the threat of the double bind. The characters and the evidence from real lives also imply that society, with all of its formidable, often forbidding structures and codes, is not nearly as immovable as it seems. It is not, in short, a dead weight that can only be lifted by some revolutionary cataclysm; instead, society is more like a "contestable process," which, by their decisions and actions, public women affect every day (Finke 155, 159).

Works Cited

Byron, George Gordon. "Don Juan Canto I." *Anthology of Romanticism*. Ed. Ernest Bernbaum. New York: Ronald P, 1948. 625–61.

Cagle, Jess. "The Women Who Run Hollywood." *Time* 29 July 2002: 52–54, http://vnweb. hwwilsonweb.com/hww/results/results_single_ftPES.Jhtml, accessed 18 June 2008.

Campbell, John. *Margaret Thatcher: The Grocer's Daughter*. Vol. 1. London: Jonathan Cape Random House, 2000.

Finke, Laura. "The Pedagogy of the Depressed: Feminism, Poststructuralism, and Pedagogical Practice." *Teaching Contemporary Theory to Undergraduates*. Ed. Dianne Sadoff and William Cain. New York: Modern Language Association, 1994. 155–59.

Hwang, David Henry. "M. Butterfly." *Stages of Drama*. Ed. Carl H. Klaus et al. New York: Bedford/St. Martin, 2003. 1378–1403.

Jamieson, Kathleen Hall. *Beyond the Double Bind*. New York: Oxford UP, 1995.

Kakutani, Michiko. "Candidate Clinton Scrutinized by Women." Rev. of *Thirty Ways of Looking at Hillary*. Ed. Susan Morrison. New York: Harper, 2008. *New York Times* 15 Jan. 2008, http://www.nytimes.com/2008/01/15/books/15kaku.html, accessed 15 June 2008.

Peck, Janice. *The Age of Oprah: Cultural Icon for the Neoliberal Era*. Boulder: Paradigm, 2008.

Shaw, G. B. *Complete Plays with Prefaces*. 6 vols. New York: Dodd, Mead, 1963.

———. *Major Barbara*. Ed. Dan H. Laurence. New York: Penguin, 2000.

———. *Man and Superman*. Ed. Dan H. Laurence. New York: Penguin, 2004.

———. *The Millionairess. Plays Extravagant*. Ed. Dan H. Laurence. New York: Penguin, 1981.

———. *Saint Joan*. Ed. Dan H. Laurence. New York: Penguin, 2001.

Sheehy, Gail. *Hillary's Choice*. New York: Random House, 1999.

"Sherry Lansing." http://www.lukeford.net/profiles/profiles/sherry_lansing.htm, accessed 19 June 2008.

"Sherry Lansing." *The Sherry Lansing Foundation*. http://www.sherrylansingfoundation. org/page.php?whPage=lansing.php, accessed 19 June 2008.

Traister, Rebecca. *Salon.com*. http://www.salon.com/mwt/feature/2008/06/08/hillary_ concession/print.html, accessed 17 June 2008.

11

The Energy behind the Anomaly

In Conversation with Jackie Maxwell

• • • • • • • • • • • • • • • • • •

INTERVIEW AND EDITING BY D. A. HADFIELD

In September, 2010, Jackie Maxwell, the first female artistic director of the Shaw Festival in Niagara-on-the-Lake, Ontario, sat down with D. A. Hadfield to discuss the emergence of women's voices in and around the works of George Bernard Shaw. The following is an edited transcript of their conversation.

I never really considered myself a career artistic director. I'm a director—that's what I am at heart, that's what it says on my passport. So when I was asked [in 2002] if I'd be interested in running the Shaw Festival, I was a bit taken aback at first. I was very aware, of course, of the Shaw's well-deserved, growing international reputation for many of the things that it has been doing right: the production values, the strength of the ensemble, the intellectual rigor of the plays, the mandate itself. But what really drew me in was a change that [former artistic director] Christopher Newton made to that mandate just before he left: he opened it to include contemporary plays about the era as well as plays by Shaw and his contemporaries. For me, this opened an exciting creative potential in the programming.

It's not that I didn't love Shaw and many of his contemporaries, but I was very intrigued by the whole notion of being able to juxtapose a play *about* the era and put it alongside a play *of* the era and watch the conversation between them emerge. It was a chance to ask questions like "Well, what have we learned?" and "How have plays changed, both in content and form?" It was also a chance to bring in a voice that hadn't particularly been part of the conversation yet at the Shaw Festival, the Canadian voice. Introducing Canadian writers and the Canadian point of view to this conversation fascinated me, but wasn't really possible without an expansion of the mandate to allow for contemporary works, because Canada for the most part has a very young theater.

There was another important voice that I wanted to bring into the conversation, and that was the voice of women, which, in so many ways, has been silenced. To me, theater is voices being heard, stories being told, and this was a major voice that wasn't there. Right from the start, I have been very overt about insisting on hearing the women's side of the conversation. I thought to myself, "Surely there must have been female playwrights in the Victorian and Edwardian times," and sure enough, there were! In my first year at the Shaw, I began a kind of archaeological digging into the world of women's plays, and frankly, I didn't have to dig very far or very deep to find these extraordinary pieces.

Shortly after I came to the Shaw, we presented a play by Cicely Hamilton, *Diana of Dobson's* [2003]. It's a wonderful piece, a beautiful comedy, but one that caused a tremendous ruckus when it was first performed in 1908. Much of the notoriety arose from the first scene, which opens to the sight of all these shop girls chatting in their rooms above the shop in their underwear. This in itself was very radical in its time, but more importantly, the entire perspective that the play presented—a thoughtful, realistic look at the life and options of a working shopgirl—was a world that had never been put onstage before. This, too, was totally radical.

Githa Sowerby [1876–1970] is another "find" that I'm particularly proud of. Sowerby is an astonishing writer. Her play *Rutherford and Son* had already been done by the National Theatre before we did it at the Shaw [2004], but it's remarkable for the way it presents power politics in a world moving toward modernism. In *Rutherford and Son* it is the daughter-in-law who topples the tyrannical father. To be sure, he's a bit of a dinosaur and on the topple as it is because the world is taking him over, but in the end, it's still the daughter-in-law who sits down and bargains with him and dictates what is going to happen. This is really quite phenomenal, to look at the whole dynastic family construct at the end of the Industrial Revolution, and for the first time see all of that from the female point of view. For me, having revelled in the plays of Granville-Barker, Galsworthy, or Shaw, it's fascinating to see the same story, but to see it from a radically different point of view.

So *Rutherford and Son* had already been rediscovered, but no one could find any of Sowerby's other works. This was the only published piece. There wasn't anything else. Here was this woman who had written this hugely successful play—Emma Goldman wrote a thesis on it—but virtually nothing was known about her or her work beyond this one play. (There's actually now a book about her since this upsurge of interest in her, but then there was nothing.) We knew that she had written five other plays, but they had simply vanished. How could this be?

Then one day I got a visit from someone I know who runs the Mint Theater in New York, a company that specializes in this kind of archaeological play programming.[1] He said, "I've got a surprise for you," and handed me a copy of Githa Sowerby's *The Stepmother*. He had found a copy of the original typescript—complete with all of Sowerby's corrections marked on it—just buried in a box in the basement of the Samuel French publishing house. I almost cried! There was a note on the typescript that said the play had been done only once, one afternoon in 1924. Those first read-throughs with the [Shaw Festival] company were very moving for us, realizing that this was the first time Sowerby's play had been read out loud since 1924.

The Stepmother is about marriage and money. Well, there are a lot of plays about marriage and money, but there are not a lot of plays about marriage and money from the point of view of the woman—and the woman who, in this case, is actually making her own living. The "step-mother" often has pejorative connotations, but in this case it's completely the opposite. Lois is a career woman who has money, and is, in fact, the primary wage earner for the family. She is loved by her two stepchildren and also another man; she seems to have it all. But she doesn't have the kind of social backing through most of the play to enable her to establish her own independence. Her husband wants her money for himself, and contrives to get it by very devious means. She seems to be moving after all toward another predictable plot position, that of the chastened independent woman who is killed, commits suicide, or disappears in disgrace—only to have Sowerby once again take things in the opposite direction. The stepmother actually ends up with her two stepdaughters and the husband is sent off in disgrace. I think many people were shocked by that ending:

it's not what we expect because it's not the ending that a strong, independent woman in a play by Ibsen, Pinero, or even to a large extent Shaw would normally get.

We were absolutely stunned at the reaction to *The Stepmother*. It was the most vocal reaction that I've heard to a theatrical presentation that wasn't a panto. People literally couldn't contain themselves. There's an amazing scene that just keeps revealing and revealing and revealing until the main character finally realizes the extent to which her husband has taken her money and spent it, and you could *hear* the audience during that scene. At some performances, people even shouted out loud, things like, "He's stolen your money!" And poor Blair Williams, who played the husband, thought he was going to need security guards to get him off the stage! The reaction was a little bit reminiscent of early Ibsen, when people stormed out into the streets all fired up by what they had seen. It was truly amazing to realize that here is a play written almost a century ago that is clearly touching a very raw nerve in our audience. Every time we performed that play, there were audible gasps from people in the audience. It was tremendously rewarding: the audible gasp is the ultimate sign of triumph for me.

It's just shocking to me how a playwright of Sowerby's stature and obvious relevance was allowed to languish, because no one with the power or money or publishing connections valued her voice enough to keep it in the public eye. Since then, in fact, we've tracked down three more of Sowerby's scripts, so you just might see more Githa Sowerby at the Shaw Festival in seasons to come.

What's perhaps not shocking but frustrating is the frequency with which this scenario seems to repeat itself with women's plays, and not just in England. The same thing happens in America. Look at the plays of Susan Glaspell, for example. She's getting much more attention now since feminist researchers have pushed her to the fore, but there she was, one of Eugene O'Neill's best friends, and they were both doing experimental drama of similar type, but his was recognized and valued in a way that hers wasn't. I don't want to suggest that he wasn't an extraordinary playwright, but that doesn't entirely explain why his work has always had so much acclaim right across the board—all of it, not just the good stuff—while it has taken so long for Susan Glaspell's work to be looked at in this same way. What has become very obvious to me in recovering these works is that these women's works are not worse than the plays that survived historically, but there are definitely significant differences. The most fascinating difference arises from a totally different point of view from plays written by men. These women are credible artists whose work needs to be put into the general conversation.

While the perspective and voices that these women playwrights bring in are clearly vital and provocative, they don't ultimately diminish Shaw's contribution to the conversation for me. If anything, it puts them in a good context. I think, to be honest, it gives him pretty good marks in terms of the ways he recognizes some of these issues in his own plays. The women are every bit as smart as the men in his plays, if not smarter and more interesting and perceptive. I certainly think that he gives them a level of complexity that not all playwrights were necessarily doing at that point. He treats his female characters very three-dimensionally, and gives great credence to their points of view. Sometimes he might tend toward somewhat of a Madonna complex in certain places—I think you find that in someone like Candida, and you've got to be careful with those kinds of women, that they don't come off too saintly or omniscient. But Shaw was also dealing in these plays with the New Woman in a society that was still coming to grips with the idea of women who demanded more independence and autonomy, and the New Woman was a little scary in many ways, even for Shaw. I think one of the things that is so brilliant about Shaw is that he doesn't sit in judgment on these characters; you continually flip to and fro. Even in the dynamics of his dialogue, Shaw creates situations where there is an informed argument going on—often between members of the opposite sex—but the combatants are intellectually very well matched. There's something very sexy about the dynamics of those moments, when the dynamics of the dialogue itself becomes kind of erotic, which is why the scenes are so interesting and so active.

He also makes the *women* active, which is relatively rare for plays of the time. For example, *The Second Mrs. Tanqueray* by Pinero is actually a fantastic play, and I've been tempted to do it, but it's very hard; not just because she commits suicide at the end, which is so depressing, but also because the women in that play simply don't—and can't, it seems—*act*, that they're somehow just *stuck*. Another example is Wilde's *An Ideal Husband*, which I just directed [2010]. It's a wonderful piece, but with Lady Chiltern, we had to work very hard to pull her out of what at times seemed to be a very priggish point of view. We really tried. The really active characters in that play are Mabel, the young girl who is moving on, and Mrs. Cheveley, a woman who's essentially out there all on her own, by her fingernails, trying to do whatever she can to get ahead—but she's also the baddie. So I think in that sense Shaw's characters are a lovely leap from that type of playwriting because they're unfettered women, especially in the first half of his career, when he wrote his really interesting and strong women. Look at *Man and Superman*, which is the ultimate love story, but it's about a woman chasing her man all across Europe.

I think his interest in women shifted over the course of his career, or more to the point, I think his dramaturgy really shifted as his career evolved, and the psychology of his characters and how they operate really shifted. *Both* the men and the women operate differently in the later plays, and I don't think that any of the women in the later plays really have the same kind of standout strength as a Candida or Vivie Warren, Mrs. Warren, or even Saint Joan for that matter.

But in that early part of his career, you have to really appreciate how front and forward he does put his women, how much responsibility he gives them in the play. Perhaps his female characters rarely win unequivocally, but for his time that would almost have been science fiction in a sense. I mean, you could argue that Candida loses to Marchbanks, that the secret in the poet's heart is something better than washing your husband's socks or ordering his meals, but to my mind, Candida ends up back in the relationship that she has *chosen* to be in, with as much control as she had before, but perhaps a little tempered and revisioned. I don't know that there's much more in that situation that is going to be able to happen to that woman, but it's significant what has happened. Or look at Jennifer Dubedat in *The Doctor's Dilemma*. There was a discussion after the play [in 2010] about how much Jennifer actually knows [about her husband's real character and how the doctor feels about her]. In playing the role, Krista Colosimo decided that Jennifer probably knows a lot, but *chooses* to know or not know because she has to survive. And Jennifer is a woman who more than survives, she actually takes charge, but she can only go so far within the construct of where they're at, societally, I think.

Even Mrs. Warren, who has lost her daughter for sure, is still in a great position of strength in her own world. Her own particular pact with her own particular devil has been shown and clarified, and she's going to go off and maintain the life that she has chosen for herself with open eyes. Same with Vivie, another one of those women who are still in their historical straitjackets to a certain degree. Yes, Vivie went to university, but she still wasn't allowed to graduate at that point, and the notion of her being a lawyer, well that's going to be a long way away yet. So not only are the women quite radical as characters, for a play of this period to have the two leads both be women, who really shoulder the responsibility for the play while the men satellite around them, that in itself is radical as well. So in a sense, they often have their power in ways that are kind of subversive.

Beyond issues of independence and power, the New Woman also always has a real emotional journey to make. Sometimes you have to really work to find that emotional journey, but it's always there. I mean, if you work on *Mrs Warren's Profession*, which is one of my favorite Shaw plays, you spend a great deal of time on those two extraordinary scenes between Kitty and Vivie, the one at the end of act 2 and the one at the end of the play. These are scenes which are all about generational struggle, generational in the sense of how the world has shifted between one generation and the other, and this is a confrontation between two women who are survivors in very different ways. This is also a love story, but it's a love story between a woman and her daughter, and I find it very moving working on those scenes, as I did a couple of years ago. I think he has a great empathy for both those women, actually, probably more a little bit for Kitty, the mom, than Vivie, but I'm not sure. At the end of the play there's this huge long stage direction and poor Moya O'Connell [who played Vivie] would say, "You know, I don't know what I'm doing there," and I'd say, "I don't think we're going to know what we're doing until we've been rehearsing this play for a long time. How do we know where you're at at the end of the play?" And we waited, and we more or less blocked it, but it wasn't really until we were almost into previews that we really got that scene happening, and started to realize that when she shuts the door on her mother it's a bit like the next door shut after *The Doll's House*.[2] It's a very obvious comparison, and the important thing is to figure out what happens in that silence after the door slam. Shaw is very clear on *what* she does—she takes the letter and she rips it up—but how much time that takes, where she's at, how confident she is and all of that, we didn't really know that until the production took us there.

That's the great thing about a Shaw play: you always spend ages on the last moments of it, and argue and argue and argue. Shaw gives us the same thing at the end of *Candida*: the two of them are sitting there, but are they OK? Are they not? The ending is sort of a question mark. *Pygmalion* is another one. Jimmy Mezon [who played Higgins] and I had *huge* arguments about it. There's Higgins at the end, after the newly emancipated Eliza gives him what-for and leaves, and he *laughs*! You have to wonder what's going on there. Is the irony so great? Has he missed his chance? Has he . . . ? You talk and talk and talk to try to figure that out, you have to fill it in. I love that about Shaw. He gives you a great road map in terms of the relationships between men and women, and there's extraordinary depth in all of those relationships still today.

On the other hand, when I worked on *Candida* with Kelli Fox [2002] we questioned whether Candida is really as all-knowing as she seemed to be. We really wanted to pull that away from her and make the situations a little more out of her control than they appeared at first. The play really warranted that, it seemed to me, because this is a woman who's been married for a certain number of years, she's by no means middle aged, but then a young man comes along. . . . To think that you can just smoothly handle that and not have any sense of questioning yourself seems a little unlikely. And once we went into that possibility, there was lots of room to play with it in the text. The play responded very well to bringing more contemporary sensibilities about women into the reading.

Contemporary actresses still *love* playing these women. In fact, one of the huge advantages for the Shaw Festival has to do with the opportunities for women. Yes, Shakespeare has some fantastic roles for women, but there aren't as many, and they are certainly hugely iconic. But in terms of setting up the classical company, because of our mandate, we can equalize the roles for women and for men a little bit more, both in terms of numbers and in terms of the responsibility that they take in the plays. In that sense, Shaw is a great springboard for us. Since we are doing Shaw and his plays, we've got his extraordinary women, and now it behooves us to keep following that model and looking for where that model continues in theater. That doesn't mean we wouldn't do *The Iceman Cometh*, which is an enormously interesting play, just because it has little to offer the women in the company, but I can balance that out, on the other hand, by doing *The Women*. I mean, ultimately, I have an entire company to program for, and that includes men as well as women, but it's interesting to be able to think of that type of balance in all sorts of the plays that we do. I'm curious to find plays that have parts for older women, too, which is another important issue for contemporary actresses. What do you do if you've been playing all these wonderful Shaw heroines, and then you get to fifty, so now where do you go? Shaw himself doesn't have a lot of them.

There's Mrs. Warren, who's fantastic, and a few others in there, like *Captain Brassbound's Conversion*, which is such a scary play for us to be doing now, but the older woman in it is fantastic. Shaw sets a tone for a kind of active, energetic woman who carries the play, and that's a very interesting thing for actors to work with.

It's so important to have the right actors in place to do particular works; for example, I held off doing *Saint Joan* until Tara Rosling was ready for it. When I did *Candida*, I cast Mike Shara as Marchbanks because Marchbanks is often presented as this weak wisp of a man, a boy, really, and I wanted Mike to play it like a rock star. I wanted a Marchbanks who would create a situation where this has to be a genuine dilemma of a choice for Candida. In *Mrs Warren's Profession*, I specifically wanted Mary Haney to play Mrs. Warren, because it requires an actress who needs to be able to put on a particular type of society show, but who, at the crucial moment, lets something else show through, so you realize that it's really all a veneer that could collapse at any moment, and Mary Haney really has that ability and makes herself aggressive when necessary. I also saw that Moya had a tremendous sense of self-possession, which was crucial for Vivie, but she also surprised us in rehearsals when she showed a vulnerability to Vivie that I hadn't seen there before. Good actors do this all the time; they surprise us with things they bring out of the character that add a whole new dimension to the role.

An actor who wants to do Shaw well needs lots of active energy. I'm often accused of "casting young," that is, casting actors that are younger than the roles they have to play. This isn't something I intentionally do, but it often happens because I find that younger actors are better at that kind of energy that a Shaw character has to have. The problem this sometimes creates is that the ideas in Shaw's plays are often really difficult ideas, and they are coming on very quickly. If the actor doesn't understand the ideas, he or she can't play the character, so it's absolutely crucial that they get the ideas straight in their heads. This means they have to be willing to put in the work so that they can understand exactly what their character is saying at every moment. Sometimes I find actors bring in an audition piece from a Shaw play that they've just learned the day before, and you can tell—they need more time to really understand what they're supposed to be saying.

One of the reasons actors sometimes have difficulty understanding Shaw is that he's not really taught much anymore. He isn't a controversial or notorious playwright like he was when he first started out. There are probably two or three generations who don't necessarily know who Shaw was, so in a sense the problem now is that he's neither mainstream nor radical, he's not even on the radar! So I think it's a big part of our job to let people know that this strange dude with the big beard and a mad suit wrote really, really progressive and interesting and thorny plays that still have lots and lots to say and still feel at times eerily prophetic, to be honest. It's one thing to enjoy the way people come to see him here at the Shaw Festival, and it's so easy for them to accept him, but I also feel that we're at a cusp—we've got to make some real moves to make sure that he is seen still as a really valid part of the conversation and that his plays still ask questions and shed light on things that are really worth looking at. And that's our job, both in terms of how we produce it and how we make people know that this is there and interesting to see.

When we did *Saint Joan*, I actually got my older daughter to write my program notes for me—I mean she's now in a creative writing course, so I know she can write—but I just thought, I've been working my ass off doing this play and I've got nothing more I can say to make people get it. The biggest problem for me was figuring out why some people find it so easy to understand or take in the idea that she heard voices and some people don't, but it was my daughter who pointed out that as a teenager, you're hearing your own voice all the time and everyone completely discounts it, so Joan's world really wasn't that far from her own. In fact, she brought loads of friends to see it, kids who were not in the theater, and they loved it. Even having to sit through the tent scene, and some really difficult ideas, they could still completely empathize with the teenage girl who hears a voice clearly that everyone else dismisses or suspects. I also remember talking to a few younger women who came to see it that were just knocked sideways by it. I think we knock down the stupid, clichéd view of Shaw, the talking heads and all that pretty fast, but it's very important for young women to understand that there are actually women in these plays that are still striding ahead in one way or another.

We have seen a change in the audience demographics, especially since we introduced the "30 under 30" program, which has hugely increased the participation of younger audiences. Now don't get me wrong, I don't care what age anybody is, and just because you're old doesn't mean you aren't smart or interested, of course, any more than just because you're young means you are! But I do think that there are edges now in the programming that can hit other groups for sure, and I'm very, very aware of that.

There's no doubt that his plays are still provocative. I think any piece that questions the nature of the status quo manages to keep itself in mode for such a long time because the status quo is so hideously unchanged in so many ways. That goes even in the theater as an institution, which is why it's been so important to me to bring more women's voices into the conversation. I've been very active about making sure that women are part of the playbill. I mean, it's not a ratio, but I've always had at least one, and often more: this year [2010] I think there were about four plays by women, and I've also been very overt in bringing female directors in, so that the productions can look at some of these issues from a female point of view. It's kind of sad, really, that this would still warrant comment, but I've had "querying" in the press, being asked whether I'm "tipping the balance," and I say women have been left out of the conversation for so long that you have to go *so* far to even get anywhere *close* to equal! I mean, there's really nothing to be said. And you know, I'm very careful, I run a whole theater company of wonderful actors, and it's really nothing to do with more actors or less actors, it's really just about opening the programming. And I see audiences responding to this, becoming very interested to see who's going to be the next "new" voice we bring in. It could be a contemporary, like Caryl Churchill or Linda Griffiths, or it could be someone we've "rediscovered," but they have to be there: it's part of the history, it's part of the world, the conversation has to be had by more than just this one male point of view.

Years and years ago there was a survey done by PACT when I was running Factory [Theatre, Toronto], about women working at Canadian theaters, and it was very depressing, back in those days. They decided to look at it again recently—and the new survey shows that it's not that much better these days—but it was really interesting to see that there had been a big statistical improvement at the "A" houses, which are the really big theaters.[3] Then somebody noticed that if you take the Shaw Festival out of it, the average goes way down: the presence of women's work hasn't increased that significantly in Canadian theaters generally the way it has at the Shaw Festival since we've actively started focusing on it. We've become a statistical anomaly, making everyone else look good! Of course, it makes us look pretty good, too, because audiences have been reveling in some of the pieces that we've been bringing out. When you're building a playbill, and building continual programming, investigative programming, you've got to keep opening the doors to different points of view. Different points of view energize.

Notes

1. From their website, www.minttheater.org/about: "MINT THEATER COMPANY commits to bringing new vitality to worthy but neglected plays. We excavate buried theatrical treasures; reclaiming them for our time through research, dramaturgy, production, publication and a variety of enrichment programs; and we advocate for their ongoing life in theaters across the world. Mint has a keen interest in timeless but timely plays that make us feel and think about the moral quality of our lives and the world in which we live. Our aim is to use the engaging power of the theater to excite, provoke, influence and inspire audiences and artists alike."

2. For a critical examination of this comparison, see "Shutting Out Mother: Vivie Warren as the New Woman" by Ann Wilson in this volume.

3. The first survey was conducted by the Professional Association of Canadian Theatres (PACT) in the late 1970s and early 1980s. Survey results were summarized in a report written by Rina Fraticelli, "The Status of Women in the Canadian Theatre" (1982). The second survey was commissioned by PACT, The Playwrights Guild of Canada, and Nightwood Theatre, a Toronto-based company dedicated to exploring gender and racial equity in it productions. The results of this survey were reported in "Adding It Up: The Status of Women in Canadian Theatre," written and presented by Rebecca Burton in 2006 and available online at http://www.playwrightsguild.ca/pgc/news_docs/womens.pdf.

Bibliography

MICHEL PHARAND

In *SHAW: The Annual of Bernard Shaw Studies* 24 (2004): 221–35, I published "A Selected Bibliography of Writings by and about Bernard Shaw Concerning Love, Sex, Marriage, Women, and Related Topics." I called my attempt to gather Shaw's pronouncements on sexuality and related topics (Section A), as well as some pertinent critical commentaries (Section B), a "preliminary compilation." Sure enough, with the publication of Charles A. Carpenter's "A Selective, Classified International Bibliography of Publications about Bernard Shaw: Works from 1940 to Date, with Appendix of Earlier Works" shortly after *SHAW* 24 appeared, new material surfaced; as a result, I published a Supplement to my bibliography in *SHAW* 25 (2005): 257–59.

Since then, further items have come to light and have been added to the combined Bibliography and Supplement. I have corrected a few errors and redundancies and added items from Carpenter's online bibliography, which is updated periodically.

References in brackets are to Dan H. Laurence's *Bernard Shaw: A Bibliography*, 2 vols. (Oxford: Clarendon, 1983), and to his *Supplement* (entries marked ['-S']) published in *SHAW: The Annual of Bernard Shaw Studies*, 20 (2000), 3–128. In the second section, "Works about Shaw," three important sources were utilized: *G. B. Shaw: An Annotated Bibliography of Writings about Him* (DeKalb: Northern Illinois UP), vol. 1: 1871–1930, ed. J. Press Wearing (1986); vol. 2: 1931–1956, ed. Elsie B. Adams, with Donald C. Haberman (1987); and vol. 3: 1957–1978, ed. Donald C. Haberman (1986) [K310-S, K311-S, K312-S]; Lucile Kelling Henderson, "Shaw and Woman: A Bibliographical Checklist," *Shaw Review* 17.1 (1974): 60–66, reprinted (and expanded) as "A Bibliographical Checklist" in *Fabian Feminist: Bernard Shaw and Woman*, ed. Rodelle Weintraub (University Park: Penn State P, 1977), 262–71 [B437]; and Charles A. Carpenter's "A Selective, Classified International Bibliography of Publications about Bernard Shaw: Works from 1940 to Date, with Appendix of Earlier Works" (2004).

Works by Bernard Shaw

"About Sex and Marriage." Ruth Adam. *What Shaw* Really *Said*. New York: Schocken Books, 1966: 37–46. [K204].

"As Bernard Shaw Sees Woman." *New York Times* 19 June 1927: 4, 1–4, 2:1–5. [C2651; see B167].

"Authors' 'No' to Sex Play Jury." *Daily Mirror* 15 June 1925: 2:4. [C2553; statement: "Should sex plays be tried by public juries before production?"].

Bernard Shaw and Mrs. Patrick Campbell: Their Correspondence. Ed. Alan Dent. London: Gollancz, 1952; New York: Knopf, 1952. [A266].

Bernard Shaw: Agitations, Letters to the Press, 1875–1950. Ed. Dan H Laurence and James Rambeau. New York: Frederick Ungar, 1985. [A316-S; on censorship: 93–105, 252–55; morality: 153–59; obscenity: 239–41; prostitution: 25–35; sex and marriage: 89–92, 106–13, 137–38, 279–81].

"Bernard Shaw on American Women." *Cosmopolitan* Dec. 1905: 247–48. Reprinted in *The Independent Shavian* 10 (Winter 1971/72): 1–5.

"Bernard Shaw Extols Divorce" (symposium). *Globe and Commercial Advertiser* (New York) 28 Mar. 1905: 4:2–4. [C1476].

"Bernard Shaw Replies" (letter). *International Journal of Sexology* (Bombay) 2 (Nov. 1948): 102. [C3825; comment on Anthony M. Ludovici's "Sex in the Writings of Bernard Shaw" in the same issue].

Bernard Shaw: Selections of His Wit and Wisdom. Comp. Caroline Thomas Harnsberger. Chicago: Follett, 1965. [see under Divorce, Man and Woman, Marriage, Women, and Sex].

"The Bishop Would Be a Nudist" (statement). *Daily Mirror* 2 Nov. 1935: 1:4, 28:2. [C3127; see "Nudism" and "Mr. G. Bernard Shaw" in this section].

"Book Ban Denounced: Eminent People Defend 'Well of Loneliness'" (letter). *Daily Herald* 22 Nov. 1928: 5:4. [C2755a; drafted by Shaw; 45 signatories supporting Radclyffe Hall's 1928 lesbian novel. See "Shaw and Wells" in this section].

"Brieux: A Preface." *Three Plays by Brieux*. London: A. C. Fifield; New York: Brentano's, 1911, 9–53. [A104]. Reprinted in Bernard F. Dukore, ed., *Bernard Shaw: The Drama Observed*. University Park: Penn State P, 1993. 3: 1188–1222. [A326-S; on venereal diseases, 1216–20].

"The Case of Dr. [Marie] Stopes" (letter). *Daily News* 3 Mar. 1923: 4:4. [C2443].

"A Characteristic Question Cabled by Bernard Shaw." *Puck* (New York) 20 Feb. 1915: 6. [C1989; on woman suffrage].

"Clothes and Sex Appeal" (lecture extracts). *The 1930 European Scrap Book*. New York: Forum P, 1930. 167–68. [B194].

"The Cleveland Street Scandals" (letter of 26 Nov. 1889). *Encounter* 3 (Sept. 1954): 20–21. [C3942; on homosexuality].

"Danakil Women" (letter). *Time and Tide* 13 Jan. 1940: 29.30. [C3353; also in *Time and Tide* see "Shaw on Danakil Women," 20 Jan. 1940: 54 (C3354) and "Bernard Shaw on Danakil Women," 3 Feb. 1940: 102 (C3358)].

"Divorce Law Reform" (letter). *The Times* 14 July 1950: 7:5. [C3921].

Ellen Terry and Bernard Shaw: A Correspondence. Preface by Shaw. Ed. Christopher St. John. London: Constable, 1931; New York: G. Press Putnam's Sons, 1931. [A205].

"The Empire Promenade" (letter). *Pall Mall Gazette* 16 Oct. 1894: 3:2. [C1038; on prostitution].

"Eve's Repugnance" (letter). *Weekly Westminster* 5 Apr. 1924: 738. [C2493; on *Back to Methuselah* and the method of sexual reproduction].

"Extend Divorce, Make State Separate Unfit. Danger, Otherwise, That Private Contracts Will Be Substituted for Marriage" (interview). *New York American* 5 June 1921: II, 5:1.2 (first edition). [C2343].

"Fifth Fable." *Farfetched Fables* (1948). *Bernard Shaw: Collected Plays with Their Prefaces.* Ed. Dan H. Laurence. Vol. 7. New York: Dodd, Mead, 1975: 449–54. [A296b; on nineteenth-century sex practices and beliefs].

"'Flog Every Brothel Keeper,' Says Shaw" (statement). *Daily Worker* 30 Mar. 1944: 3:4. [C3519; on the findings of an inquiry committee into prostitution].

"Forcible Feeding" (unsigned). *New Statesman* 12 Apr. 1913: 8–9. [C1870; see C1873 and "Torture by Forcible Feeding" in this section].

"Forcible Feeding . . . Mr. Shaw on Suicide as a Solution" (letter). *Daily Mail* 17 Sept. 1912: 5:2. Extracts reprinted as "Let Suffragists Die, Says G. B. Shaw" in *New York Times* 17 Sept. 1912: 4:1. [C1836].

"The Future of Marriage" (review). J. Percy Smith, *The Unrepentant Pilgrim: A Study of the Development of Bernard Shaw* (Boston: Houghton Mifflin, 1966): 192 [B408; fragments of an unpublished review of *The Future of Marriage* (1885)].

"G. Bernard Shaw Talks about Love, Sex, Charles Chaplin and Why Old Men Don't Matter!" (interview). *Sunday Express* 1 Mar. 1931: 14:3.7, 21:2.4. [C2899].

"G.B.S. and a Suffragist" (interview, extensively revised by Shaw). *Tribune* (London) 12 Mar. 1906: 3:3–4. [C1534]. Reprinted in R. Weintraub, *Fabian Feminist* 236–42.

"G.B.S. and Birth Control." *Manchester Guardian* 23 Nov. 1922. [C2468a-S].

"G.B.S. Wants Women Rulers" (interview). *Sunday Express* 28 Dec. 1924: 3:1–3.

"G.B.S. 93" (interview). *Evening Standard* 25 July 1949: 9:1.3. [C3864; on sex education in schools, among other topics].

"George Bernard Shaw's Advice to the New York Vice Society" (letter). In Alfred Kreymborg's pamphlet, *Edna: The Girl of the Street.* New York: Guido Bruno, 1919. 3. [B107].

"The Husband, the Supertax, and the Suffragists" (letter). *The Times* 10 June 1910: 7:1–2. [C1733].

The Intelligent Woman's Guide to Socialism and Capitalism. London: Constable; New York: Brentano's, 1928. [A187].

"Is the Servile State Coming? Bernard Shaw's Strange Suggestion." *Woman's Dreadnought* 16 Sept. 1916: 547. [C2090; reply to query on woman suffrage by Sylvia Pankhurst].

"The King, the Constitution and the Lady: Another Fictitious Dialogue." *History Today* 12 (Dec. 2006): 20. Text from a 1936 pamphlet by Shaw listed in Dan H. Laurence's *Shaw: A Bibliography* as B249 *The King and the Lady . . . Why Did Edward VIII Abdicate?* and C3168 "The King, the Constitution and the Lady: Another Fictitious Dialogue."

"Kulin Polygamy" (letter). *The Times* 5 Oct. 1907: 12:5. [C1605]. Reprinted as "Bernard Shaw for Polygamy" in *The Sun* (New York) 6 Oct. 1907: 3:1–2.

Letters from Margaret: Correspondence between Bernard Shaw and Margaret Wheeler, 1944–1950. Ed. Rebecca Swift. London: Chatto and Windus, 1992. [A323-S].

"Letters to Alice Lockett." *The Armchair Esquire.* Ed. Arnold Gingrich and L. Rust Hills. New York: Putnam, 1958. 331–39.

"Let Them Die" (statement). *Evening Standard* 9 June 1914: 2:2. [C1936; on suffragette hunger strikers].

"Literature and the Sex Instinct." From preface to *Three Plays for Puritans* (1900). Reprinted in Stanley Weintraub, ed., *Bernard Shaw's Nondramatic Literary Criticism.* Lincoln: University of Nebraska Press, 1972. 203–8. [A302].

"The Logic of the Hunger Strike." *Manchester Guardian Weekly Edition* 10 Sept. 1920: 213–14. Reprinted in *Living Age* 2 Oct. 1920: 30–31. [C2297].

"Love Affairs." Reprinted in *Shaw: An Autobiography, 1856–1898.* Ed. Stanley Weintraub. New York: Weybright and Talley, 1969. 163–71. [Excerpts from Shaw's writings].

"Love Is the Most Impersonal of All Our Human Emotions" (interview). *New York American* 20 Oct. 1929: 1E:1–3, 4E:1–8. Also as "Bernard Shaw Talks about Love," *Sunday Express* 10 Nov. 1929: 14:3–7. [C2813; this interview by G. S. Viereck was disavowed by Shaw as "a fabrication from beginning to end" (see C2822 and C2823), but a facsimile of his revisions was reproduced with the *Sunday Express* publication; see B196].

"Marriage and Its Critics" (letter). *Pall Mall Gazette* 2 Dec. 1907: 1:3, 2:1–2. [C1620].

"Marriage and Its Critics" (letter). *Pall Mall Gazette* 10 Dec. 1907: 3:2. [C1621].

"Martyrdom and Woman Suffrage" (letter). *The Times* 25 June 1913: 10:4. [C1902]. Reprinted as "Shaw Insists on Word Martyrdom," *London Budget* 29 June 1913: 5:3.

"The Menace of the Leisured Woman." *Time and Tide* 4 Feb. 1927: 106–7. [C2634; verbatim report of Shaw's summation from the Chair after 27 January debate between G. K. Chesterton and Lady Rhondda]. Reprinted in Dan H. Laurence, ed., *Platform and Pulpit.* New York: Hill and Wang, 1961. 168–71. [A281].

"Modern Novels and Sex." *Evening Standard* (London) 26 May 1922: 5:1–2. [C2397]. Reprinted in S. Weintraub, *Bernard Shaw's Nondramatic Literary Criticism* 209–10.

"Morality and Birth Control." *Physical Culture* (New York) 42 (July 1919): 17–19. [C2227]. Reprinted in *The Independent Shavian* 10 (Spring 1972): 33–36.

"Mr. Bernard Shaw on Sex Instruction." *The Times* 20 June 1914: 5. [Shaw at a London symposium].

"Mr. G. Bernard Shaw on Excessive Clothing" (letter extract). *Sun Bathing Review* 1 (Summer 1933): 6. [C3002; see "Nudism" and "The Bishop" in this section].

"Mr. G. B. Shaw on Women's Rights" (letter and statement). *Manchester Guardian* 4 Nov. 1933: 16:6–7. [C3017].

"Mr. Shaw and Girl Strikers" (cable). *Daily Mail* 7 Jan. 1910: 7:6. [C1719].

"Mr. Shaw and the Unprotected Child" (letter). *Time and Tide* 16 Mar. 1923: 305. [C2448; on venereal disease. See "The Unprotected Child and the Law" in this section].

"Mr Shaw on Morals" and "Public Morals" (letters of 8 and 15 Nov. 1913). Reprinted in Dukore, *Bernard Shaw: The Drama Observed* 3: 1303–9.

"Mr. Shaw's Newest Woman." *New York Times* 19 Dec. 1920: III:21. [Shaw detects that women have ceased aping men and are now asserting their femininity].

My Dear Dorothea: A Practical System of Moral Education for Females, Embodied in a

Letter to a Young Person of that Sex. London: Phoenix House, 1956; New York: Vanguard, 1956. [A271].

"No Need for Love, Shaw Thinks, Praising Secretaries as Wives." *New York Times* 4 Jan. 1930: 1:7. [C2888].

Not Bloody Likely! and Other Quotations from Bernard Shaw. Ed. Bernard F. Dukore. New York: Columbia University Press, 1996. [A333-S; see under feminism, homosexuality, love, marriage, men and women, nudity, pornography, sex, wives, women].

"Nudism" (interview). *Dress and Beauty* 1 (Apr. 1935): 14–15. [C3098; see B315, "George Bernard Shaw Gives His Views on Nudism," abridgment of C3098; see "The Bishop" and "Mr. G. Bernard Shaw" in this section].

"On Stage Morals and Censorship, Religion, Art, and Spiritual and Physical Love," "On Love, Marriage, the Nature of Sex, and Sex Ethics," and "On Sexual Reform." Allan Chappelow. *Shaw—"The Chucker-Out": A Biographical Exposition and Critique.* London: George Allen and Unwin, 1969: 61–102. [Excerpts from Shaw's writings].

"On the Economic Disabilities of Women" (verbatim report of 1 July 1907 speech at annual meeting of Association of Post Office Women Clerks). *Association Notes* (July 1907). Reprinted in *The Independent Shavian* 19.2 (1981): 27–31. [C3974].

"Our Morals and Our Police" (unsigned). *New Statesman* 10 May 1913: 133–34. [C1887].

"Pensions for Mothers." *The Western Daily Mercury* (Plymouth) 26 Sept. 1918.

"The Play and Its Author." Souvenir program of a production of Eugène Brieux's *Woman On Her Own* (8 Dec. 1913). [B77]. Reprinted in Dukore, *Bernard Shaw: The Drama Observed* 3: 1309–12. [on prostitution].

"Preface." *Getting Married. Bernard Shaw: Collected Plays with Their Prefaces.* Vol. 3. Editorial Supervisor Dan H. Laurence. New York: Dodd, Mead, 1975. 451–545. [A296b].

"Preface." *Mrs Warren's Profession. Bernard Shaw: Plays Unpleasant.* Ed. Dan H. Laurence. Harmondsworth: Penguin, 2000. 181–212.

"The Prosecution of Mr. [George] Bedborough" (letter). *The Adult* 2 (Sept. 1898): 230–31. [C1287; on homosexuality].

"The Rights of Women Now" (interview). *News Chronicle* (London) 17 Nov. 1943: 2:5–8. Reprinted as "Shaw Asserts British Law Handicaps Men; Finds Women Really Running Country Now" in *New York Times* 18 Nov. 1943: 27:5. [C3499].

"Romance and Real Sex." From *Table Talk of G.B.S.* . London and New York: Harper and Brothers, 1925. [A173]. Reprinted in S. Weintraub, *Bernard Shaw's Nondramatic Literary Criticism* 211–15.

"The Root of the White Slave Traffic." *The Awakener* 16 Nov. 1912: 7–8. [C1848]. Reprinted in R. Weintraub, *Fabian Feminist* 255–59.

"Scientists Plead for Birth Control Idea" (statement). *New York Times* 29 Mar. 1925: 9, 6:1. [C2544; sent to Sixth International Neo-Malthusian and Birth Control Conference, New York].

"Sex Education." Louis Simon. *Shaw on Education.* New York: Columbia University Press, 1958. 198–203. [Excerpts from Shaw's writings].

"Sex, Love and Marriage: I, II, and III." *Shaw: Interviews and Recollections.* Ed. A. M. Gibbs. Iowa City: U of Iowa P, 1990. 419–23. [I: 1914 conversation; II: 1927 interview; III: 1929 recollection].

"Shaw and Wells in Banned Book Battle." *Daily Herald* 6 Oct. 1928: 1:1–2. [C2745; on Radclyffe Hall's *The Well of Loneliness*. See "Book Ban" in this section].

"Shaw Gets Laughs as Expert on Sex" (expurgated verbatim report of speech, "The Need for Expert Opinion in Sex Reform"). *New York Times* 14 Sept. 1929: 2:6–7. Extracts from speech published as "Bernard Shaw on Sexual Reform" in *Time and Tide* 20 Sept. 1929: 1113–14 [C2805]. Reprinted in *Sexual Reform Congress: Proceedings of the Third Congress of the World League for Sexual Reform*. London: Kegan Paul, Trench, Trübner, 1930. 432–37 [B195] and in Dan H. Laurence, ed., *Platform and Pulpit* 200–207.

"Shaw Mute on Marriage" (statement). *New York Times* 24 Jan. 1927. [B145; rejects an invitation to contribute to Hermann Keyserling's 1925 *Das Ehe-Buch* (*The Book of Marriage*), where it is published in English and German].

Shaw on Women. Ed. Mary Chenoweth Stratton. Illustrated by Linda Holmes. Bucknell University: The Press of Appletree Alley Limited Editions, 1992.

"Shaw on Women: 'Monsters of Ingratitude'" (letter). *Daily News* 26 June 1928: 6:7. [C2731].

"Shaw's Garden of Love." *A Curmudgeon's Garden of Love*. Ed. Jon Winokur. New York: New American Library, 1989. 113–15. [see also at 30, 133, 164, 174, 179, 196].

"Shaw *versus* Roosevelt on Birth Control" (letters). *The World To-Day* 46 (Sept. 1925): 845–50.

"Should Wives Be Paid?" (symposium). *Sunday Express* 30 Mar. 1919: 4:3. [C2210].

"Should Women Stop War?" (letter). *Free Lance* 25 Jan. 1902: 429. [C1382].

"Sir Almroth Wright's Polemic." *New Statesman* 18 Oct. 1913: 45–47. [C1910]. Reprinted as "Sir Almroth Wright's Case Against Woman Suffrage" in R. Weintraub, *Fabian Feminist* 243–47.

"Some Opinions on Sex Training" (symposium). *New Era in Home and School* 5 (Jan. 1924): 34. [C2476].

"The 'Suffragette' Case: Messages from Public Men." *Labour Leader* 22 May 1913: 5:4. [C1889].

To a Young Actress: The Letters of Bernard Shaw to Molly Tompkins. Ed. Peter Tompkins. New York: Clarkson N. Potter, 1960; London: Constable, 1961. [A277].

"To Frank Harris on Sex in Biography." *Sixteen Self Sketches*. London: Constable, 1949; New York: Dodd, Mead, 1949. 113–15. [A259; substantially revised version of letter dated 24 June 1930; first published (slightly bowdlerized) in Frank Harris's *Bernard Shaw* (1931)]. Annotated and reprinted as "Shaw's Sex Credo" in *SHAW: The Annual of Bernard Shaw Studies* 24 (2004): 215–20.

"Torture by Forcible Feeding Is Illegal" (verbatim report). *London Budget* 23 Mar. 1913: 1–7. [C1867]. Reprinted in R. Weintraub, *Fabian Feminist* 229–35.

"Two Notable Occurrences" (letter to Margaret Sanger). *Birth Control Review* 9 (Jan. 1925): 5. [C2535; see C2763]. Reprinted in *G. Bernard Shaw on Birth-Control*. The Madras Neo-Malthusian League, 1930. [A196].

"The Unmentionable Case for Women's Suffrage." *The Englishwoman* 1 (Mar. 1909): 112–21. [C1674]. Reprinted in Lloyd J. Hubenka, ed., *Bernard Shaw, Practical Politics*. Lincoln: U of Nebraska P, 1976). [A303].

"The Unprotected Child and the Law." *Time and Tide* 23 Feb. 1923: 210–12. [C2442; on venereal disease]. Reprinted in *Doctors' Delusions, Crude Criminology, and Sham Education.* London: Constable, 1931. 234–40. [see "Mr. Shaw and the Unprotected Child" in this section].

Unsigned note on White Slave Act sentence. *New Statesman* 19 Apr. 1913: 36. [C1874].

"What I Owe to German Culture." *Adam International Review* 337–39 (Spring 1970): 5–16. [C1765; written 21 Dec. 1910, published in German as the preface to the first volume of *Dramatische Werke* in 1911]. Reprinted in Dan H. Laurence and Daniel J. Leary, eds. *The Complete Prefaces. Volume 1: 1889–1913.* London: Allen Lane, The Penguin Press, 1993. 331–44. [see comments on "moral and immoral romance," 333–38].

"What Is Mr. Asquith Up to Now?" *Independent Suffragette* 1 (Oct. 1916): 10–11. [C2091].

"What I Think of Women." *Manchester Evening News* 25 July 1936: 4:3.7. [C3152a-S; questionnaire interview].

"Why All Women Are Peculiarly Fitted to Be Good Voters." *New York American* 21 Apr. 1907: 3.2:1–5. [C1584]. Reprinted in R. Weintraub, *Fabian Feminist* 248–54.

"Why Not Personify God as a Woman?" (transcription of London lecture, "Some Necessary Repairs to Religion," 29 Nov. 1906). *New York Times* 30 Nov. 1906. Reprinted in *The Independent Shavian* 10 (Fall 1971): 1–2, and in *SHAW: The Annual of Bernard Shaw Studies* 1 (1981): 81–84. [B442].

"Why Women SHOULD Have the Vote: From Man's Point of View" (symposium). *Pall Mall Magazine* 51 (Mar. 1913): 305. [C1860].

"Wives' Ideas on Rights are 85 Years Old." *Daily Sketch* 19 Oct. 1945: 1:1–3. [C3614; debate with Married Women's Association. See C3606 and C3611].

"Woman—Man in Petticoats" (speech). As "As Bernard Shaw Sees Woman" in *New York Times Magazine* 19 June 1927. [B167; see C2651]. Reprinted in Dan H. Laurence, ed., *Platform and Pulpit* 173–78.

"A Woman Must Have a Home" (interview). *Cheltenham Chronicle* 27 May 1950: 7:3–5. [C3916].

"Woman's Charm" (statement). *Manchester Evening News* 11 Dec. 1924: 11:2. [C2533].

"Woman since 1860 as a Wise Man Sees Her." *McCall's* (New York) Oct. 1920: 10–11, 27. As "Woman Since 1860" in *Time and Tide* 8 Oct. 1920: 442–44. Reprinted in *New York American* as "Woman as I Have Seen Her," 14 Nov. 1920: 2.12:1–5, and as "Bernard Shaw Traces Woman's Evolution from Crying and Fainting to Swearing and Smoking," 21 Nov. 1920: 2.5:1–3. [C2301].

"The Womanly Woman." *The Quintessence of Ibsenism.* London: Constable, 1913. 36–45 and *passim.* Reprinted in J. L. Wisenthal, ed., *Shaw and Ibsen: Bernard Shaw's The Quintessence of Ibsenism and Related Writings.* Toronto: U of Toronto P, 1979. 124–31 [A307], and in *Bernard Shaw: Major Critical Essays.* Harmondsworth: Penguin, 1986. 54–63.

"Women and Friendship" (letter). *Clarion* 13 Feb. 1897: 49:6, 50:1. [C1191].

Women as Councillors (Fabian Tract No. 93). *Fabian Municipal Program* (Second Series), no. 4 (Mar. 1900). [A38].

"Women in Politics." *Leader Magazine* 25 Nov. 1944: 5–6. [C3556].

"Women in Politics" (letter). *Liverpool Echo* 2 Mar. 1948: 4:4–5. [C3787].

"Women in the War" (interview). *Leader* 16 Aug. 1941: 15. [C3427].

"Women Losing Voice Beauty?" (symposium). *Daily Mirror* 16 Oct. 1934: 2:4. [C3070].

"Women, Love and Marriage." *The Sayings of Bernard Shaw.* Ed. Joseph Spence. London: Duckworth, 1993. 23–28.

"Women, Socialism and Love" (letter). *Hearst's Magazine* (New York) Jan. 1923: 5, 131. [C2435].

"Women Suffrage" (letter). *The Times* 31 Oct. 1906: 8:4. Reprinted as "Shaw on Woman's Rights" in *New York Times* 15 Nov. 1906: 7:4, and as "The Influence of Women in English Politics" in *New York American & Journal* 16 Dec. 1906: 20:1–4. [C1557].

"The Women's Vote." *Manchester Guardian* 5 July 1945: 6:2. [C3596].

"Women Typists' Salaries" (letter). *Daily Mail* 26 Nov. 1907: 6:6. [C1618].

"Writers on Writing: George Bernard Shaw on Edith Nesbit" (letter to Molly Tompkins, 22 Feb. 1925). Reprinted in *The Guardian* (London) 13 Oct. 2007: 15.

Works about Bernard Shaw

Adams, Elsie. "Feminism and Female Stereotypes in Shaw." *Shaw Review* 17.1 (1974): 17–22. Reprinted in R. Weintraub, *Fabian Feminist* 156–62.

———. "Shaw's Ladies." *Shaw Review* 23.3 (1980): 112–18.

Allett, John. "*Mrs Warren's Profession* and the Politics of Prostitution." *SHAW: The Annual of Bernard Shaw Studies* 19 (1999): 23–39.

Barnicoat, Constance A. "Mr. Bernard Shaw's Counterfeit Presentment of Women." *Fortnightly Review* (New York) 85 (Mar. 1906): 516–27. Reprinted in *Living Age* 14 Apr. 1906.

Barzun, Jacques. "Eros, Priapos, and Shaw." *The Play and its Critics: Essays for Eric Bentley.* Ed. Michael Bertin. New York: UP of America, 1986. 67–88.

Berst, Charles A. "Passion at Lake Maggiore: Shaw, Molly Tompkins, and Italy, 1921–1950." *SHAW: The Annual of Bernard Shaw Studies* 5 (1985): 81–114.

Besant, Lloyd. "Shaw's Women Characters." Diss. U of Wisconsin, 1964.

Block, Toni. "Shaw's Women." *Modern Drama* 2 (Sept. 1959): 133–38.

Bosch, Marianne. "Mother, Sister, and Wife in *The Millionairess.*" *SHAW: The Annual of Bernard Shaw Studies* 4 (1984): 113–27.

Burlin, Robert B. "Shaw, Women and Opera: Determining the Voice." *Cahiers Victoriens et Édouardiens* 45 (Apr. 1997): 73–81.

Carpenter, Charles A. "Sex Play Shaw's Way: *Man and Superman.*" *Shaw Review* 18.2 (1975): 70–74.

Carter, Patricia M. "'Until It Was Historical': A Letter and an Interview." *SHAW: The Annual of Bernard Shaw Studies* 24 (2004): 11–37.

Cherry, Wymm. "A Look Back at Shaw's Feminism." *Independent Shavian* 32 (1994): 53–55.

Coelsch-Foisner, Sabine. "Spinsters versus Sinners: A Late-Nineteenth-Century Paradigm in G. B. Shaw's Plays." *Imaginaires* 2 (1997): 91–111.

Collins, Stacy Michelle. "Beastly Ftatateeta: The Erasure of the Crone in *Caesar and Cleopatra*." M.A. thesis, Stetson U, 2008. *WorldCat*, "Bernard Shaw, 2008–2009."

Conolly, L. W. Introduction. *Mrs Warren's Profession*. Peterborough, Ont.: Broadview P, 2005. 13–72.

———. "*Mrs Warren's Profession* and the Lord Chamberlain." *SHAW: The Annual of Bernard Shaw Studies* 24 (2004): 46–95.

Crane, Gladys M. "Shaw and Women's Lib." *Shaw Review* 17.1 (1974): 23–31. Reprinted in R. Weintraub, *Fabian Feminist* 174–84.

Das, Nila. "The Shavian New Woman as Outsider." *G. B. Shaw: A Critical Response*. Ed. Sudhakar Pandey and Freya Barua. Stosius Inc./Advent Books, 1992. 53–62.

Davis, Jill. "The New Woman and the New Life." *The New Woman and Her Sisters: Feminism and Theatre, 1850–1914*. Ed. Viv Gardner and Susan Rutherford. London: Harvester Wheatsheaf, 1992. 17–36. [on *Mrs Warren's Profession*, *Man and Superman*, and *Getting Married*].

Dierkes-Thrun, Petra. "Incest and the Trafficking of Women in *Mrs Warren's Profession*: 'It Runs in the Family.'" *ELT: English Literature in Transition 1880–1920* 49.3 (2006): 293–310.

Doan, William J. "*The Doctor's Dilemma*: Adulterating a Muse." *SHAW: The Annual of Bernard Shaw Studies* 21 (2001): 151–61.

Drew, Anne M. "Embracing Ambiguity: Shaw's Women." *Staging the Rage: The Web of Misogyny in Modern Drama*. Ed. Katherine H. Burkman and Judith Roof. Madison, NJ: Fairleigh Dickinson UP, 1998, 158–70.

Du Cann, C. G. L. *The Loves of George Bernard Shaw*. New York: Funk and Wagnalls, 1963; London: Barker, 1963. [K180].

Dukore, Bernard F., ed. *Bernard Shaw: The Drama Observed*. 4 vols. University Park: Penn State P, 1993. [A326-S].

———. "The Fabian and the Freudian." *The Shavian* 2.4 (1961): 8–11.

———. "G.B.S. and S.E.X.: Sexuality and Sexual Equality." *Essays in Theatre* 6.2 (1988): 81–94.

———. "Girl Gets Boy." *SHAW: The Annual of Bernard Shaw Studies* 29 (2009): 17–27.

———. "Sex and Salvation." *SHAW: The Annual of Bernard Shaw Studies* 24 (2004): 112–18.

Gahan, Peter. "*Jitta's Atonement*: The Birth of Psychoanalysis and 'The Fetters of the Feminine Psyche.'" *SHAW: The Annual of Bernard Shaw Studies* 24 (2004): 128–65.

Gainor, J. Ellen. "Lesbian Sexuality and Violence in the Plays of G. B. Shaw." *Violence in Drama. Themes in Drama* 13. Ed. James Redmond. Cambridge: Cambridge University Press, 1991. 177–89.

———. *Shaw's Daughters: Dramatic and Narrative Constructions of Gender*. Ann Arbor: U of Michigan P, 1991. [K345-S; see "Shavian Androgyny," esp. 67–94].

Gates, Joanna E. "The Theatrical Politics of Elizabeth Robins and Bernard Shaw." *SHAW: The Annual of Bernard Shaw Studies* 14 (1994): 43–53.

"G. B. Shaw Condemns Sex Appeal in Movies." *New York Times* 19 Nov. 1927: 5. [see also "Shaw Chides the Movie Producer," *New York Times* 4 Dec. 1927: Part XI, p. 2].

Gerrard, Thomas J. "Marriage and George Bernard Shaw." *Catholic World* 94 (Jan. 1912): 467–82.

Gill, Stephen. "Shaw, the Suffragist." *Literary Half Yearly* 14 (1973): 153–56.

Gilmartin, Andrina. "Mr. Shaw's Many Mothers." *Shaw Review* 8.3 (1965): 93–103. Reprinted in R. Weintraub, *Fabian Feminist* 143–55.

Glicksberg, Charles. "Bernard Shaw and the New Love-Ethic." *The Sexual Revolution in Modern English Literature*. The Hague: Martinus Nijhoff, 1973. 45–58.

Godfrey, Esther Liu. "Gender, Power, and the January–May Marriage in Nineteenth-Century British Literature." *Dissertation Abstracts International* 67.04 (Oct. 2006).

Goldman, Michael. "Shaw and the Marriage in Dionysus." *The Play and Its Critics: Essays for Eric Bentley*. Ed. Michael Bertin. New York: UP of America, 1986. 97–111.

Grecco, Stephen. "Vivie Warren's Profession: A New Look at *Mrs Warren's Profession*." *Shaw Review* 10 (Sept. 1967): 93–99.

Greer, Germaine. "A Whore in Every Home." In R. Weintraub, *Fabian Feminist* 163–66. [on *Mrs Warren's Profession*].

Greiner, Norbert. "Mill, Marx and Bebel: Early Influences on Shaw's Characterization of Women." In R. Weintraub, *Fabian Feminist* 90–98.

Hadfield, Dorothy A. "What Runs (in) the Family: Iterated Retelling, Gender, and Genre in *You Never Can Tell* and *Major Barbara*." *SHAW: The Annual of Bernard Shaw Studies* 26 (2006): 58–78.

Hanley, Tullah Innes. *The Strange Triangle of G.B.S.* Boston: Bruce Humphries, 1956. [fictionalized treatment of Shaw's relationship with Janet Achurch and her husband].

Hanna, Kim. "Lesbian Representations in *Mrs Warren's Profession*." Paper read at the International Shaw Society conference, USF, Sarasota, Mar. 2004 (unpublished).

Harris, Frank. "Shaw's Sex Credo." *Bernard Shaw*. New York: Simon and Schuster, 1931. 227–45; London: Victor Gollancz, 1931. 223–38. [See "To Frank Harris on Sex in Biography" in "Works by Shaw"].

Henderson, Archibald. "Bernard Shaw on Women (My Friend Bernard Shaw: VI)." *Sunday Chronicle* (Manchester) 6 Feb. 1927.

———. "G.B.S. on Women." *Encore* 10.23 (1946): 118.

Henderson, Lucile Kelling. "Shaw and Woman: A Bibliographical Checklist." *Shaw Review* 17.1 (1974): 60–66. Reprinted (and expanded) as "A Bibliographical Checklist" in R. Weintraub, *Fabian Feminist* 262–71.

Johnson, Josephine. *Florence Farr: Bernard Shaw's "New Woman."* Totowa, NJ: Rowman and Littlefield; Gerrards Cross: Colin Smythe, 1975.

———. "The Making of a Feminist: Shaw and Florence Farr." R. Weintraub, *Fabian Feminist* 194–205.

Kakutani, Michiko. "G. B. Shaw and the Women in His Life and Art." *New York Times* 27 Sept. 1981: Arts and Leisure.

Kelley, Katherine E. "Shaw on Woman Suffrage: A Minor Player on the Petticoat Platform." *SHAW: The Annual of Bernard Shaw Studies* 14 (1994): 67–81.

Kester, Dolores. "The Legal Climate of Shaw's Problem Plays." R. Weintraub, *Fabian Feminist* 68–83.

Khanna, Savitri. "Shaw's Image of Woman." *The Shavian* 4.7–8 (1973): 253–59.

Kornbluth, Martin L. "Two Fallen Women: Paula Tanqueray and Kitty Warren." *Shavian* 14 (1959): 14–15.

Laurence, Dan H. "Katie Samuel: Shaw's Flameless 'Old Flame.'" *SHAW: The Annual of Bernard Shaw Studies* 15 (1995): 3–19.

——. "Victorians Unveiled: Some Thoughts on Mrs Warren's Profession." *SHAW: The Annual of Bernard Shaw Studies* 24 (2004): 38–45.

Lawrence, T. E. *Correspondence with Bernard and Charlotte Shaw*. Ed. Jeremy and Nicole Wilson. 3 vols. Fordinbridge, Hants.: Castle Hill, 2000–2008.

Leary, Daniel. "Don Juan, Freud and Shaw in Hell: a Freudian Reading of *Man and Superman*." *Shaw Review* 22.2 (1979): 58–78.

Le Mesurier, Lillian. *The Socialist Woman's Guide to Intelligence: A Reply to Mr. Shaw*. London: Benn, 1929.

Lenker, Lagretta T. *Fathers and Daughters in Shakespeare and Shaw*. Westport, CT: Greenwood P, 2001.

——. "Pre-Oedipal Shaw: 'It's Always the Mother.'" *SHAW: The Annual of Bernard Shaw Studies* 26 (2006): 36–57.

Lorichs, Sonja. "The Unwomanly Woman." *The Shavian* 4.7–8 (1973): 250–52.

——. *The Unwomanly Woman in Bernard Shaw's Drama and Her Social and Political Background*. Uppsala, Sweden: U of Uppsala Studies in English, 1973.

——. "The 'Unwomanly Woman' in Shaw's Drama." R. Weintraub, *Fabian Feminist* 99–111.

Ludovici, Anthony M. "Sex in the Writings of Bernard Shaw." *International Journal of Sexology* (Bombay) 2 (Nov. 1948). [see C3825 above].

MacCarthy, Desmond. "What Is Sauce for the Goose—G. B. Shaw on Woman's Emancipation." *New Statesman and Nation* 15 Apr. 1944: 255.

Mackworth, Margaret Haig (Thomas) [2nd Viscountess Rhondda]. "Shaw on Sex." *Notes on the Way*. New York: Macmillan, 1937. 71–75. Reprinted by Books for Libraries Press (Freeport, NY: 1968).

Mansel, Mildred E. "Bernard Shaw and Feminism." *Socialist Review* 9 (1912): 50–57.

Mathur, S. C., and Akhilesh Kumar. "The Shavian Concept of Spider-Woman." *Triveni* 55.3 (1986): 71–75.

McCauley, Janie Caves. "Kipling on Women: A New Source for Shaw." *Shaw Review* 17.1 (1974): 40–44. Reprinted in R. Weintraub, *Fabian Feminist* 23–30.

McDonald, Jan. "New Women in the New Drama." *New Theatre Quarterly* 21 (1990): 31–42.

McKenzie, Carole, ed. *Quotable Sex*. New York: St. Martin's Press, 1992. [Of over 800 people quoted, Shaw comes in third (17 quotations), after Mae West (20) and Oscar Wilde (23)].

Molnar, Joseph. "Shaw's Four Kinds of Women." *Theatre Arts* 36 (Dec. 1952): 18–21, 92. Adapted as "Shaw's Living Women," *Shaw Society Bulletin* 49 (June 1953): 7–11.

Morgan, Margery M. "Edwardian Feminism and the Drama: Shaw and Granville Barker." *Cahiers Victoriens et Édouardiens* 9–10 (1979): 63–85.

——. "Shaw and the Sex Reformers." *SHAW: The Annual of Bernard Shaw Studies* 24 (2004): 96–111.

Murrenus, Valerie. "Hostages of Heartbreak: The Women of *Heartbreak House.*" *SHAW: The Annual of Bernard Shaw Studies* 23 (2003): 17–25.

Nathan, George Jean. "Shaw as a Lover." *American Mercury* 13 (Feb. 1928): 246–48.

Nathan, Rhoda. "All About Eve: Testing the Miltonic Formula." *SHAW: The Annual of Bernard Shaw Studies* 23 (2003): 65–74. ["Shaw's Eves come in a variety of guises."].

———. "Kindred Spirits: Charlotte Shaw & T. E. Lawrence." *Independent Shavian* 45.1–3 (2008): 28–34.

———. "The Shavian Sphinx." *Shaw Review* 17.1 (1974): 45–52. Reprinted in R. Weintraub, *Fabian Feminist* 30–38.

Nelson, Raymond S. "*Mrs Warren's Profession* and English Prostitution." *Journal of Modern Literature* 2 (1971–72): 357–66.

Nethercot, Arthur. "Bernard Shaw, Ladies and Gentlemen." *Modern Drama* 2 (1959): 84–98.

———. "G.B.S. and Annie Besant." *Shaw Bulletin* 1.9 (1955): 1–14.

———. *Men and Supermen: The Shavian Portrait Gallery.* 1954. New York: Benjamin Blom, 1966. 2nd ed., corrected. [K142; see "The Female of the Species," 77–126].

Nickson, Richard. "GBS and Laura Ormiston Chant: Man and Superwoman." *Independent Shavian* 37 (1999): 21.24.

Oe, Mariko. *My Fair Ladies: Untamed Heroines in the Plays of Bernard Shaw.* Tokyo: Keibunsha, 2005. [in Japanese]. Reviewed by Hisashi Morikawa in *SHAW: The Annual of Bernard Shaw Studies* 27 (2007): 229–32.

Pagliaro, Harold. *Relations between the Sexes in the Plays of George Bernard Shaw.* Lewiston, NY: Edwin Mellen P, 2004. [see "Lovers Coupled by the Life Force," pp. 61–99].

———. "Truncated Love in *Candida* and *Heartbreak House.*" *SHAW: The Annual of Bernard Shaw Studies* 24 (2004): 204–14.

Pederson, Lisë. "Shakespeare's *The Taming of the Shrew* vs. Shaw's *Pygmalion*: Male Chauvinism vs. Women's Lib." *Shaw Review* 17.1 (1974): 32–39. Reprinted in R. Weintraub, *Fabian Feminist* 14–22. [reprinted title reads "Lib?"].

Peters, Margot. *Bernard Shaw and the Actresses.* New York: Doubleday, 1980.

———. Foreword. *Shaw on Women.* Ed. Peters. Lewisburg, PA: Bucknell UP, 1992. 9–17.

Peters, Sally. "Ann and Superman: Type and Archetype." R. Weintraub, *Fabian Feminist* 46–65.

———. *Bernard Shaw: The Ascent of the Superman.* New Haven: Yale UP, 1996.

———. "From Mystic Betrothal to *Ménage à Trois*: Bernard Shaw and May Morris." *The Independent Shavian* 28.1–2 (1990): 3–14.

———. "Shaw's Life: A Feminist in Spite of Himself." *The Cambridge Companion to George Bernard Shaw.* Ed. Christopher Innes. Cambridge: Cambridge UP, 1998. 3–24.

Pharand, Michel W. "General Introduction: Dionysian Shaw." *SHAW: The Annual of Bernard Shaw Studies* 24 (2004): 1–10.

Powell, Kerry. "New Women, New Plays, and Shaw in the 1890s." *The Cambridge Companion to George Bernard Shaw.* Ed. Christopher Innes. Cambridge: Cambridge UP, 1998. 76–100.

Radford, Fred. "Domestic Drama and Drama of Empire: Intertextuality and the Subaltern Woman in Late Victorian Theatre." *Nineteenth-Century Contexts* 20 (1995): 1–25.

Rhondda, Lady. "Shaw's Women." *Time and Tide* 11 (7 Mar.–11 Apr. 1930): 300–301, 331–34, 364–66, 395–96, 436–38, 468–70.

Ritschel, Nelson O'C. *Performative and Textual Imaging of Women on the Irish Stage, 1820–1920: M. A. Kelly to J. M. Synge and the Allgoods.* Lewiston, NY: Edwin Mellen, 2007.

Roberts, R. Ellis. "The Inhibitions of Bernard Shaw." *Bookman* (London) 79 (Oct. 1930): 4–7.

Sachs, Lisbeth J., and Bernard H. Stern. "Bernard Shaw and his Women." *British Journal of Medical Psychology* 37 (1964): 343–50.

Sargent, Michael. "Shaw and the New Woman." *Shavian* 11 (2010): 5–16.

Sauer, David K. "'Only a Woman' in *Arms and the Man*." *SHAW: The Annual of Bernard Shaw Studies* 15 (1995): 151–66.

Senguta, Gautam. "New Women, New Idioms." *The Shavian* 10.3 (2006): 8–16.

Sharpe, Susan L. "Neither Sudden nor Startling: A Look at Choice in Shaw's Women." *Literature in Performance* 6.2 (1986): 22–29.

Shaw and Women. BBC-TV Production (U.S. Distributor: Peter M. Robeck and Company, 230 Park Avenue, New York, NY 10017). 16 mm black and white, 45 min. [no date; listed in R. Weintraub, *Fabian Feminist* 271].

"Shaw Favors Women on Censorship Staff." *New York Times* 12 June 1926: 4. [Support of proposal that a woman should assist the Lord Chamberlain in censorship of plays].

Shields, Jean Louise. "Shaw's Women Characters: An Analysis and a Survey of Influences from Life." Diss. U of Indiana, 1958.

Silver, Arnold. *Bernard Shaw: The Darker Side.* Stanford, CA: Stanford UP, 1982. [a psychoanalytic reading of Shaw's plays].

Singer, Irving. *The Nature of Love 3: The Modern World.* Chicago: U of Chicago P, 1987. 239–53. [on sex, love, the Life Force, and Shaw's "vitalistic Puritanism"].

Sirlin, Lázaro. "La sexología en las comedias de Jorge Bernard Shaw" (Sexology in the comedies of George Bernard Shaw). *Sagitario* (Argentina) 7 (Oct.–Nov. 1926): 50–58. [in Spanish].

Smith, J. Percy. "The New Woman and the Old Goddess: The Shaping of Shaw's Mythology." *Women in Irish Legend, Life and Literature.* Ed. S. F. Gallagher. Gerrards Cross, Eng.: Colin Smythe, 1981. 74–90.

Stafford, Tony. "'The End of Hearth and Home': The Deconstructing Fireplace in Shaw's Early Plays." *The Independent Shavian* 44.1–2 (2006): 17–30.

Starks, Lisa S. "Educating Eliza: Fashioning the Model Woman in the *Pygmalion* Film." *Post Script: Essays in Film and the Humanities* 16.2 (1997): 44–55.

Sterner, Mark H. "Shaw's Superwoman and the Borders of Feminism: One Step over the Line?" *SHAW: The Annual of Bernard Shaw Studies* 18 (1998): 147–60.

Stone, Susan C. "Whatever Happened to Shaw's Mother-Genius Portrait?" R. Weintraub, *Fabian Feminist* 130–42.

Tahir, Laura. "*My Dear Dorothea*: Shaw's Earliest Sketch." *SHAW: The Annual of Shaw Studies* 9 (1989): 7–21.

Thornton, Michael. "The Siren Who Disappeared: Uncovering the Mystery of Britain's First Sex Symbol." *Daily Mail* 27 Mar. 2008: news section.

Timmons, Ann. *Shaw's Women*. [stage play; publication data unavailable. See online at http://home.earthlink.net/~anntimmons/aet.htm].

Uttley, Diane. *Shaw's Women* and *Shaw, Women and Feminism*. United Kingdom: The Bernard Shaw Information and Research Service, no date. ["Info Subject" pamphlets sold online].

Vesonder, Timothy G. "Eliza's Choice: Transformation Myth and the Ending of *Pygmalion*." R. Weintraub, *Fabian Feminist* 39–45.

Waltonen, Karma. "*Saint Joan*: From Renaissance Witch to New Woman." *SHAW: The Annual of Bernard Shaw Studies* 24 (2004): 186–203.

Wasserman, Marlie Parker. "Vivie Warren: A Psychological Study." *Shaw Review* 15 (May 1972): 71–75. Reprinted in R. Weintraub, *Fabian Feminist* 168–73.

Watson, Barbara Bellow. "The New Woman and the New Comedy." *Shaw Review* 17.1 (1974): 2–16. Reprinted in R. Weintraub, *Fabian Feminist* 114–29.

———. *A Shavian Guide to the Intelligent Woman*. London: Chatto and Windus, 1964; New York: Norton, 1964. [K192].

Weimer, Michael. "*Press Cuttings*: G.B.S. and Women's Suffrage." R. Weintraub, *Fabian Feminist* 84–89.

Weintraub, Rodelle. "The Center of Life: An Interview with Megan Terry." R. Weintraub, *Fabian Feminist* 214–25.

———, ed. *Fabian Feminist: Bernard Shaw and Woman*. University Park: Penn State P, 1977. [B437].

———. "The Gift of Imagination: An Interview with Clare Boothe Luce." *Shaw Review* 17.1 (1974): 53–60. Reprinted in R. Weintraub, *Fabian Feminist* 206–13.

———. "Introduction: Fabian Feminist." R. Weintraub, *Fabian Feminist* 1–12.

———. "The Irish Lady in Shaw's Plays." *Shaw Review* 23.2 (1980): 77–89.

———. "Votes for Women: Bernard Shaw and the Women's Suffrage Movement." *Ritual Remembering: History, Myth, and Politics in Anglo-Irish Drama*. Ed. C. C. Barfoot and Rias van den Doel. Amsterdam: Rodopi, 1995. 33–40.

———. "What Makes Johnny Run? Shaw's *Man and Superman* as a Pre-Freudian Dream Play." *SHAW: The Annual of Bernard Shaw Studies* 24 (2004): 119–27.

Weintraub, Stanley. "Shaw's Lady Cicely and Mary Kingsley." R. Weintraub, *Fabian Feminist* 185–92.

———. "Shaw's Sculptress, Kathleen Scott." *SHAW: The Annual of Bernard Shaw Studies* 24 (2004): 166–85.

———. "Who's Afraid of Virginia Woolf? Virginia Woolf and G.B.S." *SHAW: The Annual of Bernard Shaw Studies* 21 (2001): 41–62.

West, Rebecca. "Contesting Mr. Shaw's Will; An Analysis of G.B.S.'s Final Word on Women and Socialism." *Bookman* (New York) 67 (July 1928): 513–20.

Wherly, Eric S. *Shaw for the Million*. Belfast: Gulliver Books, 1946. [see "Shaw on Sex" 35–36 and "Shaw the Gay Lothario" 37–39].

Wiley, Catherine. "The Matter with Manners: The New Woman and the Problem Play." *Women in Theatre*. Ed. James Redmond. Cambridge: Cambridge UP, 1989. 109–27.

Contributors

Tracy J. R. Collins is faculty in the English department at Central Michigan University.

Leonard W. Conolly is Professor Emeritus of English at Trent University and a fellow of the Royal Society of Canada. He serves as the literary adviser to the estate of Bernard Shaw, is a corresponding scholar with the Shaw Festival in Niagara-on-the-Lake, and is general editor for the "Selected Correspondence of Bernard Shaw" series published by University of Toronto Press. His most recent book is *The Shaw Festival: The First Fifty Years*.

Virginia Costello is a lecturer in English and in gender and women's studies at the University of Illinois, Chicago.

D. A. Hadfield is lecturer in English at the University of Waterloo. She is the author of *Re: Producing Women's Dramatic History: The Politics of Playing in Toronto*.

Brad Kent is associate professor of British and Irish literatures at Université Laval in Quebec City, Canada.

Kay Li is adjunct professor in the Faculty of Liberal Arts and Professional Studies, York University. She is the author of *Bernard Shaw and China: Cross-Cultural Encounters* and the project leader of the SAGITTARIUS-ORION Literature Digitizing Project on Bernard Shaw.

Jackie Maxwell is the artistic director of the Shaw Festival in Niagara-on-the-Lake, Canada.

John M. McInerney is Professor Emeritus of English at the University of Scranton.

Michel Pharand is director of the Disraeli Project at Queen's University, Kingston, Ontario, and the general editor of *SHAW: The Annual of Bernard Shaw Studies*.

Jean Reynolds is Professor Emerita at Polk State College in Florida and author of *Pygmalion's Wordplay: The Postmodern Shaw*.

Margaret D. Stetz is the Mae and Robert Carter Professor of Women's Studies and Professor of Humanities at the University of Delaware. She is the author of *Gender and the London Theatre, 1880–1920*.

Lawrence Switzky is assistant professor in the Department of English and Drama at the University of Toronto.

Rodelle Weintraub edited *Fabian Feminist: Bernard Shaw and Woman*, *SHAW 5: Shaw Abroad*, and the *Garland Captain Brassbound's Conversion*.

Ann Wilson is associate dean in the College of Arts, University of Guelph.

Index

Abbey Theatre, 78, 85, 87n4, 88n17

Achurch, Janet, 11; as actress, 112, 115, 117, 118, 119, 129, 131n5; substance abuse by, 118, 127, 129–30; and theater management, 115, 116, 129; as writer, 116–17, 118–32, 139. See also *Mrs. Daintree's Daughter*

Actresses: bodies of, 36n3, 117; disapproval of, 96, 98–99, 101; dubious morality of, 34–35, 129; employment difficulties for, 98, 102–3, 111n23; Shaw's relationships with, 95; and theater management, 114–15

Allen, Grant, 114, 117, 130n2, 131n9

Anarchists, xii, 11, 144–46, 156, 160–61, 164, 167nn1,5; Chicago, 147, 154–56, 157–58; feminist, 12, 146, 166

Anderson, Benedict: *Imagined Communities*, 59

Anderson, Margaret, 161, 164–65

"Angel in the House, The" (Patmore), 2, 57

Annajanska (Shaw), 31–32

Anthias, Floya: *Woman-Nation-State*, 74–75

Apple Cart, The (Shaw), 20

Arbuthnot, John: *The History of John Bull*, 87n10

Arms and the Man (Shaw), 136

Armstrong, Nancy, 113

Artaud, Antonin, 53

Ashwell, Lena, 109n3, 111n23

Audiences: challenge to, 23, 74, 160; and nationhood, 76; and pain, 10, 37–38, 45, 53; response from, 202, 208–9

Backsliders, The (Egerton), 12, 140–42

Barrie, J. M., 136; *Mary Rose*, 108

Belasco, David, 97, 109n3

Bentley, Eric, 5

Berény, Henri: *Little Boy Blue*, 100

Bergson, Henri: *Creative Evolution*, 105, 110n16

Berkman, Alexander, 148, 149–50, 152, 153

Bernard, Claude, 52

Bernard Shaw and China: Cross-Cultural Encounters (Li), 173

Bernard Shaw and the Actresses (Peters), 95

Bernard Shaw: An Unauthorized Biography (Harris), 148–53

Blackwood, Algernon, 108, 109

Blake, William, 105, 110n18

Boothe Luce, Clare: *The Women*, 206

Boxer, Barbara, 182

Brecht, Bertolt, 53

Brieux, Eugene: *Les Avariés* (trans. *Damaged Goods*), 107, 111n20

Bright, Arthur Addison, 136

Bright, Reginald Golding, 12, 136; as literary agent, 136, 137; marriage to George Egerton, 133, 134, 135, 140, 143; relationship to Shaw, 136–37, 138

Brooke, Sarah, 110n8

Brooks, Peter, 43–44
Brooks, Van Wyck, 159–60
Burton, Rebecca, 210n3
Byron, George Gordon Lord: *Don Juan*, 177

Campbell, John, 183, 184
Campbell, Kim, 182
Campbell, Lady Colin, 39
Campbell, Mrs. Patrick (Beatrice Stella), 95
Candida (Shaw), 203, 204, 205; casting in, 206, 207; productions of, xi, 119, 140
Capitalism, 68, 160–61, 165
Captain Brassbound's Conversion (Shaw), 207
Carnegie, Andrew, 163–64
Case, Sue-Ellen, 1
Castelnuovo, Shirley: *Feminism and the Female Body: Liberating the Amazon Within*, 21–23, 28
Cathleen ni Houlihan (Gregory and Yeats), 77–78, 84, 87n16
Censorship, 167n4, 174
Charrington, Charles, 116, 117–18
Charrington, Nora, 122
Chen, Wendy, 171
Chen Kit-fang, 172
Chicago Press Club, 164
Churchill, Caryl, 209
Cixi, Empress Dowager, 172
Clairmonte, Egerton, 140
Clinton, Hillary Rodham, xii, 13, 178, 184–88
Clothing, 24–25, 28, 31–33, 61
Cobbe, Frances Power, 40
Coburn, Charles, 103, 110n15
Coburn Players, 110n15
Collins, Tracy J. R., 10
Colosimo, Krista, 204
Conolly, Leonard W., 11, 61
Copley Theater (Boston), 107–8, 111n21
Corbett, Mary Jean, 118

Costello, Virginia, 12
Cotterill, Erica, 138
Crane, Walter, 158
Creative Evolution (Bergson), 105, 110n16

Daly, Arnold, 139–40
Davies, Hubert Henry: *The Mollusc*, 100
de Maupassant, Guy: *Yvette*, 120
Depression era, 3
Devil's Disciple, The (Shaw), 103
Diamond, Elin, 45
Diana of Dobson's (Hamilton), 200
DiGaetani, John Louis: *Stages of Struggle*, 20
Doctor's Dilemma, The (Shaw), 41, 95, 105, 132n10; casting in, 11, 95–96, 97–99, 102, 107–8, 109n2, 110n7, 204
Doll's House, A (Ibsen), 56, 70–71, 86, 173, 205
Domas, Louis J., 161–64
Douglas, Alfred, 148
Dreiser, Theodore, 147
Duse, Eleonora, 43

Egerton, George (Mary Chavelita Dunne), 11, 12, 115, 133; *The Backsliders*, 12, 140–42; biographical information about, 140, 141; "A Cross Line," 140–41; *Discords*, 135; "A Divided Duty," 136–37; as fiction writer, 133, 135–36, 140–41; "His Wife's Family," 137, 140; and Irish, 134, 135, 137–38, 139; *Keynotes*, 12, 133, 140; play production history of, 139–40, 142; as playwright, 136–38, 139–43; resemblance to Shaw, 134–35, 142; *Rosa Amorosa*, 141; *Symphonies*, 134
Emerson, Ralph Waldo, 159
Equal Rights Amendment (U.S., 1923, 1972), 7

Fabian Feminist (Weintraub), xi, 5, 8, 19
Fabianism, 83
Factory Theatre (Toronto), 209

Fanny's First Play (Shaw), 29–31
Farr, Florence, 42
Feminine Mystique, The (Friedan), 3
Feminism, xi, 1, 13–14; advocated by
Shaw, 2, 4–5, 9–11, 112, 114, 140, 145, 153,
194; and anarchism, 12, 166; Chinese,
13, 171–76; critiques of, 5–7, 187; and
identity, 118, 185–86; liberal, 4; and
nationalism, 172–73; and physicality,
10, 21–23; post-, 6–7, 14nn4–5; second-
wave, 3–4, 5, 7, 187, 194; and separate
spheres ideology, 1–2, 40–41, 59, 113;
and social causes, 40–41, 145, 147, 171;
and suffrage, 3, 14n2, 141, 187; and
theatrical production, 13, 200, 202–3,
209–10; third-wave, 5–6, 187; transnational, 174, 186; Victorian era, 1–3, 7,
40–41, 52, 138, 145, 194 (*see also* New
Woman; "Woman Question")
*Feminism and the Female Body: Liberating
the Amazon Within* (Castelnuovo and
Guthrie), 21–23, 28
Ford, Hugh, 109n3, 111n23
Fox, Kelli, 206
Fraticelli, Rina, 210n3
French, Richard, 40
Frick, Henry Clay, 152
Friedan, Betty: *The Feminine Mystique*, 3

Gainor, J. Ellen, xii, 45–46, 51
Galsworthy, John, 109n3, 201; *The Silver
Box*, 98, 110n9
Gardiner, E. W., 119
Garner, Stanton, 38
Gates, Joanne E., 139
Gender: challenges to, 22, 34–35, 44–45,
185; and double standards, 122, 124,
179–81, 183; and nation, 75–91, 87nn7,15,
88nn19–20; performance of, 10, 178,
183–84, 185, 189; and social anxiety,
113, 180, 182–89, 197; and suffering, 10,
44–45, 48–49, 50–52
Geneva (Shaw), 189, 190, 192–93

Gertz, Elmer, 152
Getting Married (Shaw), 4, 189, 190–91,
195, 197
Gibbs, A. M., xii, 14n2
Ginsburg, Ruth Bader, 182
Gissing, George: *The Odd Women*, 14n1
Glaspell, Susan, 202
Glassgold, Peter, 161
Goldman, Emma, xii, 12, 201; admiration for Shaw's works, 12, 146–47,
153, 156–57, 158, 159–63; biographical
information about, 144–45, 152–53, 157,
161–62; differences from Shaw, 145–46,
147, 151–52, 153; disappointment with
Shaw, 146–47, 153–54, 157–59, 166; lectures by, 145, 157, 159–65; *Living My Life*,
152, 153, 154; *My Disillusionment of Russia*, 167n5; political views of, 144–45,
147, 151–53, 156, 164, 167n5; relationship
with Shaw, 12, 144–46, 147–48, 149, 152,
154–55, 167n10; similarity to Shaw, 11,
144, 155–56; *The Social Significance of
Modern Drama*, 146–47, 157, 160, 161,
165–66; writing by, 149, 157, 160, 164
Gonne, Maud, 84
Gorki, Maxim, 162
Granville-Barker, Harley, 11, 99, 103,
109n3, 110nn9,14, 117, 200; *Prunella*, 98
Graves, Clotilde, 117
Green, Alice Stopford, 84
Gregory, Lady Augusta, 82, 102; *Cathleen
ni Houlihan*, 77–78, 84, 87n16
Griffiths, Linda, 209
Grosz, Elizabeth: *Volatile Bodies: Toward
a Corporeal Feminism*, 21
Grundy, Sydney, 43; *The New Woman*, 133
Guthrie, Sharon: *Feminism and the
Female Body: Liberating the Amazon
Within*, 21–23, 28

Hadfield, D. A., 11–12
Hamilton, Charles, 96, 100, 101, 102,
110nn4,13

Hamilton, Cicely: *Diana of Dobson's*, 200
Hamilton, Mary, 11; acting career of, 95–
  101, 106, 107–8, 109, 110nn6–7, 111n23;
  biographical information about, 96–97,
  102, 104; family pressures on, 99–100,
  102, 106–7, 109, 110n13; requests a new
  play from Shaw, 101–2
Hamsun, Knut, 135
Haney, Mary, 207
Hansson, Ola, 135
Hardy, Thomas: *Dynasts*, 105, 110n16
Harris, Frank, 144, 147; account of meet-
  ing between Shaw and Goldman by,
  148, 150–53; *Bernard Shaw: An Unau-
  thorized Biography*, 148–53; *My Life and
  Loves*, 150; *Oscar Wilde: His Life and
  His Confessions*, 155
Harris, Nellie, 147, 148, 149
Heartbreak House (Shaw), 39
Henderson, Archibald, 5
Hentschel, Irene, 96
Hepburn, Katharine, 20
Homosexuality, 58
Hong Shen: *Wai Nu Si De Zhi Ye* (*Miss
  Wai's Profession*), 174
Housman, Laurence: *Prunella*, 98
Hsiao Ch'ien, 174
"Hundred Days Reform" (China), 172
Huntington, Helen, 110n14
Hutchison, Kay Bailey, 182
Hwang, David: *M. Butterfly*, 180

Ibsen, Henrik, 43, 115, 159, 162, 202; influence on Shaw of, 112, 135; and theatrical
  cruelty, 37, 45. See also *Doll's House, A
  Ideal Husband, An* (Wilde), 203–4
Industrial Revolution, 200
Ireland: feminized, 75–76, 77–78, 79,
  81, 85; and national tale, 76–78, 82–83,
  86, 87n10; political history of, 75–76,
  77, 78, 84–85, 111n22; reality of, 82;
  Shaw's ambivalence about, 83–84, 86,
  88n24

Jamieson, Kathleen Hall, 178, 182, 188
Jewett, Henry, 107–8, 111n21
John, Angela V., 139
John Bull's Other Island (Shaw), 10–11, 138;
  barrenness in, 83–84, 88n25; courtship
  in, 79–81, 88n21; English imperialism
  in, 79–83, 84, 88nn21–22; gender in,
  78–79, 83–84; nationalist allegory in,
  79–83, 84, 86, 87n10; production history of, 78; as response to Yeats, 10–11,
  78, 81, 82; scholarship on, 73, 87nn4–5,
  88n19; stage directions in, 79
Jones, Henry Arthur, 43
Jonson, Ben, 179

Kakutani, Michiko, xi, xii, 187
Kang You-wei, 172; *Datong-Shu* (*Book of
  Universality*), 172
Kent, Brad, 10–11
Kropotkin, Prince Peter (Pyotr Alexeyev-
  ich), 155

Lane, Grace, 110n8
Lane, John, 135
Langner, Lawrence, 20
Lansbury, Coral, 38
Lansing, Sherry, 195
Lavery, John, 85
Lavery, Lady Hazel, 84
Lewis, Eric, 109n2
Li, Kay, 13; *Bernard Shaw and China:
  Cross-Cultural Encounters*, 173
Little Review, The, 161
Living My Life (Goldman), 152, 153, 154
Lorichs, Sonja, 19
Lytton, Neville, 99, 109n3

Major Barbara (Shaw), 39, 52, 142, 181;
  Barbara Undershaft in, 178, 181–82, 184,
  188, 189
Man and Superman (Shaw), 38, 52, 100,
  181; casting in, 9, 11, 95, 97–99; female
  characters in, xi, 9, 110n6, 204; Life

Force in, 104–5, 194; marriage in, 191; productions of, 11, 204

Man of Destiny, The (Shaw), 32, 101

Marbury, Elisabeth, 136

Markiewicz, Countess, 84

Marriage, 4, 30–31; choice about, 34, 58, 64, 172, 190–92, 194; laws, 43, 161, 172; and money, 201–2; and politics, 75–76, 84; as prostitution, 4, 24

Maugham, Somerset, 136

Maxwell, Jackie, xii, 8, 13; admiration for Shaw, 203–5; on casting, 207–8; on programming women's work, 209–10; on Shaw's contemporaries, 13, 199–204; on Shaw's contemporary relevance, 206, 207–9

McCarthy, Lillah, 9, 110n14

McInerney, John M., 13

McRobbie, Angela, 6–7

Melodrama, 43–45, 50, 119, 127, 201–2

Mezon, Jim, 205–6

Mill, John Stuart: "The Subjection of Women," 172

Millionairess, The (Shaw), 20, 33–34, 178, 179–80, 187, 188, 189

Minney, Rubeigh, 175

Mint Theater (N.Y.), 201, 210n1

Misalliance (Shaw), xi–xii, 39; female characters in, 26–29, 189–90, 197

Modernism, 200

Morphia, 119, 127–28

Morris, William, 155, 158

Morrow, Albert, 133

Mrs. Daintree's Daughter (Achurch), 12, 112; composition history of, 115, 119–20; daughter character in, 124–26, 129; drug use in, 127–29; economic exploitation examined in, 122–24; melodramatic conventions in, 119, 127; mother character in, 119–29, 131n9; mother-daughter relationship in, 119–20, 121–22, 124–26; production history of, 115, 117, 118–19

Mrs Warren's Profession (Shaw), 23, 45; capitalism in, 67–68, 124, 131n7, 175; casting in, 173, 205, 207; Chinese adaptations of, 174–75; composition history of, 115, 120; depiction of prostitution in, 128–29, 145, 153, 160–61, 174; ending of, 56–57, 68–71, 205; family structures in, 60–61, 63, 173; female emancipation in, 58, 60, 64–65, 118, 204–5; ideas of performance in, 10, 56–57, 61–62, 63–64, 65–66, 69–71, 207; middle-class respectability in, 4, 10, 61–62, 65, 67, 71, 124; mother-daughter relationship in, xii, 60–71, 121, 124, 135, 205; motherhood in, 60–61, 62–63, 64–67, 69, 120, 165–66; political use of, 146, 151, 153, 157, 159, 160–66, 171–75; reception of, 70, 140, 174–75; stage directions in, 56, 57, 61, 64; Vivie Warren in, 6, 10, 26, 62–63, 66–71, 121, 122, 124, 166, 173, 175, 178, 204–5

My Fair Lady (Lerner and Loewe), xii

My Life and Loves (Harris), 150

National Action Committee on the Status of Women (Canada, 1972), 4

National Organization for Women (U.S., 1966), 4

National tale, 76–77, 79–80, 86

Naturalism, 45, 49, 54n2

Nettlau, Max, 150

Newcombe, Bertha, 42, 43

Newton, Christopher, 199

New Woman, xi, 10, 11, 138, 203, 205; athleticism of, 19–36, 62; and class privilege, 57, 59–60, 70, 71; critiques of, 60, 67–68, 70, 142–43; and identity, 56–58, 59, 62, 63–64, 67–68, 113, 131n6; and writing, 113, 114, 117, 130n2, 131n6, 133–34, 136, 139. *See also* Feminism: Victorian era

New Woman, The (Grundy), 133

Nietzsche, Friedrich, xi, 159

Novick, Julius, 46, 54n5
Nu Bao (Women's newspaper), 172
Nu Xue Bao (Women's education newspaper), 172

Obama, Barack, 187, 188, 196
O'Connell, Moya, 205, 207
Odd Women, The (Gissing), 14n1
O'Flaherty V.C. (Shaw), 73, 101
O'Neill, Eugene, 202; The Iceman Cometh, 206
On the Rocks (Shaw), 189, 190, 193–94, 195, 197
Orwell, George, 37, 38, 53n1
Overruled (Shaw), 101
Owenson, Sidney: The Wild Irish Girl, 76–77

Pain, 37–38, 47–48; and gender, 10, 39, 44–45, 47–50; theatricalized, 43–45, 53
Palin, Sarah, 13, 193
Passion, Poison & Petrifaction (Shaw), 101
Patmore, Coventry, 62; "The Angel in the House," 2, 57
Patterson, Jenny, 42–43
Pearn, Violet, 109
Peck, Janice, 196
Peking University, 172
Pelosi, Nancy, 182
Pemberton, Max, 97
Peters, Margot, xii, 161; Bernard Shaw and the Actresses, 95
Peters, Sally, xii
Pharand, Michel, 53n2
Philanderer, The (Shaw), 10, 21, 23; as autobiography, 42–43, 131n6, 134; composition history of, 39, 50–51, 116; female characters in, 24–25, 131n6; pain and cruelty in, 10, 39–40, 44–55; production history of, 116, 119, 142; scholarship on, 39; stage directions in, 45, 49–50, 142

Pinero, Sir Arthur Wing, 43, 202; The Second Mrs. Tanqueray, 119, 121, 203
Plays Unpleasant (Shaw), 23
Plunkett, Horace, 75
Powell, Kerry, 114, 115, 139
Pozner, Jennifer, 14n5
Presidential Commission on the Status of Women (U.S., 1961), 4
Professional Association of Canadian Theatres (PACT), 209, 210n3
Project Shaw (New York), xiii, 8
Prostitution, 45, 122, 144; as business, 65–66, 68–70; marriage as, 4, 24; socioeconomic causes of, 120, 145, 153, 160–66
Prunella (Granville-Barker and Housman), 98
Pun Jia-sheng, 171
Pygmalion (Shaw), xii, 205–6

Quinine, 119, 127

Realism, 45, 54n2
Reece, Gordon, 183
Reeves, Amber, 20
Reinelt, Janelle, 6
Ritvo, Harriet, 41, 54n4
Robins, Elizabeth, 139
Roosevelt, Eleanor, 186
Rorke, Kate, 119
Rorty, Richard: Contingency, Irony, and Solidarity, 53n1
Rosie the Riveter, 3, 14n3
Rosling, Tara, 207
Ross, Arthur, 153
Royal Commission on Opium (England, 1893), 127–28, 131n8
Royal Commission on the Status of Women (Canada, 1967), 4
Royal Court Theatre (Vedrenne-Barker), 11, 95–96, 97, 137, 142
Russell, Annie, 142

Russell Theatre (Ottawa), 100, 101
Rutherford and Son (Sowerby), 200–201

Saddlemyer, Ann, 88n17
Saint Joan (Shaw), 157–58, 204, 208; casting in, 207; as exemplar for real women, 178, 184, 185, 188, 208; gender in, 32–33, 180–82, 189
Savoy, The, 135
Scriblerus Club, 87n10
Scully, Frank, 148, 149, 150
Second Mrs. Tanqueray, The (Pinero), 119, 121, 203
Shakespeare, William, 206
Shara, Mike, 207
Shaw, Bernard, 100, 148–49; advice to actors from, 97–98, 101–2, 108; and anarchism, 144, 146, 154–56, 157–59, 167nn1,7; and audiences, 10, 23, 37–38, 45, 74, 160; Cashel Byron's Profession, 1, 40; contemporary relevance of, 8, 9, 13–14, 208–10; cross-dressing in plays by, 31–33, 180, 189; discomfort with real women of, xii, 11–12, 113, 134, 138; disparity between works and actions, 12, 146, 150–51, 152, 153–54, 157–59, 166; female characters by, xi–xii, 1, 2, 9–11, 19–36, 74, 78–79, 112, 114, 177–82, 184, 185, 187, 188–95, 202, 203–7; female playwright contemporaries of, 11–12, 112–13, 115–20, 134, 137–40, 199–203; feminist ambivalence of, 9, 11, 12, 52–53, 112–13, 117–18, 130, 134, 138, 140–43; feminist sympathies of, 2, 4–5, 9–10, 35–36, 58, 112, 114, 145, 153, 194; influence of, 5, 7–8, 13, 175, 178, 207–8; and Ireland, 83–84, 86, 88n24, 111n22, 159; on life's purpose, 96, 104–7; and masculinity, 10, 20, 34; on medical institutions, 41–42, 129, 132n10; "My Memories of Oscar Wilde," 155; novels by, 2, 40,

114, 135; and pain and cruelty, 10, 37–55, 138; political views of, 151–52, 154–56; The Quintessence of Ibsenism, 37–38, 58; relationships with women, 11–12, 42–43, 54n5, 95–96, 112, 142, 144–46; on theater, 12, 96, 105, 114–15, 175; on vivisection, 40, 41–43, 46–47. See also individual plays
Shaw, Charlotte (Payne-Townsend), 83, 150
ShawChicago, xiii, 8
Shaw Festival (Niagara-on-the-Lake, Ont.), xii, 8, 13, 14n1; audience response at, 202, 208–9; casting at, 206–7; mandate of, 199–200, 206
Shenbao, 171–72
Silver Box, The (Galsworthy), 98, 110n9
Simpleton of the Unexpected Isles, The (Shaw), 38
Social Significance of Modern Drama, The (Goldman), 146–47, 157, 160, 161, 165–66
Song Chun-fang, 174
Soong Ching-ling, 173
Sowerby, Githa: Rutherford and Son, 200–201; The Stepmother, 201–3
Spencer, Herbert: "The Rights of Women," 172
Stage Guild (Washington, D.C.), xiii
Stage Society, 140
Stages of Struggle (DiGaetani), 20
Stephens, Yorke, 119
Stepmother, The (Sowerby), 201–3
Stetz, Margaret D., 12, 115
Sudermann, Hermann, 116
Swift, Jonathan, 75, 87n10
Switzky, Lawrence, 10
Symons, Arthur, 135

Terry, Ellen, 95, 136
Thatcher, Margaret Roberts, 182–84, 188, 192

Theater: depiction of suffering in, 43–44; women in, 13, 113, 114, 115, 134, 200, 202–3, 209–10

Tien Han, 175

Tobin, A. I., 152, 153

Tompkins, Molly, 95, 111n19

Tompkins, Richard, 107, 111n19

Too True to Be Good (Shaw), 35, 139

Traister, Rebecca, 187–88

Tucker, Benjamin, 167n1

Turco, Alfred, 42–43

Tyler, George, 142

Tyson, Brian F., 50

Vedrenne, J. E., 102–3, 108, 110n9

Vivisection: anti-, 40–41, 52, 54n4; ethical considerations of, 38–39, 50–51; in relationships, 42–43, 46–47; theatrical, 39

Volatile Bodies: Toward a Corporeal Feminism (Grosz), 21

Votes for Women (magazine), 145

Wai Nu Si De Zhi Ye (Miss Wai's Profession) (Hong and Zhang) 174

Waller, Lewis, 118–19

Wang Chung-hsien, 173, 174

Webb, Beatrice, 42, 54n5

Weintraub, Rodelle: Fabian Feminist, xi, 5, 8, 19

Weintraub, Stanley, 119

Wells, H. G., 147, 167n10

West, Rebecca, 159–60

Wexler, Alice, 145

Whitman, Walt, 159

Widowers' Houses (Shaw), 2, 23–24, 39, 45, 116

Wilde, Oscar, 135, 155, 159; An Ideal Husband, 203–4

Wild Irish Girl, The (Owenson), 76–77

Williams, Linda, 44

Wills, Iva, 110n15

Wilson, Ann, 10

Wilson, Charlotte, 167n1

Winfrey, Oprah, 195–97

Woman-Nation-State (Anthias and Yuval-Davis), 74–75

"Woman Question," 2, 9, 87n5, 112, 114, 171. See also Feminism: Victorian era

Women: as cultural symbols, 113, 186; difference from men, 9, 34–35, 118, 122, 141, 177, 179–81, 200–203; double bind for, 178, 188, 197; education of, 6, 27, 67–68, 88n20, 161, 173, 204–5; employment opportunities for, 3, 64–65, 66–67, 68, 70, 95, 98–100, 102–3, 113, 121–22, 162–63, 172–73, 182, 190, 195; equality for, 7, 171–72, 175; family pressures facing, 99–100, 102, 106, 173; idealization of, 58–59, 182; and nationhood, 10–11, 59–60, 73, 74–75, 77–82, 88n20, 183; physicality of, 10, 19–23, 29, 180, 182, 189; political agency of, 11, 59, 84–86; and public power, 13, 178, 180–97; reproductive rights for, 4; societal position of, 14n1, 166, 194; and suffrage, 3, 85, 145; Victorian conceptions of, 19, 20, 56–58, 121, 122, 132n9, 145; writers, 113–18, 133–43

Women, The (Boothe Luce), 206

Woolf, Virginia, 58–59

Wyndham Land Act (UK, 1903), 85

Wyndham's Theatre (London), 97

Xin Chao (New Tide), 171

Xing Yeh Company, 172–73

Yeats, W. B., 81, 82, 87n4; Cathleen ni Houlihan, 77–78, 87n16

Yellow Book, The, 135

You Never Can Tell (Shaw), 38, 105

Yuval-Davis, Nira: Woman-Nation-State, 74–75

Zhang Zhi-chuan: Wai Nu Si De Zhi Ye (Miss Wai's Profession), 174

Zola, Émile, 38–39, 54n2

Pygmalion's Wordplay: The Postmodern Shaw, by Jean Reynolds (1999)

Shaw's Theater, by Bernard F. Dukore (2000)

Bernard Shaw and the French, by Michel W. Pharand (2001)

The Matter with Ireland, Second Edition, edited by Dan H. Laurence and David H. Greene (2001)

Bernard Shaw's Remarkable Religion: A Faith That Fits the Facts, by Stuart E. Baker (2002)

Bernard Shaw's The Black Girl in Search of God: The Story Behind the Story, by Leon Hugo (2003)

Shaw Shadows: Rereading the Texts of Bernard Shaw, by Peter Gahan (2004)

Bernard Shaw: A Life, by A. M. Gibbs (2005)

What Shaw Really Wrote about the War, edited by J. L. Wisenthal and Daniel O'Leary (2006)

Bernard Shaw and China: Cross-Cultural Encounters, by Kay Li (2007)

Shaw's Controversial Socialism, by James Alexander (2009)

Bernard Shaw as Artist-Fabian, by Charles A. Carpenter (2009)

Shaw, Synge, Connolly, and Socialist Provocation, by Nelson O'Ceallaigh Ritschel (2011; first paperback edition, 2012)

Who's Afraid of Bernard Shaw? Some Personalities in Shaw's Plays, by Stanley Weintraub (2011; first paperback edition, 2013)

Shaw, Plato, and Euripides: Classical Currents in Major Barbara, by Sidney P. Albert (2012)

Shaw and Feminisms: On Stage and Off, edited by D. A. Hadfield and Jean Reynolds (2012; first paperback edition, 2016)

Shaw's Settings: Gardens and Libraries, by Tony Jason Stafford (2013; first paperback edition, 2016)

CPSIA information can be obtained
at www.ICGtesting.com
Printed in the USA
LVOW11s0233041116
511418LV00001B/3/P